London Rotterdam
Antwerp
•Paris

CORSICA
Naples

MOROCCO

S a h a r a

SIERRA
LEONE

Albert
National
Park UGANDA
KENYA
L.Victoria
BELGIAN Serengeti Plains
CONGO TANGAN
YIKA

ANGOLA

S.
RHODESIA

UNION
OF SOUTH NATAL
AFRICA

On Safari

Armand Denis

ON SAFARI
The Story of My Life

COLLINS
St James's Place, London

First Impression   *July*, 1963
Second Impression   *August*, 1963

To Michaela

Contents

Illustrations

Maps

Acknowledgements

I would like to thank here the people who have helped me with the production of this book.

The majority of the photographs were taken by me or by my associates, principally among them Des Bartlett. For others I am indebted as follows: to Mr. E. O. Hoppé for the pictures of Bali between pages 48 and 49; to the Explorers Club, New York, and Mr. H. W. Kitchen for the photograph of the four-tusked elephant skull between pages 96 and 97; to Alfred Gregory and Camera Press Ltd. for the pictures of Nepal between pages 96 and 97; and to Mr. W. Suschitzky for the study of the gorilla opposite page 192.

Above all I would like to thank John Pearson for invaluable help in the writing of this book.

A.D.

I *Novice*

IT IS late and the house is asleep. Tonight I had to drive the
twelve and a half miles out to Nairobi airport to get the final film
for our current television series on to the Friday night Comet,
which stops here on its way from Johannesburg to London. In a few
hours it will be unloaded at London Airport. For us another period
of work will be over, and we will be free for a few weeks before
our next expedition to the jungles of Suriname. Despite this I am
restless to-night and although it is after midnight I cannot sleep.

As I drove in from the road the moon was so bright I could see
my house with its long white veranda outlined against the great
plain beyond and the mauve of the Ngong hills heavy along the
horizon. A jackal was barking in the distance. Frogs were echoing
from the small stream beyond the track, and now as I sit here in the
long room at the back of the house that I use as my office and
film-cutting room, I can still hear them. It is the sort of noise you
never forget, and I find it one of the things I miss when I am away
from Africa for long.

For the last eight years we have lived here, Michaela and I,
using this house as a base for our different journeys around the world.
I, who for years have had a horror of houses, finally possess a house
of my own. I, who still believe the tent and the hotel to be two of
man's most sacred inventions, designed this house myself and
watched it being built. For eight years it has been our headquarters;
the place where we have planned our films and television programmes, stocked our expeditions, kept our animals and returned
to edit our films.

It is an unusual place. Our garden consists of twenty-five acres of wooded hillside, the sort of forest that once covered vast areas of East Africa—and apart from clearing a few paths we have left it as it was so that there are still wild orchids growing on our trees and at night leopards prowl by the river. It is a place of shade and silence. Zebra and antelope visit us and sometimes we wake to find a giraffe outside our bedroom window.

The house seems to suit the animals we have collected as well. At the moment, Michaela has a mongoose sleeping on the veranda, and the big ant-eater, the three cheetahs and the four Rhodesian Ridgeback dogs all seem more at ease with a roof over their heads than I do.

For me, the real advantages of our house begin when we leave it. At a moment's notice we can be off to almost anywhere we want in Africa. To the north-west we can reach Entebbe on the shores of Lake Victoria in a day's good driving. Mombasa and the Indian Ocean lie a day away to the east. Three days to the west are the forests and mountains of the Congo and to the south we can head for the rich game areas of Amboseli and Tanganyika.

During the last eight years that has been the pattern of our lives —loading the cars, driving off on safari, filming, and then working against the deadline of that Friday night plane to have our programmes ready for delivery to London. Television is a hungry medium and that film I delivered to-night was the eighty-fourth we have made since we started here. It seems impossible to believe that we have made so many, but there they are, stacked against the wall opposite me, all neatly labelled and piled in their flat film cans along the shelves.

A few of the titles catch my eye, reminding me of the incredible richness of this continent. "Baby Crocodiles at Murchison Falls," "Lassoing Rhino," "Baboons feeding on Water Lilies," "Pygmies of the Ituri Forest." The variety of Africa is inexhaustible and although I have spent so much of my life with my cameras seeking out and recording the wonders of the place, I am continually being reminded of what remains to be found. A single lifetime is not enough.

Not that I can grumble at my life; I have seen things no one will ever see again. I have taken the chances the world offered and the world has been kind to me. But as I look back, my life seems to take on a pattern I had never expected, a pattern formed by what has been happening to wild life throughout the world. It is only this that makes me think my story is worth telling, for already I am something of a survivor. Already I feel like one of the few remaining witnesses of a cataclysm, the cataclysm that has swept Africa and is sweeping the world wherever there is wild life still to be found. It is this that has caught me and changed me and made me what I am.

I have had two great passions in my life—travel and animals. As a young man, I went wherever I could, excited, enthusiastic, naïvely imagining that the wonders of the animals I saw would last for ever. Time taught me it would not. In the last few years I have realised that the animals I filmed were already precarious inhabitants of a world rapidly closing in on them. Place after place where I went before the war I now refuse to return to, knowing that the tribes and the animals I saw there once have vanished. The freedom and splendour I marvelled at barely preceded their death agony.

That is why this story of my life, although it is a record of enjoyment, the story of a man doing the one thing he really wanted to do, is something else as well. I have not just been a spectator but a witness, and I have watched thirty years of destruction. Another thirty years like those I have seen and almost everything I describe in this book will be a thing of the past. Generations will be born that will curse us for the vandalism with which, in one short century, we have squandered the wild life it took fifty million years to perfect.

I described myself as a witness. To make clear what sort of witness I am it is appropriate to adopt the method I would use with any other animal and describe my species and my habitat.

The first thing that people who know me remark on is the contrast between my birth and upbringing and the life I have led ever since. My father was a judge in Antwerp. He was a good judge, a good Catholic and the most devoted family man I have ever known. We always spoke French at home but both my father and mother were of Flemish stock, and on both sides of the family the relatives I remember were amply endowed with the traditional characteristics of all true Flemings. They were tough, stolid, obstinate, long-lived people, with a strong sense of individuality and a marked tendency to become characters in their old age. There were no less than three generals in the immediate family; one of them, General Henri Denis, was also Belgium's Minister of War, and, alas, a firm believer in the impregnability of the Maginot Line. There was my first cousin, Marguerite Denis, who had the strength of will to marry a young Chinese student she met at the university at Brussels, and to follow him to Chungking, where for many years she was the only white woman living in the immense Chinese province of Szechwan. Their daughter, who became Han Suyin the novelist, is thus my first cousin once removed.

I myself was born in Brussels but the family moved to Antwerp soon afterwards so that I found myself brought up in one of the tightest, most rigid middle-class societies in Europe. Not that I was unhappy as a child. Quite the reverse. I was particularly fond of my mother and certainly did not object to the somewhat unrelenting routine of the Jesuit school in Antwerp where I was fed a solid diet of Latin and Greek, befitting the son of an Antwerp judge. I learned easily and seem to have been a surprisingly obedient pupil.

To-day I find it hard to believe that a world such as the one I grew up in could ever have existed. With its security and its narrow-mindedness, its taboos and obligations, its profound sense of what could be done and what could not, it has sunk almost without trace. Yet there are times even to-day, when I seem to catch myself re-acting unconsciously against it all.

For example, my father, who was something of a puritan and a stern disciplinarian, decided early on that my sister and I were to be kept rigidly away from anything that could defile our childish innocence. So with typical zeal he went through every book in the house that contained pictures of primitive races. When he saw a picture of a bare-breasted woman he would either cut the whole page out or else clothe the unfortunate lady with a blot of ink. In the same way, although my sister and I were devoted to animals almost as soon as we could walk, the one part of the Antwerp Zoo forbidden to us was the monkey house, for fear that we might pick up dangerous information from the animals.

Yet despite, or perhaps because of this, I seem to have spent some of the happiest years of my life with primitive races and have always had a particular affection for monkeys.

But when I think of those early years in Antwerp, I am struck by the way the seeds of my later career were clearly planted in my early boyhood. My mother once told me that I shared my first active interest in animals at the age of three when she found me breeding flies in a matchbox, and it was certainly while I was still very young that I picked up the obsessions for travel and for collecting animals that have been with me ever since. In a way, the two interests developed together. Just before the First World War, travel was remarkably cheap and every spring and summer, as soon as the Antwerp courts adjourned, the whole family would pack and be off to the most exciting places a small boy could imagine.

One spring it was the Ardennes, and it was there that I learned to catch the small wall lizards with a long piece of cane and a noose of cotton. Another year we got to Italy and my collecting graduated to the great green lizards of the Ligurian coast. From then until almost the end of my schooldays I devoted myself with true Flemish stubbornness to my lizards. My mother, who encouraged all my hobbies, went to the Zoo and inquired at the reptile house for the proper diets for my different species and my sister was soon dragged in to help me feed them.

I must have been about fourteen when my mania became such a nuisance that my father decided the time had come to put his foot down.

We were staying that year at a fairly smart hotel on the Italian Lakes. The Lakes are a lizard hunter's paradise. At daybreak, I would already be out searching and in the evening I would get back to the hotel, tired out, with the day's catch. My father had a more than average respect for the conventions of life and must have realised that lizards were simply not the thing to bring back in great quantities to a smart hotel. So one morning just before breakfast he caught me and in the kindly, judicial way he adopted with his family, delivered his verdict: "Armand, no more lizards."

Now I was a dutiful son, and in those days honestly wished to obey my father. But I also had this devotion to my lizards. What was I to do?

Not for nothing was I a judge's son, and not for nothing was I being educated by the Jesuits. I thought a while and then proceeded to interpret my father's words according to the strict letter of logic and casuistry. He had said I was to catch no more lizards. That much was clear. He had not said anything though about the lizards I possessed already, and as he had not mentioned them I would be perfectly within my rights to hold on to them.

In my eyes, these lizards were wildly beautiful. There were several dozen of them, large, well-fed, brilliantly coloured and there were also a couple of slender olive-green grass snakes to keep them company. For safety's sake, I kept them all in a large empty pillow case beneath the bed, far from the prying eyes of parents or hotel maids.

I remember that after my father spoke to me, the rest of the morning dragged atrociously. If I could not collect lizards, what else was there for me to do? So just before lunch I went up to my room to look at the animals for consolation.

In the corridor which led to my bedroom, there was a patch of sunshine. In it two lizards were basking. Lizards are not normally found in hotel corridors, and at once I feared the worst. As I opened the door another lizard scuttled by me into the passage and when I reached under the bed for that squirming pillow case, it squirmed no longer. The seam at one end had come undone, the bedroom door did not reach to the floor, and every one of my lizards and the two snakes as well, had silently disappeared.

The silence did not last long. From somewhere in the hotel I heard someone shouting. Then a door slammed. Bells started ringing, servants running, and within a few minutes the whole hotel was in pandemonium.

It was while I was sitting there on the edge of my bed that my father came in. He was wearing his overcoat and his brown bowler hat and was looking grim.

"Pack your bag," he said. "We're leaving." And leave we did that very morning without even staying long enough for lunch. A cab took us down to the station and there, very hot in our best clothes, our cases piled beside us and my father still in his brown bowler and overcoat, we waited most of the afternoon for a slow train to Milan where we spent the rest of the holiday.

I was expecting trouble from my father, but curiously it never came. He never referred to lizards again during the rest of the holiday and never alluded to the embarrassing interview he must have had with the hotel manager. To this day I do not know if the plague of lizards which suddenly struck the hotel was ever traced to us.

It was about this time that I got the habit of travelling on my own and learned the knack I have employed many times since of planning a trip so as to see the greatest number of places for the cheapest possible fare. In those days for twenty francs you could buy a season ticket allowing unlimited travel for a full five days and nights on the Belgian Railways. As soon as I discovered this, I bought myself a ticket, loaded up with five days' supply of sandwiches and set off on the most complicated schedule, stopping off at all the intermediate stations I could find. By the time the five days were up and the sandwiches were finished I must have seen three-quarters of Belgium.

I decided then that I was going to be a traveller when I grew up. I remember lying in bed in the light summer evenings with two large, highly coloured German maps of the world on the wall opposite, and minutely planning expedition after expedition. Mentally I would trace out the routes I was going to follow, the supplies I was going to take, the places I was going to see. For some reason, there were two spots on the map that intrigued me and attracted me above all others—the Galapagos Islands and Baja California, the part of California which extends beyond the United States into Mexican territory. Several times since I have planned to go to both places, and once, long before a road was built, I actually got as far as Ensenada. But I am certain now that that is as near as I will ever get to Baja California. I have always found that a journey once abandoned never takes place.

The other accomplishment I picked up as a boy was a basic skill at photography. For some reason I never used to photograph my animals in those days. All my energies went on buildings. I col-

lected whole albums of photographs of the cathedrals and churches
of Belgium and Northern France. By pure chance I happened to
have been the only person to have photographed all the windows
and the interior of St. Martin's Cathedral at Ypres. After the war
when the ruined cathedral was being rebuilt, the architects used the
pictures I took as a boy to guide them.

War—the First World War—broke out when I was seventeen,
and in a heroic mood I joined up on the very day the German
armies invaded Belgium. At this time I was an overgrown youth of
six foot four. I had been intensively schooled in the classics but
about life I knew almost nothing. Now, for the first time, the outside world broke into the tight little world of my boyhood to
complete the deficiencies of my education.

First came the collapse of my country before the German armies,
and I who had begun the war an enthusiastic volunteer in the
Belgian Army, ended it a few weeks later in an internment camp in
neutral Holland. As no one had produced a uniform large enough
to fit me, I was still wearing my civilian trousers when I was interned;
these, together with a peasant's cast-off cap and jacket, gave me an
adequate disguise. By my eighteenth birthday I had escaped from
the camp and reached Britain. I rejoined the remnants of the Belgian
Army in France, but my health had gone and after a prolonged spell
in hospital I was accepted as a refugee student at Oxford.

It was only later that I realised exactly how lucky I was in this, for
the period I spent at Oxford was one of the turning points of my life.
I stayed, as a refugee student, in the house of Mrs. Lewis. She was a
person of considerable wit and intelligence, and her two daughters
and her two sons were all accomplished literary and classical scholars.
Through them I was thrown straight into the liberal, rationalist
world of Oxford. Scientists like F. S. Haldane and D. L. Chapman
used to come to tea. The Henry Sidgwicks and the Gilbert Murrays
were frequent guests and I remember sitting through those polite
Oxford teatimes, a gauche, gangling youth, clutching my teacup
and trying to follow the conversation as these great men held forth
on the sort of subjects I had never listened to before in my life.

Before long I had completely succumbed to Oxford, and it was

Oxford that turned me from a classical scholar into a scientist. D. L. Chapman, who was doing research work for the Ministry of Munitions Inventions Board, offered me a job as an unpaid lab. assistant and within a few months I was on the way to becoming quite a competent chemist. As has happened to so many people, I found myself rediscovering in science the faith that I had begun to lose in the Church.

But the really important thing Oxford did for me was not just to turn me into a scientist but to cause me to examine and question every one of the accepted ideas with which I had grown up. For here in Oxford was a society run according to principles that my parents and my previous teachers would have condemned as heretical and probably subversive. Yet the result was a community more tolerant, more kindly, more learned and not noticeably less moral than the people I had lived with all my life in Antwerp.

This was a lesson of great importance. I have been relearning it time after time throughout my life, whether among the head-hunters of New Guinea, the pygmies of the Congo, or in the troubled land of Kenya where Michaela and I live to-day. No single group, I am convinced, ever has a right to claim a monopoly of goodness or wisdom or political sense, still less to try imposing its views on other theoretically less enlightened people in the name of religion or politics. Societies are usually best left to work these things out according to their own traditions.

But while the impact of Oxford at this point in my adolescence was to turn me into the sceptic I have been ever since, it did not really disillusion me, as it might have done. Instead of being disappointed to find that all the cast-iron beliefs I had grown up with were at best half-truths or convenient prejudices, I felt remarkably freed. Instead of feeling lost, I suddenly wanted to know more—about other societies, other peoples, and other religions. All this went to reinforce the restlessness that was already a dominant part of my make up.

But before I could be on the move again, I had to master my new trade as a chemist. I was to study in Oxford for several years at the end of the war and take an honours degree there in chemistry, but while the war was still on I was anxious to do something more immediately useful. I jumped at the chance of joining the experimental Aircraft Establishment at Farnborough—then still known as the Royal Aircraft Factory.

I worked there as a chemist for nearly two years, experimenting on aircraft fuel, lubricating oils and acetate dope. This was the great period of Farnborough. Some of the most brilliant scientists in Britain were there—men like Lindemann, Aston, C. T. R. Wilson and Sir George Thomson—and for me the experience of working among them was decisive. These men were heroes. They were not just experimenting in laboratories, but were risking their lives daily, test flying the prototype aircraft of the First World War and as I watched them walking on to the airfield or performing their precarious aerobatics above the drab landscape of Aldershot, I made up my twenty-year-old mind that this was the sort of life I wanted too. From now on I tended to look down on purely academic scientists. The scientist I admired had to be a man of action as well. My first experience of flying was at Farnborough, and I still shudder to think of the planes we flew in and the liberties we took with them.

Curiously, it was during this period at Farnborough that my interest in animals, which had lain dormant ever since I left Belgium, began to revive. It was hard to get anywhere to live close to the factory. Farnborough and Aldershot were full of soldiers and their families, so in the end I took a room for five shillings a week with an old woman who owned a cottage at Blackwater on the edge of Yateley Common.

In those days, the Common was a wild, still virtually untouched stretch of country, and every day I used to walk the four miles through the pine woods to and from Farnborough. In this way I got to know the countryside in spring, in autumn and when it was deep under snow, and I still think that the English countryside is completely unmatched in the variety and combinations of colour it offers through the seasons.

It was on these daily walks that I started observing the wild life. There were times in the evenings when I would spot a badger in the woods and spend hours following him. I began studying the birds and discovered a family of foxes living barely two hundred yards from the cottage.

That summer I spent much of my spare time getting to know their habits. It was then that I realised just how much I missed the close contact with animals that I had enjoyed before I came to England. But even lizards would have been impossible to keep in that tiny room at Yateley, and I had to wait for the end of the war and my return to Oxford before I could resume that close relationship with living animals that is almost an instinctive need of my being.

Not that Oxford itself gave me any chance of keeping animals as I would really have liked. But the vacations, and especially the four-months' long vacation in the summer, were heaven-sent opportunities for travelling and studying animals. The allowance from my father was not great, and like most students I was usually in debt, but when the vacations came I always seemed to find enough money for third-class railway tickets and cheap hotels somewhere or other in Europe.

My first long vacation I spent with my friend, Alister Hardy, at the Oceanographical Institute at Naples. He was later to become Professor of Zoology at Oxford and was already known as a brilliant young zoologist. But as I watched him working in the Institute, I realised just how different my interest in animals was from that of the professional scientist. He was working on a study of the diet of several Mediterranean fish at the time, and would spend hour after hour in his laboratory sorting over the partly digested stomach contents of a particular fish. He would have his raw material in large trays, and worked away, quite oblivious of the nauseating smell, his pipe between his teeth. He was so absorbed that on one occasion I actually saw his pipe fall in among one of his pails of fish gut. Without seeming to notice what he was doing, he picked it up, put it back in his mouth and went on with his work.

This attitude of his naturally impressed me, but was something I could not hope to follow even if I had wanted to. To me, an animal was interesting only so long as it was alive. While it lived it was a thing of wonder. When it was dead it was immediately repellent.

It was this above all that prevented me from ever becoming a zoologist myself. My interest in animals lay in watching them live, not in discovering what happened when you changed their hormone secretions. Nor could I ever convince myself that the dividing up of animals into minor sub-species was of outstanding interest or importance.

In those days I felt that chemistry, physics and mathematics were the subjects that really mattered because they were concerned with ultimate truth. Animals, on the other hand, were something to be enjoyed. If I am honest I suppose my attitude to them was sentimental rather than scientific, and compared with a dedicated scientist like Hardy, I was a mere enthusiast and dilettante, following the things that interested me rather than spending hours in the laboratory methodically pursuing truth. During this time at Naples, I spent most of my days at the aquarium, watching the life of the squids and octopuses, or else I would be out in the Bay with the fishermen in their feluccas.

Another of my expeditions led me to the great caves of Postumia on the Yugoslav side of Trieste. This time I was in search of a rare type of salamander that lived in the waters of the deep underground lakes. In the continual darkness of the caves it was blind and colourless and my friend, Julian Huxley, wanted several specimens for an experiment. According to his theory, this salamander was similar to the Mexican axolotl, a type of salamander that reaches sexual maturity without developing a land form. With the axolotl, it had proved possible to induce the aquatic form to complete its development into a land animal by feeding it on thyroid extract and Julian wished to see if the same was possible with the salamanders of Postumia.

Once again, it was not the idea of the experiment that interested me, so much as the animals themselves and I spent many days wading through the dripping caves of Postumia with a net and an acetylene lamp, searching for salamanders.

But the salamanders must have known I was coming, and although I got very wet and explored the network of caves from one end to the other, I came back from Postumia empty-handed.

It was the following year that I took my degree at Oxford. I was now a qualified chemist, but there was still a great deal I intended to do and see before I settled down. First I felt I had to make sure that I really had rejected religion as decisively as I imagined. So a few days after I had taken my finals, I packed my suitcase, put a copy of Plato in my raincoat pocket, and with an old trilby hat on my head, set off for Italy.

My objective was an ancient monastery on the Ligurian coast, very near to the now fashionable village of Portofino; the Certosa di Cervara. I had seen it several times before when I had passed through this part of Italy on holiday. It was in a magnificent position on the brow of a hill and belonged to the Carthusians, one of the strictest orders in the Church, and a few days after leaving Oxford, I was talking to the Father Superior and asking him to accept me as a novice monk.

He was an old Frenchman of great saintliness and simplicity and was understandably baffled by my request. For I explained quite frankly that I was an agnostic, but that instead of dismissing religion, I actually wanted to expose myself to it. If God did make His presence known to me I would not hesitate to accept Him.

At first he was against having a non-believer within his walls, but I argued that this was possibly a chance for him to save a soul, and finally he agreed to accept me on condition that I came to his cell for two hours every day to discuss religion.

I knew that the monastery had a reputation for strictness, but it was not until I was actually a novice monk in my cell that I realised quite how harsh the regime was. At midnight we would be awakened and for the next three hours, cold and bleary-eyed, we would chant the office in the damp chapel of the monastery. We would get to bed again at three and be called for prayers at six. There was one meal a day.

Not that any of this particularly worried me at the time. I was young and fairly strong and my days passed not unpleasantly. Part of the time I read Plato. Part of the time I discussed God with the Father Superior. And part of the time I spent in Rapallo or Santa Margherita, for I was given the job of going to market to buy food for the monastery.

In this role, I was not a complete success and the Father Superior felt obliged to relieve me of my marketing duties after I bought a dolphin from some of the local fishermen. It looked all right, but dolphin often appears better than it tastes and although I thought I had a bargain, the fish finally became an object of considerable dissension among my brother monks.

Every day my discussions with the Father Superior would continue, but after a while I realised we were getting nowhere. The subject might be personal devils or the virgin birth. We would argue until we had reached a state of complete deadlock, and the old man, obviously very upset, would say, "I can't argue. I just know I'm right but I can't argue any more. We must go to the Superior of the Capucini. He's a better theologian than I. He'll put things straight."

The Capucini had a monastery two or three miles away, and the Father Superior and I would get into his broken-down old carriage. The gardener would be summoned to harness the horse, and while he was muttering beneath his breath about the way the monks wasted his time when the vegetables needed so much attention, we would be driven over to the Superior of the Capucini.

Here, after a glass of liqueur, the argument would continue. I would explain my difficulties. My Father Superior would put his case. And then the Father Superior of the Capucini would deliver his verdict as a good theologian should.

Unfortunately, I soon realised that through these visits, I was beginning to get my monastery a bad name. The old Father Superior was being criticised for harbouring a heretic, and so finally one bright November morning, I put my Plato back into my raincoat pocket, thanked the Father Superior for his kindness and caught the morning train to Naples.

2   *A Hot Tortoise*

IF my period as a novice monk had any effect on me it was to make me more certain than ever that my life was to be dedicated to science, and I left the monastery feeling that the moment had probably come for me to take a job and settle at last. So I spent only a few weeks in Naples, and most of the time I seemed to be catching up on food and sleep.

Naturally I revisited the Oceanographical Institute, but much as I loved the fish and the other rare sea creatures in the aquarium, I realised again that by temperament I was no theoretical zoologist. By late autumn I was near the end of my allowance. There was just enough money to pay my hotel and buy a third-class ticket to Antwerp and I was home by Christmas.

My appearance must have confirmed my parents' worst fears about me. I was thin, bedraggled and looked like a tramp who had been on hard times. So it was a great relief to everyone when, early in the New Year, I announced that I had a job as a chemist with an engineering firm in Brussels, who specialised in the design and building of metallurgical coke ovens.

Coke ovens may not sound particularly romantic, but I enjoyed this period of my life immensely. My company was building a huge coke plant in the desolate colliery country near the French-Belgian border and I found I was perfectly happy working in that atmosphere of dust and sulphur, for there was considerable scope for a research chemist. People had been making coke for years without really studying how it happened and there seemed to me endless ways of increasing the chemical efficiency of the process. It was to study this that I finally left the firm I was with and obtained a job as research assistant to a Professor Charpy at the Ecole des Mines in Paris. Not that I saw a great deal of the good professor, for I got into the habit of working at night. The professor, not unnaturally, continued to work by day, and most of our contact was by the notes we left each other in the laboratory.

While I was working in Paris I made one of the most unexpected friendships of my life. This was with Dr. Marie Stopes. For as well as being an expert on sex, love and marriage, Marie Stopes was also an acknowledged international authority on coal, and it was in this secondary role that I knew her. I met her at a Congress of Industrial Heating in Paris, a tall commanding figure in a tweed suit, and I helped her with an impromptu translation of her paper on the microstructure of coal. I think that few of the scientists at the Congress can have known who she was, but I found her one of the most animated and intelligent conversationalists I have ever met. Rather to my regret, the only subjects I can never remember discussing with her are sex, love and marriage.

Apart from meeting Marie Stopes, the most memorable result of my research on coal was to get me to the United States. For after two years in Paris, I was feeling the urge to be on the move again and when the chance presented itself of a research fellowship in America under the auspices of the Belgian Relief Commission, I jumped at it.

I must admit that in the mood I was in by now, I was more interested in travelling than studying. Suddenly I wanted to get as far from Europe as I could. Consulting my atlas I found that the California Institute of Technology at Pasadena in California was located just about as far from the eastern seaboard of the United States as it was possible to go. So I set to work preparing an elaborate research project that could be carried out only at Pasadena. It was accepted without a murmur and early one September morning, accompanied by twenty-two other sober and industrious young Belgians, I set sail for New York.

I managed to take seven weeks over my journey from New York to Pasadena. Repeating the trick I had learned with my five-day season tickets on the Belgian railways, I succeeded in seeing an astonishing amount of the United States, including the Grand

Canyon on the way, and when I finally called on Dr. Robert Millikan, the Nobel prize-winning physicist who was head of Caltech at the time, I was a good month late. He told me that everyone had given me up for lost.

Even at Caltech I could not work. It was not laziness so much as sheer excitement at being in America. I had been cramped in Europe so long that the breadth and scope of this new continent went to my head. It seemed criminal not to cram as much travel and experience as possible into my time there. I saw everything avidly, from Hollywood to the Rockies, and then, five months after I arrived, remorse caught up with me.

I told myself that this was not what I had been given my fellowship for and I wrote to the C.R.B. Foundation offering my resignation. To my relief their reply suggested that since I seemed bent on travelling, the Foundation would be willing to give me a proper travelling fellowship. They knew I was interested in the co-operation between American industry and the research departments of the universities and told me to visit any institutes and universities I liked and then write a report.

Had this plan worked I would probably have ended my days teaching physics or chemistry in some Belgian university. Luckily for me it did not. I visited my universities, travelling for this purpose to almost every State in the Union ; I wrote my report ; I returned with it to Belgium and no one was remotely interested. I was told that the projects I put forward were visionary and unworkable—although everyone agreed that they worked perfectly well on the other side of the Atlantic—and after several weeks of continual discouragement, I decided that I needed the elbow room that I felt I could find only in America.

This time when I came back to America, I returned intending to stay. I took a job as a research chemist in a laboratory at Cambridge, Massachusetts, close to Harvard University, and the Massachusetts Institute of Technology, and for several years I felt that I really had found the life I wanted. For at last I seemed to have the chance of reconciling my work as a scientist with my interest in animals, and suddenly the mania for collecting animals I had as a boy made its appearance again. It began unexpectedly enough one afternoon

29

when I was driving through Connecticut and had to stop the car to avoid crushing some young turtles that were swarming across the road from a nearby pond. When I got out, I found that they were the common American *punctata* turtles and were only a few inches long, but there were hundreds of them around the pond and I could not resist taking half a dozen home with me in the back of the car.

This was only a start. Once I actually had animals like these in my house all my collector's instincts revived. I began to be as interested in turtles as I had once been in my lizards, and found it fairly easy to build up a sizeable collection of them. For New England is fine turtle country and I was soon spending my week-ends driving off, net and waders in the back of the car, to search for some sub-species that I still needed. There were Muhlenberg's and Blanding's turtles and the delicate wood tortoises. And I was particularly interested by the remarkable box tortoises and turtles. These boasted hinged flaps front and rear and so were able to retire into invulnerable isolation when startled, by withdrawing into their shells and drawing up their flaps.

Turtles and tortoises make agreeable pets and there are so many species and sub-species that they are a fascinating study for a serious naturalist. But I doubt if my collection would have grown at the rate it did had it not been for Dr. Harry Wegeforth. Dr. Wegeforth was a San Diego physician who founded the San Diego Zoo. He was also to become my deadly rival for he was the outstanding turtle lover in the United States. I soon got to know him and he was such an eager and devoted collector that I felt impelled to compete.

Both of us used to have private arrangements with the fish merchants in Fulton Street in New York to send us any unusual specimens that came their way and there was always a great battle to see which of us came off best. I would rage when I found something had been sent to him, and he would rage when he heard of something being sent to me.

Under these conditions of acute competition, my collection was soon completely out of hand and life was becoming impossible. Every bath, every tub, every wash-basin in the house had its resident turtle. Had I been strictly rational about my turtles, I would have thinned my collection out, but no real collector is entirely rational. My love was an all or nothing affair, and rather than reject some and keep others, I finally decided they would all have to go. But there was one tortoise I would not part with under any circumstances. His name was Jake. He was a very large, very handsome, very rare and very valuable tortoise from the Galapagos Islands, and I was devoted to him. But there was another reason why I felt I could not get rid of him: in police court terms, Jake was hot.

I had acquired him in an unusually roundabout way from a junior member of an expedition organised by the New York Aquarium in the 1920s to collect a number of these tortoises—already then, as now, threatened with total extinction—from the Galapagos Islands. This man had had some disagreement with the expedition and as a sort of revenge had walked off the ship at New York carrying Jake. For a while he kept him, but he had not reckoned with the serious difficulties involved in keeping a giant Galapagos tortoise in a New York apartment, and before long he wanted to get rid of him. He could not very well return him to the New York Aquarium, so I was offered him in a sort of black market deal, and was so excited at the chance of owning a thirty-pound Galapagos turtle of my own that I accepted him at once, promising absolute secrecy, and asking the minimum number of questions.

For several years, our relationship was ideal and the subject of Jake's semi-criminal status never arose. He stayed with me long after the rest of my tortoises and turtles had been dispersed and his weight grew steadily from the thirty-pound adolescent he was when I first had him, towards the three-hundred pounds which would be his normal adult weight. He was an expensive pet to keep, and I fed him on great quantities of vegetables, although his greatest partiality was for fruit, melons, paw-paw and apples, particularly apples.

It was when Jake was confronted with an apple that his personality would appear to best advantage. The one thing nobody, not even the most ardent tortoise admirer, can claim for the tortoise, is a high level of intelligence. But Jake had other qualities to compensate, the most outstanding of which was pertinacity. He would never give in, and least of all with an apple. If I gave him a particularly large apple, just too big for the spread of his jaws, he would think nothing of spending five or six hours chasing it around the room until he could wedge it in a corner where he could really bite into it. He would exhibit much the same perseverance when he got stuck under a piece of low furniture as he often did. He would not consider giving up and backing out. He would just go on, trying to push forward until the piece of furniture moved or he clawed himself a hole in the carpet or even in the wooden floor. Sometimes he would get under the chair I was sitting on, and solemnly trundle me around the room until I decided I had had enough.

Trouble began with Jake after I had moved from Massachusetts to an apartment in New Jersey. Normally he would lie quite torpid on the hot air outlet that warmed the room. Suddenly he would wake up, to embark with vast enthusiasm on some expedition around the room ; then realising the drop in temperature, he would go thankfully back to his hot air outlet. This was routine behaviour. But one day when he awoke I realised he was sick. His nose was running, his eyes were closed, and he hardly had the energy to get around the room. Jake had pneumonia.

It was now that his illegality as a tortoise suddenly mattered; he was so rare that I could not admit his existence to any of the experts who might have been able to help him without breaking my oath of secrecy.

I did my best for Jake. I nursed him through the afternoon and the evening, but his condition got steadily worse. By two in the morning, I knew that unless I got help straight away, Jake would not survive.

So I took the risk I had been avoiding all day. I rang Dr. Ditmars, the Head of the Reptile Department of the New York Zoological Society and asked his help. If he had wanted to be difficult he could have been very easily. For all the Galapagos tortoises in America were theoretically in zoos and any investigation would inevitably have involved me in extreme embarrassment. So when he came to the telephone and sleepily asked what I wanted at such an unearthly time of the night, I said, "Dr. Ditmars, I prefer not to disclose my name for reasons you will understand, but I have a Galapagos tortoise critically ill with pneumonia. Can you tell me how to save his life ? "

Well, he was magnificent. He spent the next twenty minutes telling me in great detail how I should keep my tortoise warm, how to give him an inhalant to keep his nasal passages clear and how to try camphorated oil on his throat. When he had finished, he made no attempt to find out who I was or what I was doing with a Galapagos tortoise. He just said, "Good night. Good luck to you," and hung up.

For nearly a week I followed his instructions and slowly—for tortoises take their time over everything—Jake recovered and was soon slumbering happily on the hot air duct and digging holes in my carpet again.

It was as well that he did recover, for Jake's most important role in my life was still to come. To understand how this came about it is necessary to add a little more to the story of my life as a research scientist.

As early as 1926 I had become interested in radio. To start with, I was only the merest amateur, but my interests have always had a habit of growing out of hand, and before long most of my energies were going into this new hobby. During the day I was still earning my living as a chemist, but in my spare time I was building experimental circuits and soaking up as much knowledge about radio as I could from magazines, pamphlets and even illustrated catalogues.

In these early days the whole field of radio was so wide open that an amateur like me, granted some luck and ingenuity, could still hope to stumble on a discovery of some value between breakfast-time and dinner. In my case things did not happen quite so swiftly as this and it took me eighteen months to perfect an idea I had. But by plodding away, rather as Jake did when he was pursuing an apple, I finally produced a method of automatically controlling the volume on a radio set that has been universally used on radios ever since.

Stupidly, I did not realise the full commercial value of my invention. I applied for patents of course, and then turned down a fifty-thousand dollar offer for my patent application. Instead I preferred to accept six thousand dollars for an option on the invention from a firm in New Jersey who dazzled me with promises

O.S.   33   C

of unlimited facilities in their research laboratories to develop my invention to production level.

To start with, things went well, but before long I found that I was not getting the facilities I wanted and was being led away from my own work to problems of mere routine production. The hours I was having to work grew steadily longer, and development of my invention was virtually at a standstill. It was a frustrating and a maddening situation to be in, but as I had surrendered the option on my invention there was little I could do about it.

One decisive Wednesday morning I told myself I had had enough, collected my six thousand dollars, and shook the dust of the research laboratory off my feet for ever.

This was my great escape, and the start of the sort of life I have been living ever since. But at the time it did not seem like that at all. At first, all I planned for myself was a good long holiday, as far away from cities and research laboratories as I could get. Of course I had been thinking about getting away for several months before I finally made the break and had been trying to discover the ideal place to go to.

I knew quite well what I wanted. It had to be somewhere, preferably an island as far from America as possible, that was completely untouched by the civilisation of the West. I wanted the chance of a good long sea voyage on the way, and I had decided that I was going to stay there as long as my money lasted.

My requirements may sound simple enough, but there seemed to be something wrong with almost everywhere I could think of. After a lot of inquiries, I decided that the one place in the world which would give me the peace I wanted was the island of Bali.

In those days, Bali had not been heard of by one person in a thousand. It was barely sixty miles long. It lay in the Pacific close to the western tip of Java and if everything I heard of it was true, it was an earthly paradise. The scenery was spectacular, the climate perfect, and the people were said to be a carefree, spontaneous race with a unique art of their own. Several writers commented on their natural skill as actors, and when I read of their wealth of legends and folk stories, I decided that here was all the material a film maker could ever need.

This decision of mine to make a film began as an attempt to justify to myself the highly irresponsible way in which I proposed to get rid of the first and last six thousand dollars I possessed in the world. I had done a lot of still photography, but was virtually ignorant of movie cameras. This trip, I felt, would give me a good chance to learn.

So I bought myself a pair of second-hand wooden de Brie cameras from a shop off Broadway. They cost me eight hundred dollars and included a pair of tripods and set of lenses. It was only later that I realised quite what antiques they were, even for those days.

The other equipment I needed was more cumbersome. At that time, film makers had to process their own film as they went along, so I needed things like drying racks and wooden developing tanks that were big as well as expensive. I bought only one each of these and decided that I would save money by getting them copied by local carpenters when I reached Bali.

Within a few weeks I was ready to go. I had practised filming some of my friends at home just to get the feel of my cameras and the results seemed surprisingly good. I had also remembered to have two brief lessons from a Broadway make-up artist I knew and bought a large box of assorted stage make-up for the stars of my film. There was only one problem that remained—Jake the tortoise. As I have explained, I could not give him away if I had wanted to, and I knew no one who would accept the burden of looking after an illicit eighty-pound Galapagos tortoise for me for seven or eight months. Clearly if I was going to Bali, Jake would have to come too.

Just one month after I walked out of the laboratory, I was in Boston harbour standing on the deck of the *Silver Prince*, a round-the-world freighter due to call at Bali in two months' time, and watching Jake being carefully swung aboard by one of the ship's derricks.

3 *Escape to Bali*

AS a travelling companion, Jake presented few problems. For a few days after leaving New York he stayed retired from the world in the warmth and peace of my cabin, but as we steamed into warmer latitudes his courage grew. So did his appetite. I never seemed to stop feeding him and after several false alarms when I thought I had lost him only to find him in the galley searching for food, I decided the only place for him was on deck. He enjoyed that. The crew made a fuss of him and when there was no one else to show off to and no more apples to chase, Jake would lie, day after day, watching the long wake of the ship from the shade of the awning at the stern.

All the places we stopped at he took in his stride. At Panama I took him ashore for a little exercise while the ship was being re-fuelled, but he did not appreciate that and refused to budge a step farther until I turned and started back for the ship. At Hawaii nothing would persuade him to land, and at Yokohama when I went ashore, I just left him in his favourite place on deck, well stocked with fruit. He was still there when I came back several hours later.

The real crisis of Jake's life came a few nights later when we were steaming south through the China Sea and hit a typhoon. These were the days before radar, and nobody knew about the storm until we were in the middle of it. I was flung violently out of my bunk at about three in the morning and thought at once that the ship was going down. Then, seconds later, the first officer burst into my cabin.

"What are you going to do about Jake?" he shouted. "He's

36

up on deck and he'll be battered to pieces if we don't get him pretty quickly."

The ship was bucking alarmingly and I thought the safety of the ship should be the first officer's more urgent concern than the safety of my tortoise. But he was one of Jake's most devoted admirers and there was no arguing with him. I followed him up to the after-deck, with the gale screaming in our ears and the ship plunging so deeply after each enormous wave that I thought it could never come up again. If it had not been for the first officer Jake would certainly have been washed overboard or battered against the side of the ship. As it was, we were only just in time.

In the middle of a typhoon when you are under water most of the time, an eighty-pound Galapagos tortoise is not the easiest animal to control. Somehow we managed to lasso him, then lash him down against the deck, and hope that the ropes would hold for the night. Next morning when the typhoon had passed, the first officer and I went together to release him. He was exactly where we had left him, completely unperturbed by his adventures and more anxious than ever for his breakfast.

When we reached Bali, I found that none of the extravagant praise I had heard before I left had quite prepared me for the beauty and strangeness of the island. Since then it has been developed and commercialised out of all recognition, but in those days it was still practically untouched. I lived in one of the villages on the lower slopes of the spectacular Mount Batoer and was enchanted with the life from the moment I arrived. In the mornings I would watch the ducks being herded through the village in great flocks like sheep by a man with a bamboo pole. There were primitive chickens there that had retained their ability to fly, and I would have to keep my eyes open for the great, apparently placid water buffaloes being pushed around by tiny Balinese boys. These would become un-accountably wild if they so much as smelled a European.

I even found lizards to remind me of all my collecting as a boy, although the Balinese lizards were far bigger and grander than any I had ever had.

But the greatest impression that Bali made on me was through its people. From my first contacts with them, I could see that all my preconceptions about them were entirely wrong. The Balinese were not a primitive people in any sense. They were highly civilised, but their culture and their morality were utterly different from anything I had ever known before. Essentially, they were a race of artists. In my own small village there were painters, sculptors, dancers, actors and musicians, but it was characteristic of them that when I inquired, I was told that their vocabulary contained no word for "artist." Since they were all artists and treated their art as something inevitable and instinctive, they had no need for the word.

Bali was my first real contact with a tropical country and the climate and the way of life suited me so well that I was soon having to remind myself that I had come to make a film as well as to take a holiday. So I began to unload my equipment from the packing cases in which it had arrived. Luckily there were good carpenters in the village and I soon had them building me a dark room on to the side of the hut where I lived. I also needed extra drying racks and developing tanks and again found no difficulty in discovering local carpenters who could build me perfect copies, in teak, of the equipment I possessed already.

At first, I intended simply to film scenes from the life of the Balinese people, but as I lived among them I began to learn something of the wealth of their legends and folk tales. Their whole mythology was so intricate and impressive that I decided to draw on it for my film and one of their own stories was easily adapted to form the plot of what finally became the film "Goona Goona." When I made this decision it was with all the rashness of the complete novice, but I was saved by the remarkable acting skill of the Balinese who provided me with my stars, my extras and my full supporting cast.

As it happened, Jake, the tortoise, was to play an important part in helping me find the actors and especially the actresses I needed. For, of course, I had him with me in the village and to stop him getting lost I had a small enclosure built just outside my hut. The day after I put Jake inside, I saw a procession of local girls arriving with bowls of bananas and breadfruit on their heads.

For a moment I thought that I was being honoured but the girls walked on past my door and halted solemnly by Jake's enclosure.

Jake stared at them suspiciously through his black beady eyes. Then one of the girls stepped forward, knelt reverently in front of him, and offered him her bowl of fruit. The next girl followed, and the next, until Jake was faced with a small mountain of fruit. Then the girls knelt before him once more and ceremoniously departed.

All this seemed to be something that Jake instinctively understood and he ate as I had never seen a tortoise eat before. The same thing happened in the evening, and again the following morning. From then on, twice a day, Jake was devotedly fed by processions of respectful maidens, just as if he were some local deity. I found out that this was exactly what the girls thought he was. His fame spread and the whole village was soon visiting him. Prayers would be said before him, mats were woven for him, and every day the pile of fruit and vegetables offered by the faithful seemed to increase until even Jake was finding it difficult to keep pace with it. He began getting cracks between his scales from over-eating and I had to try rationing him to stop him bursting out of his shell from sheer gluttony.

What puzzled me for some time about this cult of Jake was that there were no tortoises on the island and as far as I could find out there never had been. Later I learned the answer. The Balinese are not Malays or a Polynesian race like most South Sea Islanders. Instead they came originally from India and brought with them the old animistic rites of early Indian religion. The animals they worshipped included the tortoise, although in Bali it soon became an entirely mythical creature that was represented in Balinese carvings as a sort of large egg with three holes at each end to represent the legs, the head and the tail.

This explained the veneration Jake received the whole time I was on Bali. It was as if I had arrived in Europe with a centaur or a unicorn and I found that I was beginning to share some of Jake's prestige. By Balinese standards I suppose I ranked as his prophet or high priest, and this status of mine assured me of all the help I needed for my film.

It was not until I started preparing my camera for filming that I realised quite what an antique I had bought. The legs of the wooden tripod swelled in the tropics and I spent hours trying to sandpaper them down to make them work properly. To focus the camera there was an elaborate process of taking the back off and then punching a small hole in the first frame of the film through which you peered through the lens at the object you were filming. Then you would draw lines on the ground in front to show the actors the areas in which they could move and still remain roughly in focus. I had, of course, no light meters in those days, and had to judge the aperture completely by guesswork. But despite all these apparent handicaps, this old de Brie produced results which to-day I would never imagine possible with such primitive equipment, let alone when operated by a novice like I was.

As I worked with the local Balinese who had volunteered as actors in my film, I began to understand something of the unusual psychology of the Balinese people and how different their entire make-up was from anything I had been used to in Western civilisation.

The plot of the film was a traditional Balinese love story, about a Balinese prince and the beautiful wife of a poor coolie. The climax came when the coolie returned to find evidence of his wife's unfaithfulness in the form of the prince's richly jewelled kriss lying by their bed. Immediately, the coolie became incensed with jealousy, pursued the prince to the seashore and, after a terrific fight, stabbed him to death with his own kriss. Then, horror-stricken at having killed a royal prince, the coolie used the kriss to stab himself.

All this made for a lot of action and colour and the Balinese excelled themselves in the fights and the crowd scenes. But although the young Balinese who was playing the part of the coolie was a most accomplished natural actor, I found it impossible to make him register anger or jealousy against the prince. He would grimace in a half-hearted fashion, but although I rehearsed him several times he was quite unconvincing. I soon realised that this was because the whole idea of jealousy in this situation was completely foreign to him and to the Balinese in general.

"But just think," I said to him, "you have a young wife whom you are very much in love with. You go away on a journey. You come back and you find out that she has deceived you with another man. What would you do?"

He stared blankly at me and shrugged his shoulders.

"But you'd have to do something," I said, getting impatient. "You couldn't just accept a thing like that."

By now the young man was clearly trying very hard to be helpful and thought for a minute or so before replying.

"I know what I would do," he said. " I'd go out and get myself another wife."

I soon found that this summed up the attitude of the Balinese, not just to morality, but to life in general. They were warm, they were kindly, they were immensely tolerant, but most of the passions and extremes of emotion and ambition which plague Western man were totally incomprehensible to them.

On the whole I admired this. It certainly made life far easier and probably more enjoyable. But at the same time I always felt that there was something missing in them. Their characters lacked depth and mystery and the idea of ever forming a lifelong friendship with a Balinese was impossible.

On the other hand, superficially at any rate, Bali itself was the most beautiful place on earth. Living was easy. The people were as beautiful as the country and there seemed to be nothing to upset a way of life that had proceeded undisturbed for centuries.

But it soon dawned on me that none of this richness of culture was going to last. Almost everything on the island I so admired— the carving, the music, the decoration—was already doomed. The signs were everywhere. Bali had survived untouched for as long as it had mainly because it possessed little to attract the traders who were drawn to Sumatra and Java and the other islands of the Dutch East Indies. Now, at last, the traders had arrived and were firmly installed. Already the Balinese were eagerly buying their first bicycles and cars. Corrugated iron had begun to scar the villages. Machine-woven cotton goods from abroad had already made obsolete the old hand looms, and cheap Swiss dyes were being imported by the industrious Dutch to take the place of the rich batik dyes that had been made in Bali for centuries. The wealth of the island was beginning to drain abroad as the Balinese traded the gold that had remained in their families for years to pay for their imports. The serene isolation of Bali was about to vanish for good.

This was my first real experience of what progress means when thrust on a people like the Balinese. As a scientist I was theoretically on the side of progress and I had always been impatient of the sort of sentimentalists who always crop up to defend whatever is picturesque or inefficient or out-of-date. But gradually I realised that what was happening in Bali was something different. Progress was not replacing here—it was simply destroying. Wherever it penetrated, the old way of life seemed to crumble, and however much I tried to convince myself of the benefits that progress would bring the Balinese, I knew in my heart that their contentment would go. Their culture would degenerate into a caricature of their former civilisation to amuse the tourists. This whole rich, unique way of life around me would be turned into one more bad imitation of America.

It was this sense of loss that gave me my first real doubts about my role as a scientist. It also turned my mind to the problem of preserving and recording societies that were as valuable and as imperilled as the Balinese. From what I knew of animals, I already understood how final is the loss of a species once it becomes extinct. The world is that much poorer, the variety of nature is that much less and no amount of sorrow or ingenuity can ever restore it. With a people the loss suddenly seemed even greater and more absolute, and it appalled me to think that within a few years something as vital and as beautiful as the culture of Bali could vanish from the earth as decisively as the dodo or the great auk.

I had my cine camera, and after a fashion the film I made became an irreplaceable record of the world of Bali that has now gone for ever. But I had no sound recording equipment. My cameras were inadequate for the sort of task I had in mind, and I decided then that if I had the chance again to visit other unusual human groups, I was going to be properly equipped to place them on record for ever.

But while I was in Bali it was impossible to remain too worried by the future for long. All the time I was shooting "Goona Goona" I was learning my future trade as a film-maker, and when I was not occupied with this, there was the animal life of the island for me to discover.

Almost before I knew where I was I had three grey Java monkeys living in the hut as pets. One of them called Sakiet became my inseparable companion. Sakiet is the Balinese for "ill," "depressed," and this young monkey had a look of perpetual unhappiness. But he was the most amiable of all the monkeys I ever had. Normally, a monkey is not particularly trustworthy, and the moment always comes, sooner or later, when he loses his temper and buries his teeth in your arm in an access of sudden rage. But this never happened with Sakiet. Something of the easy-going tolerance of Bali itself seemed to have rubbed off on to him, and even when I had taken him back with me to the States, he still remained his sad, kindly self.

Monkeys were by no means the only animals Bali had to offer. West Bali, in contrast to the mountain country where I was making my film, had a terrain of rich parkland and in those days there were still tigers to be found there. I planned to go there several times and finally got my chance when an American yacht arrived at Bali manned by a crew of students from Yale and Harvard.

They were anxious to see the whole of the island, especially when I mentioned the tigers to them, so I joined the boat for a few days and set sail for the virtually uninhabited western coast of Bali.

When we landed we spent a long time looking for tigers but without success. Wherever the tigers of Bali were remained a secret that the combined resources of Yale and Harvard could not uncover. But when we had given up our search I discovered something far more exciting. As I walked along the beach on the way back to the yacht, I noticed the tracks of a startlingly large animal coming out of the sea and disappearing into the bushes at the top of the beach. These tracks were enormous, with a five-foot spread between them and when I followed them I saw that they led into a sort of tunnel through the bushes. I hesitated a while and listened carefully in case the animal was still around but there was no sound. So I crawled in myself and followed for thirty or forty yards until it opened out to a pool of fresh water standing amid the trees.

The tracks I had followed were those of a giant sea crocodile; I had heard the local fishermen speak of them with considerable awe and say that they often came up from the sea and spent some time ashore in fresh-water pools before returning again to the sea where they lived. As the tracks pointed only one way, I knew that my crocodile must still be there. But although I peered into the water I could see no sign of him and decided that the only way to set eyes on him would be to wait until he returned seawards of his own accord.

I knew I was probably in for a long wait. So I told the boys on the yacht and together we kept up a vigil for the rest of the afternoon and the whole of the night. We had brought blankets with us and made ourselves comfortable. Finally, all of us must have nodded off.

I woke just before dawn. The crocodile had come and gone while we slept. In a neat circle round the place where we had been lying went the huge footprints I had seen the previous day. When I followed them I saw that they led back to the sea. In the early morning the crocodile had come out of the pool, seen us, walked round to investigate and then gone on his way. I reminded myself of the passage in Boulanger's authoritative book on reptiles, in which he states that the marine crocodile is the only one of the crocodile family that will attack a man on land without provocation.

I woke the students and we raced down to the edge of the surf. It was light by now and we could actually see the crocodile about a hundred yards off-shore, floating like the trunk of a very large tree. He was lying there peacefully, and as far as I could judge was between twenty-five and thirty feet long. We climbed aboard a native canoe and paddled out cautiously towards him, but when we got close one of the students disturbed him by trying to stand up to take a photograph. With a flip of his great tail he submerged, swimming right beneath us so that I could see the dark olive-grey of his skin. That was to be my last sight of a marine crocodile for nearly twenty-five years.

4   *An Interlude with Snakes*

BALI was the nearest I ever got to paradise. I found the peace and beauty of the island growing on me, and I sometimes wonder whether I would ever have left had the *Silver Prince* not called again four months after I arrived to remind me that it was time to be getting back to America and reality.

I had my film to sell and my career as a research scientist to pick up. So, reluctantly, I said good-bye to my actors and actresses, packed the old de Brie cameras and climbed sadly aboard the *Silver Prince* with my three monkeys. I had not the heart to take Jake away from an island where life was so good for a tortoise of such sanctity.

It was during the slow journey back to Boston with time to think over the events of the last four months, that I began to realise how much Bali had changed me. When I had gone there I had been a scientist. All my attitudes had been those of a scientist and nothing had previously made me doubt the supreme importance of discovering and inventing and progressing as fast as possible.

Now I still felt that my career would have to continue in science but all the old urgency had gone. Progress was not as important as it had seemed before, and to me it hardly mattered whether a particular scientific advance came this year, or in ten years' time. What did seem important was to find a means of halting the destruction progress seemed to bring with it and preserving the fullest possible record of places like Bali before they were lost for ever.

While I was thinking about this, the *Silver Prince* was steaming steadily across the Indian Ocean, and suddenly I had a minor scientific crisis of my own on my hands. A brine pipe that went through my cabin sprung a leak shortly after breakfast and by the time it was discovered the whole cabin was awash in a foot of salt water. When I went in to see what had happened, the first thing that met my eyes was a tangled mass of film negative floating on the surface of the water. The tins containing my precious film were afloat, and half a dozen of them had burst, spilling their contents into the brine that was sloshing gently from side to side with the motion of the ship. I was lucky to discover what had happened before the disaster was complete.

As it was, everyone aboard came to my aid. The bathtubs were filled with fresh water and all the film that had been affected by the brine was hurriedly washed. Even so, a few rolls were irretrievably damaged as the emulsion had already started to slough off in great patches. But I could see that most of the film could still be saved if only I could find an effective way of drying it.

To do this, I planned to stretch ropes from rail to rail across decks of the ship, winding the film from rope to rope to dry. When I tried this, however, I soon found that there was a stiff breeze blowing and that it was carrying up enough spray on to the deck to spot the film and make it useless.

When I pointed this out to the captain, he was most upset and insisted on turning the ship round and steaming downwind for more than a hundred miles until the film had been completely dried and rewound. By now I thought my troubles were over for that day, but I was being altogether too optimistic. As I was re-winding the film on to the spools, I noticed something peculiar about it. Although the film had been properly developed, the dark-ness of the negative fluctuated regularly every five or six feet. In-stead of being developed uniformly as it should have been, it seemed that the whole of my film suffered from these strange variations.

I soon realised what had happened. To develop the film in the dark-room in Bali, it had been wound vertically on to large wooden racks and then dipped into deep wooden tanks full of developer. After a while, I had trained a team of three Balinese who did all the developing for me, and I had left them to get on with it. I used to check that they were working properly, but one thing I had ob-viously forgotten to remind them about was to stir the developer in the tanks. Obviously a considerable difference in temperature had gradually appeared between the bottom and the top of the tank. The section of film at the bottom of the rack had been getting developed far more intensively than that at the top and had produced these disastrous fluctuations.

No audience was ever going to sit through a film that flickered from light to dark every few seconds. But as I thought about it, I began to see that there might be a way of saving my film after all. Essentially, this problem of the variations of intensity on the negative was similar to the changes of volume on a radio set that I had had to deal with when I invented my automatic volume control eighteen months earlier. Once we started printing, if I could only vary the light automatically to match the degree of darkness on the negative the result would be a perfect print.

I became convinced that we could do this, and spent the rest of the voyage working out the electronic circuits I would need.

By the time we docked at Boston, I had the solution in theory. To put it into practice, I needed the help of one man. His name was Dr. Mees and he was head of the research laboratories of Eastman Kodak at Rochester.

But by this time I was almost completely broke. I had sold everything to make the film and the film was now the only capital I possessed. If I was to do anything with it, I had to get to Rochester and Dr. Mees straight away.

It was snowing in Boston, and when I had spent my last dollars buying tickets for the three monkeys and myself, I found that I had to get them aboard the train to Rochester in the teeth of a howling blizzard. It was a harsh homecoming.

If you seriously intend keeping animals, you soon learn to stop worrying about being considered an eccentric by the public at large, but during that journey I felt myself sympathising with my fellow passengers when they saw me, huddled in one corner of the compartment with three frozen monkeys.

I had never met Dr. Mees before, although I knew of him by reputation and had written to him for advice about my film and equipment before leaving for Bali. But from the moment I reached Rochester and telephoned him to explain my plight, he was help-

47

fulness itself. He discussed my plans for automatically correcting and printing my film with obvious scepticism, but he nevertheless put laboratory facilities at my disposal and, with great kindness, offered to lend me money to pay for my hotel.

For six weeks I worked non-stop to perfect a machine that would save my film; in the end I succeeded. The machine produced a perfect print of all the footage which had been saved from the brine bath. More important still for my immediate purposes, the Eastman Kodak Company became interested in the automatic printing device, and on the strength of it Dr. Mees offered me a job in his research laboratory. It meant coming back to the laboratory routine I had escaped from when I went to Bali, but I knew I would not be independent until I had edited my Bali material into a saleable film, and gratefully accepted.

As it turned out, the arrangement was to be most satisfactory. I moved to a company-owned cottage that was ideal as a home and ideal for the animals. At the same time, I got the chance, through Dr. Mees, of working on a line of research very close to my heart. The Eastman Kodak Company was concerned at the time with developing new methods of recording sound on film; I had the basic knowledge for this and was soon able to become something of a specialist in sound recording techniques.

Rather to my surprise, I found that I settled down to life in Rochester. This was partly because I got on so well with many of the unusual people who made up the staff of the laboratory. In the room next to mine, for instance, were two young musicians—not chemists or physicists, but musicians—who were working away on a project that had been unofficially christened "Dr. Mee's Folly." Leopold Godowski was a virtuoso violinist. Leopold Mannes was a pianist. While they had still been at music school, they had become obsessed with photography and had formed the absurd idea—absurd to anyone but themselves and apparently Dr. Mees—that they could invent a system of colour photography. I used to lunch with them most days when I was at the laboratory and although I enjoyed their company I never fully made up my mind whether they were geniuses or misguided optimists. Little did I know, when Mannes and Godowski made me look through a magnifying

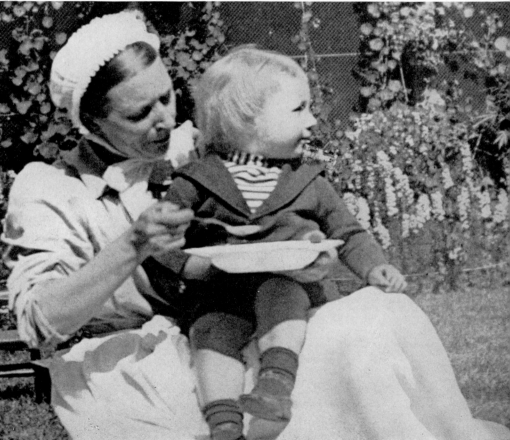

Below, the author with his nurse at Ypres. Above, his parents:
"my father was something of a puritan and a stern disciplinarian"

Balinese landscape. The Balinese were natural actors with a wealth of legends and folk stories which were the basis for the author's film 'Goona Goona'

Bali. "I saw a procession of girls"

The author and Frank Buck. "At this time Frank Buck was one of the heroes of America"

Two African elephants

Elephants "like some solid grey army on the march"

An African elephant. "You start off by thinking they are very large and very simple. Then you gradually realise that however long you study them you will never entirely understand them"

On the 'Station de Capture et de Dressage des Eléphants' at Gangala-na-Bodio in the Congo, almost the only place where African elephants were taught to work

glass at experimental bits of coloured film, that I was actually witnessing the birth of Kodachrome film.

Since 1942, when I changed from shooting my film in black and white to colour, I must have used over three-quarters of a million feet of their film myself, and I often think of those two young musicians I used to have lunch with in the Eastman Kodak canteen and how much I have depended on their invention for my own living during the last twenty years.

Another reason why I found the routine of life agreeable at Rochester was that the hours suited me. I had previously been in the habit, when engaged on a research project, of working late at night and as there seemed little point in returning home at three or four in the morning, I often worked through the night and into the next day. I had no regular hours of sleep, for work or for meals, and certainly not for leisure. This sort of thing was not encouraged by the Eastman Kodak Company—it was not even permitted. At 5.30 you were supposed to go home, and home you went, even though you felt that a momentous discovery was just around the corner.

So, for the first time in my life, I had leisure—long evenings and long week-ends. The inevitable consequence was a renewal of my interest in animals.

The neighbours complained when I began building a large cage for the monkeys in my back garden, but luckily, about this time, the Eastman Kodak Company decided to offer me $5,000 for the patent of the automatic printer. I accepted, and on the strength of this I was able to move into a larger house just outside the town where I could give my animals the sort of accommodation they deserved. I had a large, centrally-heated study and the three monkeys had a room to themselves. At last I felt free to collect any animals I wanted and for my new collection I decided on snakes.

Although I had had grass snakes as a boy, I had never been able to collect snakes seriously before because of the shortage of space, and the prejudice of people round about. Most people have an entirely illogical horror of snakes that I have never really been able to share or understand. For I have always had a weak spot for them. I find their movements graceful. I admire the neatness of their construction. Their efficiency appeals to me and I think of the texture and the decoration of their skin as the nearest nature gets to jewellery in an animal.

Of course, you need patience with snakes, and with those rather less common varieties which are provided with venom and fangs you do have to exercise a great deal of care, but the United States are a snake collector's paradise and there are probably more snakes per square mile in New York State than in any tropical area of the world.

There are not only the garter snakes with their widely diversified markings on olive skins, but the startling milk snakes, with the silver and mahogany of their colouring forming a brilliant pattern. There are also the green grass snakes, the ring-necked snakes, the red-bellied snakes and many others.

The local poisonous, and decidedly dangerous snakes are the copperheads and the rattlesnakes, as forbidding looking and as handsome as any of the tropical snakes although, in my opinion, they are less aggressive and far less frequently fatal. Often when people have died as the result of a rattlesnake bite, it is because they have literally been scared to death, or else because they have drunk so much whisky as a supposed antidote to the venom, that their natural resistance has gone.

I captured my own rattlesnakes and copperheads, of course, and was rather proud of them.

Then unexpectedly, my interest in snakes became quite useful. A subsidiary of Eastman Kodak, called Eastman Teaching Films, heard of my collection and commissioned me to make a film on the reptiles of North America. They reached this decision just as the northern New York State winter began in all its harshness; hardly the season for snakes. But I made the film with my old de Brie camera, in my double garage which I converted into a studio. In the middle of the garage I rigged up a stage with sand, pebbles and cactus plants borrowed from a local flower shop to imitate the landscape of Arizona and the Painted Desert. Luckily the house was already full of horned toads, gila monsters, hog-nosed snakes, and alligators, and I managed to obtain specimens of the other poisonous snakes of North America—coral snakes from Florida and cottonmouth moccasins from Georgia.

Every evening I toiled away in my improvised studio, muffled up to the ears in heavy overcoat, woollen scarf and sheepskin lined boots, with the snow blowing in through the cracks around the doors, several oil stoves going full blast, and 2,000 watts of artificial sunshine pouring down from a pair of sun lamps upon the hapless lizards in my synthetic cactus garden.

For a crested iguana I had to send all the way to Snake King's Reptile Emporium at Brownsville, Texas; the poor creature arrived at my house during a particularly cold spell, and when I opened his box I found him stiff with cold. I felt sure he had succumbed to the rigours of the journey, but placed on the stage under the heat of the 2,000 watt lamp, he surprisingly revived—not only well enough to play his part in the film quite creditably, but to become a pet who lived in my household for many months and apparently thrived— all five feet of him. He was emerald green in colour, with a mag- nificent scaly crest and a kindly, gentle disposition.

By the time I had finished the Eastman film, my collection ran to well over 200 specimens. I had enjoyed making the film and had learned a great deal about reptiles of North America in the process.

But a film like this was a poor substitute for the sort of filming I had already had a taste of in Bali, and it was while I was making this teaching film that I began to get my first twinges of restlessness again. One plan I had which, if successful, would set me travelling again involved old Mr. Eastman himself. I had got to know him quite well during the first months I was working for the company. By then, of course, he was aged and ill; I suppose he was already suffering from cancer. He was giving away much of his immense fortune to build Eastman Dental Clinics in different cities throughout the world. But he was still interested in travel and while I was editing my film from Bali, he had specially asked to see some of the footage. I showed it to him in the private cinema in his house.

He liked what he saw, and after this used to invite me to his house quite often. He had, in his lifetime, given away millions of dollars to music. He had his own private organist—you always heard an organ playing inside his enormous mansion when you entered—and it was this that persuaded me to mention the music of Bali to him. There was just a chance that he might forget about his dental clinics for a moment.

"Music has always meant so much to you, Mr. Eastman," I said. "Why don't you arrange to record the music of Bali. It's unique and it's not going to last. If someone like you does not have it recorded, it will be lost for ever."

The old man looked at me thoughtfully.

"Tell me, Mr. Denis," he said at last. " These Balinese of yours. What are their teeth like?"

Without thinking what I was saying, I replied, "Their teeth are fine, Mr. Eastman. They have no dentists. The Balinese will lose their music long before they lose their teeth."

That was the end of the conversation, and of my chances of getting to Bali on a recording trip sponsored by the Eastman Kodak Company. But luckily my friendship with Mr. Eastman survived and it was through him that I met the two people who were truly the pioneers of what I would be doing myself within a few years. Their names were Martin and Osa Johnson. Martin Johnson was a gentle, dedicated man who had been a small town photographer in Kansas before going to sea with Jack London as a cook on one of his voyages. This had given him an insatiable love of travel, and after he had married Osa, the two of them had formed a husband and wife team driving across Africa and Asia and filming as they went.

The two of them became close friends of Eastman. He used to back their trips and they would always visit him at Rochester to show him their latest films after one of their journeys. I met them there several times and saw many of their films in Eastman's private cinema. I admired the Johnsons greatly, but I also felt sure that if I could only get enough backing and experience, I could make better films than theirs. If I could do this, nothing should stop me having their sort of life and travelling wherever I wanted.

For by this time, despite my animals and my friends at the laboratory, I was feeling my old urge to travel again. For the first time in my life, I began to resent the size and sameness of America. There was nothing wrong with Rochester. I still think of it as one of the most agreeable provincial towns in the States. But on a Friday night I would plan a week-end vacation, load my old Packard and drive five or six hundred miles, only to arrive at exactly the same sort of town as the one I had left, with the same church, the same bank, the same Woolworth ten-cent store and the same people.

In Europe, or in the parts of Asia I had seen on my way to Bali, a drive like that would have taken me through several countries and shown me an endless variety of race, of architecture, of custom. Here it was as if I had stayed on exactly the same spot and suddenly this physical sense of the size and uniformity of America seemed to sum up the effect that science and progress were having everywhere throughout the world. Richness and variety were constantly succumbing to sameness and uniformity and I suddenly felt an almost obsessive compulsion to see what was left of the world before it was too late.

Something inside me told me that if I went on playing it safe, I would regret it for the rest of my life and I made up my mind that I would gamble on any good chance that offered. The chance came sooner than I expected.

For several months after I settled in Rochester I had been working in my spare time on the film I had shot in Bali. I had had to teach myself film editing by watching other films at the local cinema, so that the whole process of cutting the material into a complete eighty minute performance, took far longer than it would to-day. I had an old Moviola viewing machine that I kept in one of the bedrooms, and I would work laboriously away at, it running the reel of films through one by one and over and over again, and snipping out the footage I wanted with a pair of scissors.

But finally my film was complete. All I had to do was to sell it. Here, of course, my absolute ignorance of the film world began to show. I had not the slightest idea how to sell a film, or even how much it was worth. I had to learn the hard way. For several months I had a terrible time travelling into New York whenever I could find the time from the laboratory and doing the rounds from the agents to the film companies and from the film companies back to the agents again.

I sat through "Goona Goona" countless times in the attempt to sell it, but the reaction always seemed to be the same. It was "too arty" for America. It was very pretty, "But hell, who's interested in a place called Bali?" and I would take the train back to Rochester with my cans of film, unsold and apparently unwanted.

Then, when I had really given up all hope about the film, I heard from an agent I had seen several months before. He wanted a print of the film. He wanted it in a hurry, and the next thing I knew was that he had sold the distribution rights in France for $35,000, and "Goona Goona" was showing for sixteen weeks at the Marigny Theatre on the Champs-Elysées.

After this, the story of "Goona Goona" in America was even more remarkable. The agent sold it for American distribution on the strength of its success in Paris. The film made a lot of money—really a lot of money—for some people. If I had not been so green and ignorant of the film business, it would have made a lot of money for me too. But I watched, appalled and slightly dazed, as the film companies turned on a super-heated publicity campaign to exploit the film on Broadway. When I went to attend the opening and saw that they were selling "Goona Goona" milk-shakes in the milk-bars around Times Square—there were also "Goona Goona Sundaes" in the drugstores; recipe: two scoopfuls of chocolate ice-cream, side by side, topped by two maraschino cherries—I knew that I had finally arrived.

5 "*Wild Cargo*"

IT was several months after I had sold "Goona Goona" that a telegram arrived at my house in Rochester, asking me to come to New York at once. The signature was that of a prominent film backer, but I was sceptical of film men by now and did not bother to reply. A few days later, another telegram arrived from him, more urgent than the first. There were several things I wanted to do in New York and this seemed as good an excuse to go as any other, so I cabled back that I was coming and took a couple of days off from the laboratory.

I had no experience of film moguls at this time, and at first was rather puzzled by the man I met. He was a tall, sad-looking individual with an office in Wall Street and he spent the first ten minutes of our conversation saying how much he had enjoyed "Goona Goona." But I knew he had not paid my fare to New York merely to be polite about a film he probably had not even seen and I waited to find out what he really wanted.

There was a slight pause in the conversation, and I gathered the preliminaries were over.

"What d'you know about Frank Buck?" he asked, watching me carefully.

"Buck?" I said. "I've never met him, but if half of what I've read about him is true he must be quite a man."

This was something of an understatement, for at this time Frank Buck was one of the heroes of America. The Buck legend had started with a series of articles in Colliers Magazine with the rousing title of "Bring 'em Back Alive," describing how this tough, resolute adventurer with the tropical helmet and the Errol Flynn moustache

roved the jungles of the world to bring back wild animals to the
zoos and circuses of the United States. The articles were well written.
They captured the popular imagination and Frank Buck had been
an overnight success.

"We've just finished a film with Buck called 'Bring 'Em Back
Alive'," said the film man. " He's making a million. We want him
to start on another straight away. There's big money in Buck.
We'd like your help."

"What sort of help?" I said.

"I'd like to be honest with you, Mr. Denis," replied the film
man, puffing at his cigar. "Don't misunderstand me. Frank's a
wonderful fellow and he's going to be great box office. He knows
how to act, but, confidentially, we think he's taking too many risks
with these animals of his."

"But isn't that his job?" I said innocently.

"Sure," replied the film man. "I tell you he's a wonderful guy.
But he's worth a lot of money to a lot of people. We want someone
to keep an eye on him—someone like yourself who knows about
animals. This new film of his has locations all over the world and
we don't want anything to go wrong, if you understand what I
mean."

Our eyes met and I understood what he meant all too well.

"What you need is a director," I said.

"Sure," he said easily. " If you want to be a director, the job's
yours."

"You say the film's on location around the world. Where?"

The film man waved airily with his cigar. "Everywhere there's
wild animals. Ceylon for elephants, India for tigers, Malaya for
cobras. If you know where to find a sabre-toothed tiger outside the
Natural History Museum, you can go there as well."

It all seemed slightly absurd, but a year around the world at a
film company's expense was too much to resist. So when I caught
the train back from New York that evening I carried a signed contract to direct Frank Buck in a film called "Wild Cargo" at two
hundred and fifty dollars a week, plus a substantial percentage. It
was only during the months to come that I discovered what the
contract really involved.

To start with, everything went at a great pace. Nobody in Rochester seemed particularly surprised when I announced I was leaving to make another film, and when I explained that I would be working with the great Frank Buck they were reassuringly impressed. Of course, my animals were something of a problem. I had to take the snakes and lizards to suitable places of the woods to release them. As for the three Balinese monkeys, they seemed quite happy to find a home in the Rochester Zoo, and less than a month after I had signed my contract I was back in New York, meeting Frank Buck and all ready to sail on the "Wild Cargo" expedition.

I found Buck something of an enigma. He seemed very much on his dignity from the start. He was every bit as good-looking as his photographs, but whenever I asked him about any of his animals, he would usually manage to change the subject. I remember asking him what equipment he would be taking for the jungle. "Jungle?" he said. "I intend to stay at the Raffles Hotel in Singapore and I think they'll have most of the equipment I need there already."

On the voyage across the Atlantic we kept out of each other's way and agreed to split the party after we had arrived at Southampton. Buck embarked straight away on a P. & O. ship sailing to Singapore, and gave his address as the Raffles Hotel. I took the camera team with me—Roy Phelps and Nick Cavalieri—and made separate arrangements to travel to Ceylon, fixing a date six weeks ahead when we would all meet again in Singapore to complete the film.

This suited me excellently, for apart from giving me a chance to get used to the camera team on my own, it also allowed me to spend a few days in Antwerp before crossing Europe by train to pick up a boat at Genoa. This was the first time I had seen my parents for several years and I was glad to find them completely unchanged. My father, of course, made a great show of pretending to disapprove of what he called "my Americanisation" and also of my films. His attitude was that it was not quite dignified for a judge's son to allow himself to get mixed up with the cinema.

But at the same time he was clearly fascinated by what I was doing. During the four days we were in Antwerp we made a short film on the city and my father insisted on helping. He even consented to act as an extra for us and I filmed him buying some flowers from a stall in the flower market, but I noticed that as soon as we had finished filming, he handed the flowers back to the woman and got his money back. I should explain that my father was not mean. He was what the French call "économe." He believed that money should be prudently laid out for certain definite ends, and that to waste money was not only immoral, but one of the highest forms of stupidity.

From Genoa, we had a leisurely journey out to Ceylon and to start with, everything about this new life of mine seemed perfect. Buck was several thousand miles away in Singapore. I had excellent cameramen who proved to be loyal and good companions, and Ceylon itself seemed to be overflowing with suitable scenes of wild life for our film.

First we filmed the Keddha, the spectacular annual round-up of wild elephants from the forest. This was my first sight of elephants in the wild and I was fascinated as I watched them being stampeded into the great stockade where they were sorted out, the young ones released and the most likely looking animals selected for training.

But what impressed me even more than the wild elephants were the tame ones the elephant owners used to train the new arrivals. Each freshly captured elephant was assigned a mahout and a reliable "monitor"—an elephant specially trained to look after the new capture and accustom it to the ways of men. I was soon to see an example of just how intelligent these monitor elephants could be.

Once a year in Kandy, the capital of Ceylon, a great celebration is held to mark the day when the temple acquired the tooth that is said to be the tooth of the Buddha himself. It is all intensely colourful, with pilgrims flocking in from the whole of southern India. The climax of the day consists of a great procession in which as many as a hundred and fifty elephants take part, and I decided that here was a scene that could have been made for our film.

The only trouble was that the procession took place at night and in those days I had had little experience of night filming. Of course I knew how to do it in theory. In those days, you used large magnesium flares that burned like fireworks. What I did not know was just how fiercely these things ignited, throwing out showers of sparks and clouds of white smoke, and that once they had been lit nothing on earth could extinguish them until they had burned out of their own accord.

Our luck seemed to be in when I discovered that the procession was due to pass directly in front of our hotel. So a couple of hours after sunset we stationed our cameras on the balcony, set up the flares and waited. We still had some time to spare although the crowds below became steadily denser, and it was nearly midnight before we heard the noise of the procession approaching. First came the men with the drums and the torches. Then followed the dancers, the acrobats, the jugglers and the holy men. And last of all, with great dignity, making their stately way to the temple, came the elephants, richly caparisoned, carrying elaborate howdahs in each of which stood three or four priests or dignitaries. This was the moment I wanted and when the largest and most impressive of the elephants was right in front of the balcony, I gave the signal to light the flares and start the cameras.

If I had realised how dangerous this was going to be I would never have done it, for not only did I completely underestimate the brilliance of the flares, but I also failed to notice the two younger elephants walking on either side of the great bull I was so keen on getting in the centre of my picture. These two elephants had been captured less than a year before and were still not properly trained. Hardly had the flares been lit when they began to panic.

They stopped dead. They began to bellow. Their ears went forward, and I thought that at any moment one of them would charge. The crowd thought so too, and there was pandemonium as everyone tried to disperse through the narrow alleys and the crowded side streets.

It was a terrible thing to watch, knowing that I was responsible for the situation, and that there was nothing I could do about it. The flares were burning away with a loud hissing noise, and were completely inextinguishable. If one elephant charged I knew that hundreds of people would be crushed to death, and all I could do was to watch, powerless, from my balcony, hoping that someone would manage to calm the elephants before it was too late.

At the last moment, the elephants were calmed but not by anyone in the crowd. I saw the old bull elephant that I had been so anxious to film, calmly raise his trunk and place it reassuringly on the neck of the young elephant on his left. Then he did the same with the one on his right and they calmed down just as horses will when someone they know pats them on the shoulder. Those flares seemed to burn for ever, but all the time the old elephant kept calming the two others, and the procession went forward without any trouble.

Luckily we had recorded the entire scene on our cameras so that when we left Ceylon for Singapore a few days later, I was certain that "Wild Cargo" was already well on the way to becoming a great success. But I had reckoned without Frank Buck.

I called on him as soon as we arrived at Singapore. Although he was very affable, he seemed to have not the remotest interest in the film we had shot in Ceylon. He had a projector in his suite and we ran several of the best scenes that afternoon but he kept shaking his head.

"It's no good, Armand," he'd say as the elephants thundered in through the stockade at the Keddha. "There's just no kick in this stuff. It's not what folks pay their money at the cinema to see."

Well, I thought, he should know what he is talking about. So when the scenes were finished and Buck suggested taking me out to his camp to show me the arrangements he had made for the next day's filming, I went along in the hope of finding out what he thought an animal film should be.

"Armand," he said, when we were sitting comfortably in the back of his car, " that stuff of yours was fine but tame. Far too tame. Now I've a wonderful idea."

He leant back and puffed at his cigarette.

"Now how's about a fight to the death between a tiger and an orang-utan?"

I thought he was joking and started to laugh before I realised he was in deadly earnest.

"Well," I said cautiously, " orang-utan occurs in Borneo and Sumatra; there are tigers also in Sumatra, so it is not inconceivable that an orang-utan and a tiger could meet—but surely if they did, they'd just avoid each other. Animals don't normally fight to the death for nothing."

"Don't they, eh?" replied Buck. "When I'm around they do."

Buck's camp, which I had imagined to be somewhere in the heart of the jungle, was a great disappointment to me. It was a hundred yards or so off the main road, in Johore Bahru, just across the causeway from Singapore, on the edge of a rubber plantation. The camp was indeed conveniently near to the Raffles Hotel, the race track and the other amenities of Singapore, but it was not even faintly reminiscent of jungle. It consisted mainly of a few cages containing a variety of despondent-looking animals, and of a number of enclosures more or less ingeniously camouflaged and in which obviously the animals were to be placed for various scenes to be photographed. With a sinking heart I began to realise what was expected of me.

The best example of how things would be staged was a scene involving Frank Buck and a tiger. The general idea was that somewhere deep in the jungle, Frank Buck had set a trap for a huge man-eating tiger. The trap was to be a carefully concealed pit and after several days of waiting, the tiger was to fall in. But then there was to be trouble. Because of torrential rain, it was to prove impossible to bring out the infuriated animal by normal means and Buck was to be lowered into the pit himself to bring out the tiger single-handed. Armed with nothing more lethal than a lasso and a whip between his teeth, he was to truss the man-eater up like a chicken and then watch him being dragged harmlessly out.

Buck proudly explained the theme to me soon after I arrived in Singapore, and took me out to the camp one afternoon to show me the arrangements he had made to shoot the scene. The location was on a stretch of low-lying waste land near the causeway connecting Singapore and the mainland. The pit had been dug. The location was lined all round with a dense mass of bamboo and undergrowth specially brought to make it look like a patch of deep jungle and Buck told me that the tiger would be brought over to-morrow for the shooting to start.

I was puzzled to see a large red fire-engine standing close to the pit, its engine chugging away, and asked Buck what part it had to play in the scenario. He explained that they had had trouble with the pit filling with water which was seeping in faster than it could be bailed out with buckets. He had had the idea of telephoning the Singapore Fire Brigade who had obligingly lent this engine of theirs to keep the pit pumped dry. The pipe was well concealed and all seemed well.

Shooting was due to begin next morning, and Roy Phelps, Nick and I were out at the location early. The fire-engine was still there chugging away, and a few minutes after we arrived, a large truck drove up. Inside was one of the stars for the day's filming—a large placid old tiger specially hired from a local animal dealer. As he was taken out of the truck, I thought he had one of the kindest faces I had ever seen.

While we were waiting for Buck to arrive, some of the men started fitting the tiger into a special harness that had been made for him. This was to keep him in check during the film whenever Buck approached him, and the success of the film would depend on the skill with which the film editor cut out the excessively revealing parts afterwards.

The old tiger submitted to all this in an amiable sort of way and when he had been carefully buckled up and lowered into position in the pit, Frank Buck arrived.

He really was most impressive with his gleaming boots, his immaculate jodhpurs, and his great rhinoceros-hide whip. He did not speak much, but the cameramen knew what to do and the filming of the preliminary scenes started. The tiger was filmed in his apparently desperate attempt to get out of the pit. Buck's assistants appeared, cowering with fright, and then Buck himself was shot peering down at the tiger and calmly evaluating the situation.

We were just about to get on with the real climax of the film where Buck descended into the pit, when we had an interruption. It began to rain—a sudden torrential downpour.

Further filming was out of the question, and we all had to take refuge in the camp until the shower was over.

When the rain cleared and we returned to the pit, disaster had struck. The heavy rain had washed great chunks of mud into the pit, choking the pump of the fire engine. The water level inside the pit had risen several feet and the old tiger, held as he was in his harness, had quietly drowned.

In my innocence, I thought that would have to be the end of the scene or certainly of shooting for that day until we got another tiger, but Buck had other ideas. The pump was cleaned out and started again. Then, when the pit was pumped dry, Buck gave the signal for the shooting to start.

It was quite a scene and Frank Buck was at his most impressive. He advanced towards his adversary, and for breathless minutes he did battle with the corpse of the drowned tiger. When I saw the finished film on the screen back in New York a few months later, I was surprised to find the battle with the tiger remarkably convincing.

If I had been free I would have walked out of "Wild Cargo" soon after I arrived, but I had signed a contract to make the film and Buck, given the privilege of choosing all the locations, animals and episodes, was virtually the boss.

So I stayed on in Singapore for several months until the filming of "Wild Cargo" was finished. There was no particular cruelty to the animals. The tiger was the only casualty of the entire film, but most of the time I felt as if I was working on a Marx Brothers comedy, instead of what was supposed to be a deadly serious film about the wild.

There was the strange case of the East Indian rhino that I was surprised to find in a large stockade in the camp. One of the episodes of "Wild Cargo" was to include an adventure between Buck and a rhino and this animal had been procured for us at great expense from the jungles of Nepal, brought overland to Calcutta and shipped out to Singapore. Even in those days, the East Indian rhino had been hunted so savagely that it was already one of the rarest animals in the world and the whole species was faced with extinction. Because of this, our rhino arrived with a special attendant, an elderly Nepalese who had obviously been told that his life would not be worth living if anything happened to his precious charge.

The old man was devoted to his rhino. He never left his side but fed him and watered him himself and at night used to sleep alongside him in his box. Even so, his presence had not entirely guaranteed the safety of the rhino. Already on the journey from Raxaul to Calcutta, someone had managed to gouge a substantial chunk out of the animal's horn and someone else had made a determined attempt to slice off its ear. For the obsessional faith the oriental world maintains in the aphrodisiac qualities of a rhino's horn also extends—although to a lesser degree—to the rest of its body. Several more attempts were made on the rhino in Singapore and in the end we had to build a kind of fortified enclosure around it and engage the services of a pair of Indian policemen to keep watch alongside the old Nepalese.

At first we all felt sorry for the exacting life the old man seemed to be leading, but then one day we discovered that his job had a lucrative side to it. In Singapore that summer, the heat was intense and several of us kept a stock of beer in one of the huts near the rhino compound, so that we could have a cool drink with our lunch. But one day when I opened a bottle I had a surprise. For the bottle contained something quite different from the drink I had been looking forward to all the morning. The fuss I made soon brought out the old Nepalese from the other side of the hut and from the look of guilt and embarrassment on his face I could see that he had something to do with the disaster. He soon admitted everything.

Ever since his arrival he had done a roaring local trade in rhino urine. He carefully collected the stuff night and morning and sold it as an aphrodisiac to the Singapore Chinese at 50 cents a bottle—our bottles. For the old man had marketed the precious fluid in our empty beer bottles, hence the confusion when his stock and ours had become mixed.

One thing that could be said for the old man was that he firmly believed in the quality of his wares. Every night and morning, when he had filled his bottles, he would personally drink a full pint of the rejuvenating liquid and he told me that it was to this that he ascribed continued good health and potency at his advanced age.

Unfortunately, the entirely unfounded but apparently unshakable belief of the East in the aphrodisiac properties of the rhinoceros

64

is not usually as harmless as this. The demand for rhino horn seems to be insatiable and the high prices paid for it have created a market for the horns that has brought rhinos in many places to the verge of extinction. For it is not only the East Indian rhino that has nearly been hunted out of existence for its horn. Even in Africa, where poaching of both the white and black rhino has reached the most serious scale, the horn invariably ends up being sold to the merchants of the East.

Towards the end of the time we were working on "Wild Cargo" I think I would have found the whole film even more intolerable than I did if it had not been for Singapore itself. But I soon found that it was a surprisingly good centre for buying animals. In those days its animal dealers were among the best in the world, and with my collector's mania, I was soon finding their wares quite irresistible. For several weeks I actually kept a baby orang-utan in my bedroom in the Raffles Hotel. He was a most affectionate pet and adapted perfectly to hotel life. He slept on the bottom of my bed, and did extremely well on a diet of fruit, raw eggs and cream. But although I loved him dearly, I finally decided that he was already becoming too rumbustious for the long journey back to the States aboard the luxury Japanese liner that was due to take me back to New York, and sadly gave him to a friend to keep.

A still more unusual pet that I acquired at this time in Singapore was a large Malayan fruit-eating bat. These animals have a wing-span of five feet and are considered a great table delicacy among the Malays. I first saw them after they had been shot, hanging in great bunches for people to buy on the stalls in the market place, and told one of the men selling them that if he could get me one alive I would pay him five times the price he got for a dead one. A few days later he turned up at the Raffles Hotel with a large cardboard box under his arm. Inside, extremely nervous, but in excellent condition, lay my enormous fruit bat.

At first I thought he was going to be difficult to train, but I soon found him one of the most intelligent animals I have ever had. He had brilliant black eyes, a head rather like a small jackal and enormous wings. He soon became surprisingly affectionate. He normally spent all day asleep, hugging the curtains as close as possible to the ceiling, but as soon as I entered the room he would clamber down, scramble clumsily across the floor, and climb up my legs and on to my shoulder. Although he meant well, this was painful, as he had needle-sharp claws on the ends of his wings and it was these he used for climbing, digging them right through my clothes and putting all his weight on them until I seemed to be bleeding all over. At first he used to bite a good deal too—not aggressively so much as out of sheer nervousness—and his teeth, like his claws, were amazingly sharp and he seemed to have three rows of them extending all the way round his mouth.

After a few days he lost his nervousness and stopped biting. At night he would sleep hanging from the mosquito net above my bed and he would make a dreadful mess: a fruit bat, like a monkey, is not really conscious of his intestinal functions and can never be effectively house-trained. During the day his company was delightful and I would often take him out walking with me. He would fly ahead, sail up into a tree, and then, when I called he would come back at once and alight on my arm or my shoulder. To make sure that nobody tried to shoot him for dinner, I had a collar made for him and a thin chain and whenever I had any business in Singapore I would leave him tied up in some safe place so that I knew where he would be when I came back. Although I did not know it, this was to be his undoing.

Early one afternoon, I had to visit someone on the outskirts of Singapore and arranged to tie up my bat in the shade of a tree in the garden. Everything seemed all right. The bat was happy, and went to sleep hanging from a low branch. Unfortunately, I was away much longer than I meant to be, and although the bat was still fast asleep when I came back, the sun had moved so far that he was no longer in the shade and his wings had got badly sunburned.

For a fruit bat, sunburn is no minor matter. His wings started to peel and after a few days there was hardly anything left of the membrane covering them. He was perfectly well in himself, but his wings lost all their skin and he was soon looking exactly like an old umbrella that had lost its cover in a gale. The skin showed no sign of growing again, and the sad thing was that he never seemed to realise he had lost the power of flight.

He was as cheerful and as affectionate as ever, but he would clamber up into a tree, launch himself confidently into space and tumble sadly to the ground. He was remarkably game and survived any number of falls, although I did my best to stop him hurting himself. But in the end he caught one of the exposed ends of his wings in a nail projecting from a wall and he was in such pain that I had to destroy him.

It was shortly after this that "Wild Cargo" was mercifully finished. As I have explained, I had already got rid of my baby orang-utan, but I was determined not to leave Singapore without an animal of some kind. So just before we sailed, I bought two young gibbons and succeeded in smuggling them aboard the ship.

The gibbons themselves were the most beautiful creatures. They were golden gibbons, the most graceful and appealing of all apes or monkeys. They came from the Malayan jungles and, with their huge wide-apart eyes, always seemed to have the most soulful expression on their faces.

I think everything would have been all right on the journey home if my passage had not been booked by the film company in true film company style. The shipping people assumed that I was some top Hollywood film mogul and as I was aboard the *Tatsuta Maru*, the crack Japanese liner of those days, I was actually given the Emperor of Japan's suite.

It may have been a great honour, but attention on this scale was the last thing I wanted, although for three days I struggled to keep my two gibbons under cover in the imperial bathroom. I hung a couple of towels from the hot water taps and trickled water down them until the atmosphere was as humid as the jungles they came from. For myself, I made do with another bathroom I found at the end of the passage.

Of course it could not last, and I think that in the end one of the stewards must have betrayed me. The captain came in person to find out what I was up to and was obviously deeply shocked to hear that I was keeping monkeys in the bathroom of the Emperor of Japan. I tried to bluff him off, but he was as determined a little man as a Japanese can be, and refused to budge and insisted on peering into the bathroom.

Now gibbons are essentially friendly creatures. They like people and as soon as they saw the captain looking in through the bathroom door, one of them took a fancy to him and started showing his affection in the only way a gibbon knows. He threw his arms around his neck and hugged him as if his life depended on it. The captain was horrified. Not only was this a dreadful loss of face to himself, but these "monkeys" as he kept calling them, were desecrating a bathroom that had been hallowed by his Emperor's divine presence.

But the gibbon hung on tight and slowly I saw the captain's expression change. To my surprise, he actually began stroking him, and when he started saying "Nice monkey, nice monkey" to him, I knew that everything would be all right.

It still took some time to assure the captain that the gibbons would do the Emperor's bathroom no permanent harm, but once I had convinced him that they were clean and well-behaved, he seemed satisfied. From then on, there was no question of having to get rid of them and they actually spent the rest of the voyage playing on deck. Long before we reached America, the two gibbons were the most popular passengers on board.

When I was back in America, I found myself in the position I had always wanted. Much as I disliked the film, "Wild Cargo" was a great success, and through it I had earned myself enough money to secure my independence for some while ahead. There was no question now of going back to my old job with Eastman Kodak, and almost straight away I began planning a new expedition of my own. I knew enough of the techniques of film making by now to be sure that I could make a professional job of a feature film, and the experience of working with Frank Buck made me more certain than ever of the type of film this was to be. There was no need to fake or to think up impossible adventures with animals as he did. The truth was far more exciting. The world was full of peoples and animals that needed recording and film was the one way to do it. Just as soon as I could raise the money and get together an expedition of my own, I intended to be off on my travels again.

6 Expedition to the Congo

I SUPPOSE I had always taken it for granted that one day I would get to Africa. For anyone as interested in recording wild life and primitive tribes as I was, it was the one continent that clearly had the most to offer, and even while I was filming "Wild Cargo" I had started planning an expedition of my own to get there.

To-day, Michaela and I reckon that we can be ready to mount a filming expedition to almost anywhere in the world within a week. Film and sound equipment is compact and airlines have made the world almost too accessible. But in the early 1930's things were different. First I had to get the right financial backers who would leave me free to make the kind of film I wanted. Then I had to collect the right equipment with which to make it. Altogether this took two years, and cost me everything I had made directing "Wild Cargo."

During the first months of my return to America I found I had an unexpected hindrance. It took the form of one of the gibbons I had brought back from Singapore, for gibbons, as I was to discover, have one great drawback as pets. They are so affectionate that they can become excessively dependent on their owners, and with one of the gibbons called Playboy this dependence became so extreme that in the end it was a burden to us both.

This devotion had begun in Singapore. Every night he would find his way under the mosquito net and curl up beside me on my pillow. On the ship his utter dependence on me was no trouble as he was the liveliest and most amusing of companions and I had nothing else to do all day except play with him and make a fuss of him. But once we got back to the States his anxiety began to get completely out of hand.

69

He continued to insist on sleeping beside me and during the day wherever I was inside the big house where I lived in Connecticut, Playboy would always be outside at the window, peering in to make sure he did not lose me. If I moved into another room he would swing along the ledge outside until he found me again, whilst if he lost me at any time he would become frantic with worry and scramble all over the house whimpering like a child.

Of course he was not like this all the time. His playfulness continued, especially when I could find time to be with him in the garden. He would often tease me unmercifully if visitors came, and then scamper away, climb up into the trees and pretend to hide.

But there was never any difficulty getting him back. All I had to do was to lie motionless on the ground with my eyes closed. Within seconds he would be out of his hiding place and down beside me, crying, stroking my hands, and trying to blow into my mouth, terrified that I might be hurt. He never seemed to learn that I was only pretending, and on these occasions he used to get so upset that in the end I decided it was simply not fair to take advantage of him in this way.

Another thing that always upset him was the act of crossing a bridge. For some reason he hated this. If we were in the car together he would always seem to know when we were crossing even the smallest stream and immediately begin to cry and cling to me.

For a while I managed to go on giving Playboy the sort of attention he needed. I had a small collar and chain made for him and used to take him with me to restaurants and on train journeys and even to the theatre. In theatres he would curl up on my lap and go to sleep, while in restaurants I would tie his chain to a leg of the table and he would wait quite happily until the meal was over.

As I became more and more involved in the preparations for my expedition, coping with Playboy became increasingly difficult. I was becoming paralysed by his dependence, and hardly dared leave the house without him.

Finally the time came when I had to go to New York for several days. I had people to see and equipment to buy and there was no question of taking Playboy this time. So I was as firm with him as I could be. I gave him the run of the large, centrally heated basement of the house, and after making him as comfortable as I could left him with the caretaker.

I had to stay in New York longer than I intended and on the sixth day the caretaker rang my hotel.

"It's Playboy," he said. "We're very much afraid he is going to die. He hasn't eaten since you left. All we can get him to take is a little milk and he sits all day hunched up in the corner. The only time he moves is when he hears a car, and it's terrible to see his disappointment when he realises it's not yours."

I hurried back as soon as I could. When I entered the room he was sitting forlornly on the table, and he walked to the edge and tried to jump to me as he always used to. But he was so weak that he fell to the ground between us. When I picked him up he just clung to me and nothing would loosen his grip. I had to spend the rest of the evening coaxing him to eat and feeding him small pieces of banana one at a time.

It was then that I decided that this obsessive friendship between us could go on no longer. Luckily I knew that the Rochester Zoo already had several gibbons of their own and that he would get the best possible attention there. Finally I persuaded the zoo to accept him. Once the break was made, it was not as painful as it might have been. I used to visit Playboy every day and always received the same enthusiastic welcome from him. But in the end he settled down and accepted life in the zoo quite happily, whilst I have never kept a gibbon, as a personal friend, since.

With Playboy comfortably settled in the zoo, preparations for the expedition could go forward more swiftly, but there was still a formidable amount to do. First I had to find my backers; to my surprise I discovered more assistance and generosity than I would ever have believed possible. All sorts of people helped. The Chrysler Company specially adapted a couple of experimental four-wheel drive trucks for the expedition and backed me handsomely on the understanding that I would make a short film for them on the journey. The Texaco oil company guaranteed all my fuel, contributed ten thousand dollars to my expenses and offered to set up depots of petrol at pre-arranged locations for our contemplated crossing of the Sahara in return for general publicity rights over my journey. I even had the luck to meet a mining executive with interests in Nigeria who commissioned me to make a brief film record of any tin mining I saw on the way, in return for a five thousand dollar contribution. It soon appeared that finance was going to be the least of my worries.

When the preparations were well under way I got my biggest stroke of luck. It was completely unexpected, but it helped settle the question of the parts of Africa I was to visit. It also provided an invaluable boost to the morale and position of the whole expedition.

As a boy in Belgium I had a friend called Gaston de Witte. He had shared my passion for snakes and lizards and when I set off on my travels, he had stayed behind in Belgium to become a distinguished naturalist. From time to time we had corresponded, and now, quite out of the blue, a letter arrived from him telling me that the King of the Belgians, Leopold III, and the Belgian authorities were anxious to have a scientific documentary film made about the great Albert National Park in the Congo. He had suggested me for the job, and I had been accepted.

This meant that I would have more than enough to do. I was now commissioned to make three films, quite apart from anything I wanted to do on my own account. My expedition that had started as a simple journey by road through Africa had become a large-scale operation that was clearly going to keep me in Africa for a year or more, and there were times when the preparations for all this became so complicated that I thought we were never going to get away.

I realise now that I made the beginner's mistake of providing against too many eventualities. To-day I would regard this expedition of mine as overstocked and over-equipped. For instance we carried a complete set of spares for the trucks so that if necessary we could have completely rebuilt an engine or carried out any major overhaul. It was the same with the cameras and the sound equipment. I duplicated everything possible and as a result we had so much sheer equipment that we had to have a specially built trailer to carry it all.

I was also determined that if necessary, the expedition was going to be virtually self-sufficient for its food. We carried a month's supply of everything except water, and this grocery list took weeks to work out. Again I made mistakes. I bought a lot of chocolate that was soon to melt in the heat of the Sahara and stick to almost all the other stores we carried. I thought that figs and dates would provide a welcome change of diet only to find later that they picked up the sand that percolated into the trucks and always seemed to taste of petrol.

What probably took the longest time of all to prepare was the sound-recording gear. I decided to make my own equipment, as there was nothing on the market really suitable for recording in the tropics. I knew that we were going to have to rely on this gear under extreme conditions, and I wanted to know exactly what was inside it.

So I took great care over it, making double joints on all the wiring, buying the highest quality components I could find, and practising how to replace any defective part of the equipment until I felt I could do it with my eyes shut.

In these days of transistors and miniaturised equipment it seems strange that I was then relying on glow lamp recording on film requiring 700 volts of biasing D.C. voltage supplied from a suitcase full of dry cells—and that I am still making use of the recordings I made with this home-made equipment in the Congo in 1935 and 1936.

At last by the beginning of 1935, I was satisfied that we had left nothing to chance and we loaded our two trucks, our trailer and our sixteen tons of equipment aboard a freighter in Brooklyn Harbour.

There is nothing to equal the excitement of setting out on your own expedition and I have never forgotten that early spring morning when we sailed down the Brooklyn River bound for Antwerp.

As soon as I reached Brussels I had to go to the Ministry of Colonies to receive an impressive diplomatic passport.

There was even more to come. The following day the entire expedition was summoned to the Royal Palace at Laeken to be received in audience by King Leopold and Queen Astrid, and for over an hour we talked about the animals of the Congo, about Albert National Park, and the great wild life reserve which had been founded there by Leopold's father, King Albert.

After this royal send-off I was feeling decidedly over-confident for so inexperienced a traveller, and it needed a few of the minor disasters of the journey south to bring me back to reality. In Biarritz I succeeded in leading the entire expedition down a blind alley at three in the morning and it took us hours to extricate ourselves.

In Spain we had our spare tyres, all thirty-two of them, stolen from us as we slept. But it was when we were actually in Africa, crossing the Atlas Mountains on the magnificent new military road the French had just built, that the most unexpected trouble of all occurred. We were descending through the thick pine forest on the far side of the mountains when we got caught in the snow and it was so thick that we had to spend the night there.

Next morning the trucks were frozen. The last thing I had thought of providing for an expedition to the Congo was anti-freeze for the radiators and it took us nearly the whole morning to get moving again. Less than two hours later we were driving through the Ziz valley in a temperature approaching 110° and just about to get our first glimpse of the Sahara.

It was not until we reached the Sahara that I really felt we were in Africa. I had been prepared for Morocco but here was something quite different. For the first time I felt the hugeness of the continent. I felt its silence and its immense age, and I was excited by it in a way I had never been by any other country.

We planned to drive due south across the Sahara through Colomb-Bechar, Adrar, In Salah and Tamanrasset to the northern tip of Nigeria and in those days the trail was far rougher than it is to-day. In many places the trail did not exist. The French had marked the route with empty petrol drums every ten kilometres or so; much of the time they were all there was.

What interested me most about the Sahara was the amount of wild life we were able to observe. I had set out with the firm idea that the Sahara was an area completely devoid of life. That was what

74

all the books on the subject had told me, but the first thing that made me think they were probably wrong was the number of flies we saw. We were plagued by them right in the middle of the desert and I knew that flies could not exist on rock and sand alone. They live and breed on the carcases of animals.

The first explanation was that they lived on the countless birds that cross and recross the Sahara during their yearly migrations and die *en route*. Of course our chances of seeing the body of one of these birds were remote, but flies are guided by a sense of smell that would always send them to any carrion in the desert.

Finally, I did find some birds myself. In one area the French had signposted the trail with corrugated iron markers looking rather like small huts raised on stilts six inches or so off the ground. As we passed one of these I happened to look down and saw two minute birds huddled in the shade it offered—the only shade for miles around. Presumably they were waiting for the cool of the night, to continue their journey. Almost every subsequent marker I looked under seemed to have a few inhabitants waiting for nightfall.

Then there were other animals. There is hardly a spot in the Sahara that is without a stray tuft of coarse grass somewhere around, and I often noticed that these tufts would be surrounded by the tracks of minute rodents. These rodents presumably kept themselves alive on the roots and seeds of the grass and were obviously nocturnal. One evening when we made camp rather later than usual we saw some of them. They were very small sand-coloured mice. They scuttled out of their burrows to see us and were so absurdly tame that they soon started climbing on our shoes and up our legs and ended by sitting on the table and sharing our meal with us.

The overland journey to the Congo took us nearly three months. Almost every minor disaster that could afflict an expedition through Africa afflicted ours and long before we reached our destination we had become inured to the hardship and excitement of this sort of travel.

Even so, nothing could quite destroy the thrill of arriving in the Albert Park. We had been driving all day across the high plateau that provides the eastern border of the park. By evening we knew we were so near that we just kept on driving. We started our

descent of the Kabasha escarpment, by moonlight, down the great
road leading to the Rwindi plains. It was eleven o'clock when we
saw the first post beside the road marked *Parc National Albert*, and
knew we had reached our goal.

The six months we spent filming in the Albert Park offered a
unique introduction to the big game of Africa, for the park was
enormous—well over two million acres—and as it was long and relatively narrow, it stretched through an extraordinary diversity of
landscape and vegetation. In the heart of it, in a triangle of heavy
forest between the three great mountains, Karisimbi, Bishoke and
Mikeno, lay the almost inaccessible jungle where the rare mountain
gorilla was rediscovered at the beginning of this century.

The Belgian authorities were most reluctant to allow anyone
into this area and we were permitted to enter only after I had
solemnly promised to make no attempt to approach or photograph
the gorillas. This was naturally a great disappointment, but the
Belgians were worried, not so much for the safety of my party, as
that a gorilla might try molesting one of us and then be shot in self-
defence.

Originally the park had been created solely as a sanctuary for
these gorillas, but by 1935 it had been extended enormously and was
particularly rich in elephants, hippos, lions, leopards and various
kinds of antelope. But as far as the park authorities were concerned,
these were not the only animals I was to film. They felt that earlier
expeditions had already done enough photography of the big fauna
and that my "scientific" film should concern itself more with the
small fauna like birds, squirrels, lizards, frogs and insects.

None of us ever quite decided what a "scientific" film was.
According to some of the instructions I received from Brussels it
sounded as if the zoologists there imagined that it meant a record
of the animals I encountered, without any selection of material,
of viewpoint, of lighting or of composition.

Finally I had to make the film according to my own judgment.
Even so I found it a hard and exacting job. For six months I travelled,
most of the time on foot, through tough and mountainous country.
There was considerable danger. Everything had to be carried by

porters, and in the end I sent off 40,000 feet of film to Brussels. The Belgians were pleased with it, but as a film maker I was far happier about the less scientific but decidedly more palatable film on the big animals of the park that the authorities had permitted me to take on my own behalf.

The time I spent in the Albert Park was really my first serious attempt to feature wild animals in their own habitat, and despite the confidence with which I arrived in Africa, I found it far harder than I had ever imagined. The first problem was simply to get close enough to the animals to provide a picture remotely worth looking at.

I soon found that a wild animal looks a great deal closer and more interesting to the human eye than it does through a movie camera. The elephant that had seemed thirty feet away when shooting the picture, appears to be a hundred yards away when the film is projected. The obvious solution seemed to be to build a hide in a likely spot and wait there until the animals obligingly walked past. But our hide was always in the wrong place and no animal ever seemed to come within one hundred and fifty yards of us.

So the next stage was to fix our Akeley camera on to one of the trucks and try following the game. This proved scarcely more satisfactory. The camera would vibrate too much while we were moving to allow us to film, and by the time we stopped and were prepared to shoot, the animals would have disappeared again.

This happened several times with the hippos of the Rutshuru River. In theory they should have been the easiest animals in the world to film since there were said to be six thousand of them in six miles of river. We would see them every day lying, sunning themselves on the sandbanks at the edge of the river and try to film them. But it only needed us to approach with our cameras for the hippos to break off their siesta and plunge back into the river, and we never seemed able to get really close to them without panicking them.

Gradually we began to learn from our mistakes. By trial and error we learned to know where to expect a particular animal or a certain tribe, and we had a great deal of beginner's luck. Altogether we spent another fourteen months in Africa after leaving the Albert Park, travelling right across to Nairobi and the Indian Ocean before retracing our tracks and driving up through Northern Nigeria and across the Sahara to Europe again.

The scenes we shot during this time were so rich and varied that with the footage we already had from the Albert Park, I finally had enough material to make into a full hour's film for Chrysler and also to produce a successful full-length feature film of my own called "Dark Rapture." During our travels, I even managed to shoot some footage on tin mining for my kindly mining executive.

I was relieved to find that my sound-recording gear stood up to the wear and tear of the tropics for we used it hard. We were the first to record authentic sound in the middle of Africa on any scale and our recordings included the royal drums of the giant Watusi, the stick music of the forest negroes and the large percussion orchestras of the Manbetu tribe that often boasted more than thirty players.

The Watusi in particular gave us splendid scenes for our film. They were an ancient race, living on the Ruanda plains and were one of the mystery peoples of Africa. For these immensely tall warriors—a Watusi in his prime in those days would be six feet eight or nine tall—were ethnically totally different from all the surrounding tribes. They were dark skinned but they were a Hamitic race, not a negro one, and it has been this that has made some experts advance the theory that the Watusi originally migrated to this distant corner of Africa from ancient Egypt. Certainly to me their art and some of their customs seemed to echo those of the Pharaohs. For instance the kings of the Watusi formed a dynasty quite apart from their subjects and were compelled by custom to marry their sisters just as the Pharaohs had done.

But while the ceremonial of the Watusi court, and the dances of the warriors, provided the sort of shots a film director dreams of, the most unusual scenes of all that went into our film "Dark Rapture" were the ceremonies of circumcision and flagellation that we filmed with one of the forest tribes of the Congo.

These ceremonies occurred once every five or six years and were normally among the most secret and jealously guarded of the tribe's secrets. Outsiders were rigidly banned from them and if a woman of the tribe was rash or careless enough to glimpse any part of the circumcision ceremony she would be instantly put to death.

For the two ceremonies of circumcision and flagellation were the supreme male rituals of the tribe; on the night before the circumcision was due to begin, the witch doctor would creep round the village uttering the most fearful cries in imitation of the male devils who were supposed to eat any women or children who ventured out of the huts the following day. We were lucky enough to be told about the ceremony by a Belgian district officer who was known and trusted by the tribe, and it was through him that the chief gave me permission to attend and film the whole event.

The key figure in the circumcision was the witch doctor. At dawn he was standing at the appointed place in the forest, in all his finery of shells and feathers and skins and as he called, the men of the village formed up in procession behind him. First came the chief and the elders. Then followed the fathers with their sons who were to be the centre of the day's proceedings. I felt particularly sorry for these boys. The Belgian official who had witnessed the ceremony before, told me that in this tribe they were circumcised between the ages of six and eleven and that they were expected to show no sign of pain. Their fathers would be with them and if the boys cried out or even grimaced, it would reflect serious dishonour on the family.

But apart from the boys it was clear that everyone was out to enjoy himself, and when the procession set off we got some excellent scenes of the milling tribesmen dancing and shouting after the witch doctor and surging t hrough the forest. This excitement continued when they reached the river. The boys were given a drink of some herbal brew from a gourd to help deaden the pain and one by one they were pushed forward by their anxious fathers to where the witch doctor was waiting at the edge of the river.

I had to admire the stoicism of these small boys, for the knife the witch doctor was using looked frighteningly rough and, whatever it was that the gourd contained, the pain for the boys must have been extreme. Yet here they were, taken away from their mothers for the first time in their lives and standing alone before the men of the tribe with the honour of their fathers depending on how they behaved. There were fourteen of them. None of them cried. One or two did show a flicker of emotion, but some of the boys actually managed to summon up a shout of triumph as they climbed out of the river. Then the elders would nod approvingly and the father beam with pride.

The flagellation ceremony usually takes place later when the men have returned to the village. This is the second of the manhood rites this tribe inflicts on its males; this time those involved are not the young boys but the older men, circumcised long ago, who voluntarily submit to flagellation in order to demonstrate their toughness and their contempt of pain before the whole tribe.

The ordeal was rather a formidable one. One by one the men stood in the centre of a circle formed by the whole village, and submitted uncomplainingly while they were lashed by members of the tribe. The men were naked except for a thin strip of wood they held in front to protect their genitals, and the whips, wielded without restraint, were saplings, eight or ten feet long, that could inflict a murderous slash. The stoicism of these men was remarkable. During the flagellation the victim would have to hold a small bell and keep ringing it to show that his courage was undefeated and that he could take more punishment. While we were filming we never once saw a man who failed to ring his bell.

After fourteen months in the Congo and with scenes like this on my film I was beginning to feel that I knew my new trade of film-maker. I also thought that I knew something about wild animals—a most dangerous illusion. For my sort of beginner's confidence was exactly the sort that causes accidents, and I count myself lucky that I learned my lesson when I did.

It happened on our way back through the Congo, shortly after we filmed the circumcision. I had been on my own filming hippo again. By now I had learned the secret of using a portable 35 millimetre camera which allowed me to stalk to within a few feet of the animals and I knew I was getting much more successful pictures than on my earlier attempts with these large elusive animals.

Then suddenly in the very middle of a shot, my camera jammed. It could not have happened at a worse moment as the hippos were just beginning to suspect my presence and I was getting the action I wanted, as the first of the old males lumbered off his sand-bank and into the river. But a jammed camera was useless; if I wanted to do any more filming that day I would have to find somewhere sufficiently dark to enable me to open the camera and clear the film track.

It was then that I remembered the fisherman's hut. It was about a quarter of a mile along the path by the river; an abandoned, tumbledown place built of mud and reeds. One of our Africans had warned me about it. "Bad place, bwana" he had said. I had asked him why, but he had just shaken his head muttering, "bad place, bad place for wild animals."

Warnings like this were all very well, but I was in a hurry. I needed somewhere dark where I could work at the camera, and the hut was the only place.

When I reached it I found it was empty. It smelled old and musty inside, but it suited my purposes and I was soon at work in the darkest corner. To open a camera as I now had to do, without spoiling all the film inside, you place it inside a thing called a changing bag. This is a large black satin bag rather like an old-fashioned muff. As well as having a zipped opening for the camera to go in by, it has two heavily elasticated apertures each side for your hands. The idea is that when you put your hands inside the bag the elastic grips your wrist tightly enough to stop any light entering, and you are able to open the camera without exposing the film.

This was what I did now, and I had nearly finished adjusting the camera when I saw a dark shadow cross the door of the hut. I was so engrossed in what I was doing that I took no notice, but a moment later I realised what the shadow was. It was the head and shoulders of a fully grown male lion.

The African's warning had been all too true and probably this particular lion was looking for shade to lie up in and had picked on the hut. Luckily he was not on the lookout for a large man with a jammed camera and was clearly as surprised to see me as I was to see him.

The hut was very small, and there was no time even to extricate my hands from the changing bag.

In situations of sudden danger like this, I have often found that people tend to do the right thing by instinct, and that by acting instantaneously they come off far better than if they had had time to think. Certainly I had no time to think; I found myself gripping the camera as tightly as I could within the changing bag and then bringing it down with all my force on the lion's head.

I shall never know if it dazed him or merely frightened him, but he jumped back snarling and bounded away into the bush. From that day to this I have always taken good notice of any warnings that local people give about wild animals in the district.

7 *Elephants of the Congo*

THE older I have got, the more interested I have become in elephants. In a way, they are like Africa itself. You start off thinking they are very large and very simple. Then gradually you realise that their life is not simple at all, but immensely complicated, and that however long you study them, you will never entirely understand them.

During this first visit of mine to the Congo, the elephants were still one of the splendours of the country, and were to provide many of the most impressive scenes for my film "Dark Rapture." To the north, by the Garamba and the Sudan border, there were several herds more than a thousand strong. We spent many weeks following them and filming them, and the scenes of these great herds, moving like some solid grey army on the march, were to provide some of the most successful parts of the film.

But in those days I still had a lot to learn about elephants, and my first attempt to study an individual elephant on my own at close quarters was nearly my last.

It happened when I was driving across the Rwindi plain, on the lookout for suitable animals for the camera team to film later in the day. About half a mile from the road, across some extremely rough country, I saw a very big elephant. He was a fine old tusker and he was alone.

Now, it is not a bad rule, if you wish to observe large game animals and stay alive, to avoid the old isolated one and stick to the herd. This is especially the case with elephants. In old age the head of the herd becomes driven out by his successor; he is often the one who gets a bad name as a rogue elephant and he is usually more aggressive and difficult to deal with than the rest of the herd.

Of course, I had heard all this several times, but the sight of this great elephant, so close and apparently so peaceful, was too much to resist. I had a loaded portable 35 mm. camera with me, so I stopped the car and cheerfully set out after the elephant on foot. Downwind of him ran a fairly substantial range of bushes. I judged that if I could once get behind them and then work towards him, I would be able to get some really exciting close-ups of the old monster.

All this seemed to work very well. I got behind one end of the bushes without being spotted and worked forward. But by the time I had got to the front of the clump and parted the branches, I saw that the elephant had come closer as well, and was now less than twenty yards away. This was better than I could ever have expected, except for one thing. From where I was sitting, there was yet another small bush directly in my line of vision that kept getting into the picture, no matter how I moved.

Finally, I decided to risk it. The elephant seemed more concerned with the foliage he was eating than with me, so I stepped out into the open, sighted my camera, and prepared to take some of the best pictures of my life of a big tusker at close quarters.

It was the clicking of my camera that did it. As soon as he heard the noise, out went his ears, up went his trunk, and I could see him feeling the air, listening for the next sound.

Curiously, the fact that I was so patently visible did not matter. To any other animal, I would have been as large as a house, but elephants have poor eyesight and at that age rarely notice things that stand still. At least, I had the sense not to move while I was photographing.

But trouble began the instant I stopped the camera. It was the change of sound that presumably irritated him and told him where I was. Determinedly he started moving towards me. I moved away. He accelerated and then at last I realised that I was actually in danger. This was the beginning of a charge.

It was then that I started to run in earnest, but to my horror I found that I could hardly move, because the ground was so rough, whereas this scarcely bothered him at all. He came lumbering on, unerringly on my track by now, and there was nothing I could do except blunder hopelessly forward clutching my camera.

Then, incredibly, he stopped and I looked back. He was standing on the exact spot where I had been when I filmed him. Obviously he had got my scent so strongly that he thought I was still there. He was going exclusively by scent and hearing, not by sight, and soon started pounding the ground there with his great feet and charging with his tusks. It was then I noticed what I should have seen earlier on: his far tusk was broken half-way off. This is a bad sign with an elephant. He may have broken it off in a fight or by hitting a tree; if the nerve was exposed, he may have suffered a painful abscess. It is always best to give a wide berth to an elephant with a broken tusk, as his behaviour is likely to be abnormal and unpredictable.

The one thing that probably saved my life was his weak eyesight. I managed to cover a good fifty yards before it struck him that it was only earth he was pounding, not me. Twice more this happened on the way back to the car. Twice more he got my scent and started to pound the ground. Thanks to this, I made it, but only just. When I reached the car the old elephant was not far behind me, and it was lucky the car started first time, for the car was something that even he could see. Once I had got going I kept at top speed for the next ten miles.

For me, the most interesting elephants I saw during our journeys through the Congo were undoubtedly the elephants of Gangala-na-Bodio. They were unique among all the elephants of Africa in that they were the only ones trained to work.

I should explain something of the differences between the Asian and the African elephant, for these are not just physical. Anatomically, of course, they are very different, and it is a long way back in the course of evolution that the two species diverged—the African elephant with his flat skull and enormous ears, and the Asian with his far smaller ears and heavy protuberances on the front of his skull. But they are every bit as different in temperament. The Asian elephant is more peaceable, more reliable, more trainable, whereas the African elephant, with the best training in the world, seems to remain moody and undependable. I have always been scared of African elephants, however well trained they were supposed to be.

85

I do not believe in allowing myself to get into a tight corner with one.

Asian elephants show almost unbelievable intelligence and common sense. Recently, Michaela and I watched them working in the teak forests in Vietnam. There the elephants are trained to pull the three- and four-ton teak logs out of the mountainous forest area where they grow. The country is too rough, and the trees too far dispersed for any sort of trucks or tractors to do the work, and we marvelled to see the elephants sliding these great baulks of timber down the sides of the mountains.

In theory, the mahouts, perched up behind their ears, told them what to do, but as far as we could see, they were normally too drugged with opium to know what was going on, and it was the elephant who seemed to know when to loosen the chain on his log at a difficult point in the journey and get behind the log and push it. Nine tenths of the work seemed to be done at the initiative of the elephants themselves, even to the extent of calling to another elephant for help if stuck tight at a particular spot.

It was presumably this sort of example of what the Asian elephant could do that persuaded the Belgians to start trying the same. In 1900, King Leopold II sent to India for several mahouts and their elephants to be shipped to the Congo.

This was the start of the *Station de Capture et de Dressage des Eléphants* at Gangala-na-Bodio. The Indian elephants soon died—the diseases in Africa were more malignant than in their native land—but the mahouts stayed on, and when I was at Gangala I recognised the Indian elephant song, which they were using to soothe their animals and put them to sleep. But, apart from this, the African elephant trainers soon developed methods of their own, very different from anything I have ever seen in India.

When we arrived, the place was being run by a remarkable man called Commandant Offerman, who was later to become chief game warden for the whole of the Congo. He was the last sort of man I would ever have expected to find in charge of elephants. By training he was a cavalryman in the Belgian army, and he was one of those spare, volatile, rather dashing men who always seem to look best on horseback.

He ran this elephant station deep in the middle of nowhere with the discipline and precision of a good cavalry barracks. There were thirty-five elephants there at the time; the camp stood on a cliff overlooking a river, with the elephant lines laid out exactly like cavalry lines behind. Twelve or fourteen of the elephants had been captured during the previous year and were still under training; others were rented out to neighbouring planters for agricultural work, such as pulling ploughs and logs and uprooting trees.

I had arranged to arrive at Gangala-na-Bodio in time for the capture season—just as Commandant Offerman and his men were setting off to capture fresh wild elephants for training during the coming year. It is economically far more sensible to catch elephants wild and train them, than to breed them in captivity like horses. It is not merely that a female elephant's pregnancy lasts twenty-two months, and that she would be practically useless for work for more than a year on the occasion of each pregnancy. More important than this is the fact that, once her baby is born, the mother elephant can think of nothing else, and thereafter, for a period of years again, is always dropping whatever she is doing at the moment to go trumpeting off in rage or anxiety to discover what has happened to her offspring.

Rather than put up with this sort of thing, Offerman and his men would submit to the incredible hazards of their annual elephant round-up. The capture party would leave early in the morning. There would be thirty or forty men and eight or ten big elephants, two or three pairs of which would be yoked to heavy, wooden-tyred wagons, similar to those used by the Boers when they trekked up into the Transvaal. The wagons would be loaded with heavy ropes and chains and supplies for several weeks.

They would head north across the river and up into the rough savannah country where there are still some of the biggest elephant herds in Africa. All the time they moved, trackers were out ahead, looking for signs of elephants, and once they found a herd of reasonable size, the rest would come up as close as they could and set up camp for the night.

I remember going out with Offerman before dawn the morning after our herd had been sighted, accompanied by the men who were going to make the captures. Each one carried a bundle of heavy rope on his back and was dressed in his roughest, oldest clothes.

They worked down-wind of the elephants; in the dim light just before the dawn, I had no idea where the herd could be. From time to time I would hear distant trumpeting, although this was deceptive in this sort of country. But the men were amazingly expert in moving without being seen, and when the foremost of them stopped, Offerman took me by the arm and led me forward to the edge of a low clump of bushes. There, feeding peacefully, was a herd of several hundred elephants—the nearest barely fifty yards from us. One of Offerman's most experienced men came forward with us. He and Offerman stayed to pick out the elephants they wanted. Meanwhile, a few yards back, all the men were binding sacking and thick canvas puttees around their legs, to protect them from the thorns of the bush during the hunt. When Offerman joined us again, he issued each man six blank cartridges for his rifle.

Guns are used only for scaring the elephants, and the noise of the blanks is all that the men use to break up a charge.

When everyone was ready, Offerman climbed on his horse and, like a starter at an old-fashioned horse race, fired his pistol into the air. For a moment I was reminded of an infantry attack in wartime. From all sides the men rushed towards the elephants, shouting and firing off blanks. Immediately the elephants panicked, exactly as they were meant to, and the hunt was on. It lasted for hours, and was a terrible test of endurance for the men.

Our cameras were mounted on our four wheel drive truck, but even so we had a job to keep up, for stampeding elephants, despite their weight, can maintain a remarkable speed across country. Offerman's men, on foot, with their heavy ropes and their rifles, managed to do what we could not. With unfailing stamina they kept with the herd for more than three hours before the first capture was made.

The way they worked was to run alongside the elephants until they saw a gap in the herd. As soon as they found one, they would try to slip inside and then, by firing their guns practically into the faces of the stampeding elephants, divert enough to split the herd up. We saw the men make several attempts at this and fail each time. Then one man who, I thought, must surely be killed, managed somehow to duck right under the legs of an elephant to fire at the one behind.

This went on time after time. At first some fifty animals were split off from the herd. These were narrowed down in their turn until twenty remained, and by luck these twenty included three of the animals selected for capture. We followed a group of four men who had their eye on one heavy young bull. By now the pace was beginning to slacken a little. I could see now the way they were hoping to work, although to me it appeared too far-fetched to be even remotely possible.

The men were carrying a long noose, and the foremost of the men was actually trying to slip this over the animal's hind legs as he was running. Twice he threw it and failed, while the elephant trumpeted and broke off in another direction. Finally they managed it.

The elephant stopped like an angry battleship. With trunk erect and ears out, he tried to charge his pursuers. They were ready for him. With the sort of good sense I would have shown several hours earlier, the men let go of the rope and ran for it. But they did not run far. As soon as the young elephant had trumpeted uselessly once more and set off again, with the rope trailing behind him, the four men reappeared, grabbed the rope and followed.

By now their tactics were clearer. The first move was to get the rope firmly tied round a tree large enough to take the weight of the elephant. This took some time, and a lot of manœuvring, but in the end they managed it, the men keeping well out of range as he turned around the tree, lashing out furiously at the men with his trunk. Then a man in front started teasing him, to hold his attention, while the rest of the hunters laid nooses of rope on the ground, in the hope that when he finally charged, the elephant would put his feet into them, thus allowing them to tie his front legs as well.

After several false tries, this succeeded too, and finally at two-thirty that afternoon, eight and a half hours after the hunt started, we saw the first capture laboriously roped by all four legs between two large trees. I felt completely exhausted with the extreme heat and with the mere effort of keeping up with the hunt, but the four men who had caught the elephant looked almost as fresh as when

89

they started. I had with me only some very soft chocolate and half-a-gallon of warm water; the least I could do was to share it with them, if only to show my admiration for one of the most courageous feats I had ever seen.

Although the elephant trumpeted forlornly from time to time, he too seemed grateful that all the effort of the chase was over at last.

We all lay around in what shade we could find for about half-an-hour. Then Commandant Offerman arrived on his grey horse, still immaculate, as if in some eighteenth century parade. I was naturally excited by what had happened, but he took remarkably little notice, mentioned something about the monitor elephants arriving soon, and galloped off again in search of more elephants.

The monitor elephants turned out to be a pair of the old, trained elephants we had brought with us from Gangala-na-Bodio. They were gently led, one each side of the newly-captured male. The effect was immediate. The old elephants had scarcely touched his side before he calmed down. He stopped waving his trunk around and trying to uproot the trees he was tied to, and I watched as the biggest of the elephants put its trunk on the younger one's shoulder as if saying quietly, "It's all right. It's going to be all right."

The men seemed to know what to do without a word of command being spoken. The ropes that were round the captive's neck were untied and refastened to the neck ropes of the two monitors. Then the leg ropes were untied, and slowly, like a newly launched ship being manoeuvred into position by a pair of tugs, the newly-captured elephant was turned round in the direction of Gangala-na-Bodio, and the long march back to camp between the two monitors began.

I did not particularly pity this elephant. I had seen far too many animals in the wild that were desperately hungry or ill or afraid, to share the general view that a captive animal must always be pitied. The elephants at Gangala-na-Bodio, once they were trained, led an easy life and were physically better off than facing the dangers and hardships of the wild.

At the start of their training, all that could be done was to accustom them to the sound and voices of men, to the smell of the camp and the smell of the other elephants. The emphasis was on patiently establishing a routine.

I remember how the animal I had seen captured was brought by the monitors his first evening in camp, and then tied, fore and aft between a pair of large trees. Here he stayed for the night. He could stand but he could not really move, and all the time the men hung around him, talking and eating their food near him, to get him accustomed to people and to the idea that humans do not necessarily bring danger.

All night, of course, he was fed. For, like all elephants, he spent most of the night eating, and when I woke in the morning I was just in time to see him being led away by his two patient attendants, down to the river where he could bathe and throw water over himself and talk to the other elephants.

In this way he was accustomed to the routine of the camp, and after six weeks Offerman would decide it was time to dispense with one of the monitors. A few weeks later, when he was completely used to the sights and smell of men, training would begin.

As far as training goes, elephants are peculiar creatures. Although they can ultimately become so reliable, they are probably of all animals the most difficult to train. In this they are completely different from rhinos, who may be hard to catch, but within 48 hours of being captured, I have had one taking food from my hand. By then he was no longer trying to batter himself to bits and did not go through any subsequent period of depression and frustration.

With elephants it is the exact opposite. For months after capture they are depressed, and struggle against the idea of accepting human domination, so that the training demands day-long patience month after month from their trainers. Unlike the Indian system, where a single mahout is assigned to the elephant immediately he is captured and stays with him for life, the system here was to train the elephant to take orders from anyone and this was more difficult to achieve.

The methods we watched at Gangala-na-Bodio were painstaking in the extreme. We saw the new elephants being taken by the monitors and led to their places along the elephant lines where their hind legs were tied to heavy stakes in the ground. The front legs were tied to long ropes, each rope held by three men. As soon as he stopped struggling, the new elephant was given the order "Lie down." This would be repeated several times, whilst the men pulled hard at the front leg ropes.

This might go on several hours until tired, exasperated, and perhaps just beginning to understand what was expected of him, the elephant decided to lie down.

At once the man would shout "*Saba, saba*" (good) at him, and give him carrots and big sunflowers full of the fat seeds elephants love. And so, slowly, laboriously the elephants would begin to understand what was required of them.

Although I admired the patience of Offerman and his men and spent several weeks in their camp filming the elephant training in detail, I have to admit that I never really trusted their elephants as I trusted the elephants in Burma or Ceylon. Riding an Asian elephant is one of the stateliest experiences I know. You are so high up that you feel you dominate the world. It is slow and assured and as the elephant walks it is rather like floating over the jungle in a balloon.

Riding an African elephant on the other hand I always found an extremely nerve-racking affair. I used to travel a lot on the elephants at Gangala-na-Bodio; for a while all would be fine, then I would see a tree coming towards us with a horizontal branch sticking out at just about the height of the elephant's back. I would look at it. The elephant would look at it too, and both of us would know what was going through the other's mind.

If he could run just a few paces to the left he would pass directly under the branch and I would be swept neatly off his back. This was usually the point at which I would jump off, but I did see several mahouts, braver men than me, end up hanging on to the elephant's tail.

For the truth is that despite all the efforts of Gangala-na-Bodio I have yet to be convinced that it is possible to make an entirely satisfactory job of training an African elephant.

In areas where elephants are not hunted or pursued, they quickly lose much of their fear of man, and humans and elephants learn to live peaceably together in surprising intimacy.

On our last visit to the Albert Park, Michaela and I came upon a temporary village being used by thirty or forty road workers and their families, and as we drove up I said to Michaela, "This is very odd. There are three elephants in this village."

"Surely," she said, "there couldn't be."

But there were—three fully-grown wild elephants, standing on their feet in the midst of the village in the way elephants do when they are half asleep, and everything else was going on around them. Some children were even playing in the sand less than twenty yards away from them, and no one seemed to pay the slightest attention to the elephants.

Then while we watched the elephants woke up and began to move. Lazily they lumbered over to a potato patch and started digging up potatoes. When the villagers got annoyed and pelted them with clods of earth to drive them away, the elephants just looked round as if to say, "O.K., we know when we're not wanted," and wandered off into the bush.

I find that sort of thing a bit disappointing. There should always be a slight thrill of danger when you approach a herd of elephant, and generally there is, but that group were practically house-broken, and might possibly have eaten out of our hands if we had given them a chance.

Wild elephants have an instinct and wisdom I have often found uncanny. During drought, for instance, the African elephant is the only animal with the intelligence and ability to dig for water. We watched this—although we never managed to film it properly—during the great drought in Kenya in 1960. Most of the rivers dried up completely, although water continued to trickle underground through the gravelly bed, often several feet beneath the surface.

Of course the Africans have always known about this and during drought it is their standard practice to dig water-holes in the dried-up beds of rivers. But the uncanny thing was that the elephants knew this as well, and working partly with their tusks, partly with their feet, and partly with their trunks they would burrow up to three feet below the surface in their search for water. We would see them early in the morning, their feet down in the sand and their head and trunk almost buried, waiting for the water to seep in. An elephant drinks up to forty gallons at a time and to satisfy a thirst like that during a Kenya drought might take several hours.

As soon as they saw us they would become alarmed and move away with a reproachful look in their eye. But if we stayed down-wind of them they would soon be back, tormented by their thirst. Once we stayed in hiding near one of their water-holes all day. When the elephants had gone they were followed by animal after animal from rhinos and gazelles down to mongooses, lizards and snakes. Unquestionably during the drought the elephants and the water-holes they dug saved the lives of untold numbers of other animals.

Any number of legends have grown up around wild elephants but there was one above all which I had never believed until 1950 when I had positive proof of its truth. This was the legend of the wounded comrade; of the elephants risking their own lives to come to the help of a wounded companion, to try to put him on his feet and head him away to safety.

I had come back to Africa in 1950 with Michaela as technical adviser to Metro Goldwyn Mayer in the making of their film "King Solomon's Mines," while Michaela was to double for Deborah Kerr in the scenes involving dangerous animals. The usual army of Hollywood camera men and technicians descended on East Africa and I then discovered to my extreme annoyance that the script called for the shooting of a fully grown charging male elephant. It was exactly the sort of film scene that I disapprove of most strongly but my opinions carried little weight againt MGM's and the killing was arranged.

There was nothing I could do so I kept well away. But I learned afterwards that when the old bull was shot, two younger elephants out of the herd came forward and tried to lead him away. It must have been a very moving, very shaming sight for those film hunters with their high velocity rifles. But incredible though it seems, hardly anyone at MGM seemed to have realised that here was one authentic and quite unique sequence that had never been filmed before. As far as I was concerned this one scene would have been worth all the rest of the film put together. But I do not know to this day if a print of this unique scene was ever preserved.

8 *The Camp of the Pygmies*

THE address was easy to remember—"Putnam. Putnam's Camp. Epulu"—and I had written there twice before I left the States. There had been no reply, but I was not too worried about that, for I knew something about Pat Putnam and his habits. All I wanted was to be sure he knew I was coming to the Congo, for I was going to need his assistance, if an important part of my programme was to succeed.

While I was in the Congo I was determined to film the life of the pygmies of the Congo Forest and I knew of Putnam as one of the greatest experts on them in the world. He was an American anthropologist who had built this camp of his at Epulu in the middle of the great Ituri rain forest of the eastern Congo, and already he had become something of a legend.

I had never met him, but I knew several people who had, and at one time I knew his parents very well. His father was a doctor who lived in Bedford Village, near New York in New York State. He was a very lively, interesting old man and the last time I saw him was at a tremendous party he gave at the age of 82 to announce that he was going into hospital the following morning for a prostate operation. He was in hospital twenty days and when he left I am told it was to marry his nurse.

Putnam's mother, whom I had known earlier, was even more of a character. I had been introduced to her because she shared my enthusiasm for monkeys, but I soon found that her concern for them went to far greater lengths than mine. In those days she used to keep two homes going—one for herself and Dr. Putnam, and the other, the better of the two, for the monkeys. She employed a man specially to look after them, and in the house the central heating was kept on the whole year round. She doted on her animals to such an extent that one of her chimpanzees completely dominated her. As I knew only too well, you have to be extremely firm with chimpanzees, but she never had the heart to be. This particular animal used to refuse to leave her, and there came a time when the only way she could get away from it was to have it lightly chloroformed.

This was the family of the man I had written to and it was perhaps inevitable that he should have been something of an original himself. He had begun his professional life at Harvard as an ordinary student of anthropology, where he was highly thought of and was said to have a great future ahead of him. Then one day, still in his early twenties, he was chosen to go with an anthropological expedition to the Congo, and this was the end of his career at Harvard. Almost as soon as he arrived he had become as obsessed with pygmies as his mother had been with chimpanzees, and when the rest of the expedition returned, he decided to stay on in the Ituri Forest to write the great definitive work on the anthropology of the pygmies of the Congo.

He had little money at the time, but he was a determined fellow, and supported himself in many ingenious ways including working as a medical officer for the Belgians. Finally he decided he was not getting enough time with his pygmies, so he created this camp of his right in the middle of the forest. To provide himself with an income he built a hotel there and actually tried encouraging tourists to take a vacation in the middle of the Congo Forest.

Putnam was a persuasive man and a very determined one. Somehow he got the Belgians to give him a concession for his hotel —a most unusual thing in those days—and he set about constructing Putnam's Camp. It never ceased being constructed. For Pat Putnam was a visionary. He thought big, and Putnam's Camp had to be worthy of him. Naturally I had heard a lot about all this from his parents and before I had left for the Congo I had read several of the brochures on his hotel that had been printed for the tourist trade. But nothing had quite prepared me for the first sight of Pat Putnam himself.

We had finished filming in the Albert Park, and I had sent him a telegram as soon as I arrived at Stanleyville. Two days later the

*Training an elephant like this freshly captured youngster at Gangala-na-
Bodio was a long painstaking business taking many months*

"*I have yet to be convinced that it is possible to make an entirely satisfactory job of training an African elephant*"

The author with two pygmy grandmothers

The end of the hunt for the four tusked elephant of the Ituri Forest—the Explorers' Club in New York with Mr. Pallister, a president of the club

The pygmies of the Ituri Forest will do almost anything for a ride

"Everything had to enter Nepal on foot or be carried on the backs of porters"

"Despite all its romantic associations, I found Katmandu a thoroughly dreary, decaying place without a scrap of charm or interest." Royal statue outside a Katmandu temple

East Indian Rhino. "These huge animals are quite distinct from African Rhino and first reached Europe in Roman times. They were later used by Dürer as models for his famous engraving"

receptionist in the hotel where we were staying rang my room to tell me I had a visitor. I came downstairs to find a tall, gaunt man with a black beard and hair down to his shoulders. It was Pat Putnam.

I took to him immediately. There was a boundless enthusiasm about him and I like enthusiasts. He also had immense charm and a rich, warm voice that conveyed simplicity and great sincerity.

"Armand Denis," he said in tones that made what he said sound like the will of God himself, "You must come and make a great film on my pygmies and on my camp. There is nothing else like this in the whole of Africa and I want you to make a film that will show the world what we're doing."

We drove east from Stanleyville and the journey took two days. All the time, Putnam was talking about his hotel and his pygmies so that by the time I arrived I thought I knew what I was in for. But no description could have prepared me for my first sight of Putnam's Camp.

The humidity was intense for this was the very heart of the equatorial forest. The trees were six and seven feet in diameter. It rained solidly most of the time, and in this moist green twilit world the forest had a quite extraordinary resonance. Much as I love tropical forest, I am sure that if I had had to stay there long the darkness and the shut-in feeling would have driven me quietly mad. Putnam had not made things any better by his firm refusal to cut down a single tree.

The camp was just beyond the spot where the road from Stanleyville to Irumu crosses the rapids of the Epulu river and the huts had been so carefully fitted in between the great trees that Putnam's Camp looked as if it had just grown out of part of the jungle itself. It was all planned on the most ambitious scale. During the journey Putnam had been telling me about his swimming pool, his museum and his library and as soon as our truck swung in through the gate, he had jumped down from the cab and was eagerly waiting to show me round.

We had been two days on the road and I could have let the conducted tour wait, but Putnam with his long hair and his eager eyes was not to be cheated of his audience.

ON SAFARI

"You must realise that things take time in this part of Africa," he said, "but I feel the important thing is to make a start. There's always time to finish things but it's the original plan that matters."

I soon saw what he meant. The swimming pool had been laid out and the diving board was in position, but only a third of the actual pool had been dug out of the red soil of the forest. It was the same with the museum. Putnam led me proudly towards a long shed with an impressive padlock on the door.

"My collection," he said modestly.

Inside the light was dim and there was an overpowering smell of carrion. A trestle table ran the length of the room and on it lay the entire remains of a partly dissected male buffalo.

"Oh, I'd forgotten about him," said Putnam. "I was trying to find out what he died of but your telegram arrived from Stanleyville before I could finish." He started picking up parts of an early motor-cycle from where they lay in the corner and placing them carefully on the table beside the buffalo.

"You know the trouble with this part of Africa?" he said. "Never any time. Always so much to do."

He had a tendency to philosophise, but was interrupted by a handsome woman in slacks and a khaki shirt, who burst indignantly into the room.

"Where have you been, Pat?" she said in a sharp Boston accent.

"To the city, my dear. To the city," replied Putnam with a great show of dignity. "I had to meet Mr. Denis."

"Well, you could have told me," she said. "You've been away five days. I was getting worried."

"Five days," said Putnam looking pained. "As long as that? Surely, dear, you must be exaggerating."

This was Putnam's first wife, Mary. I got to know her well and admired her immensely. I think she married Putnam while he was still at Harvard. She came from a wealthy and highly respectable family who, I suppose, imagined that their daughter had a comfortable future ahead of her as the wife of a distinguished Harvard professor of anthropology.

What she thought when this turned into life among the pygmies in the middle of the Ituri Forest I never cared to inquire, but Mary

98

Putnam was certainly the only source of whatever order and efficiency Putnam's Camp possessed. These unannounced departures of Putnam's were quite common. One morning he would decide he wanted to go to Stanleyville or Irumu or somewhere else, and he would go down to the road, wait until a truck came along and hitch a lift to wherever he wanted. If he remembered, he would ask an African child to run back and tell his wife. If he forgot it was just too bad.

We stayed in Putnam's Camp over a month and enjoyed every minute of it. There was always something unexpected happening. Putnam seemed to have no real stocks of provisions and when, totally unannounced, a party of tourists arrived expecting the sort of amenities promised so extravagantly in his brochure, he would turn to with his cook and improvise something for lunch.

You would sit down and eat, not quite certain what was in the Irish stew, and all the time Mary Putnam would be anxiously watching the faces of her guests. Then at the end of the meal Pat Putnam would casually ask one of the visitors how she had enjoyed the wild-cat, or the lizard, or whatever animal he had decided to rob the Putnam zoo of for the benefit of the Putnam kitchen.

There were animals all over the place. Originally the zoo had been part of Putnam's ambitious plans, but it had inevitably got out of hand and in various ways overflowed into the hotel. You would go into your bedroom and possibly find a baboon already occupying your bed; but the real scourge of Putnam's Camp were the chimpanzees. Pat Putnam shared his mother's enthusiasm for them; one, called Fataki, seemed always to be exercising his sense of humour at the expense of the guests.

One evening we were all sitting round after dinner when in came Fataki, trailing behind him several rolls of film, completely unwound. At first everyone thought it was a great joke until the owners, a party of tourists from the Middle West, realised that these were all the films they had taken over the previous three weeks.

Another time a party of tourists arrived which included a very straight-laced elderly New England spinster. She must have left the door, or a window, of her bedroom open, for Fataki appeared when we were at dinner that night, with a pair of her bloomers solemnly draped around his head.

The pygmies were of course the most fascinating thing of all about Putnam's Camp. They trusted Putnam and would trade animals and plants with him for cigarettes. Towards evening they would come into the camp in twos and threes and I had my first chance of getting to know them.

They were nomads. They had no real possessions and most of the time life was hard for them. But everything they got was such a delight to them and they were as carefree as birds.

Putnam had much in common with them and was one of the few white people capable of really understanding them. He spoke their language. He lived with them for periods deep in the forest and for me he was an unbeatable guide and adviser for my film-making. It was through him that I learned of their strange way of life.

They live in small tribal groups but have no villages of their own. Instead, each tribe is virtually owned by an African village on the edge of the forest. These villagers are their patrons and defenders and it is from them that the pygmies obtain whatever they cannot find in the jungle.

Putnam believed that this arrangement originated with the negro invasions which drove the pygmy peoples into the depths of the forests. For the negro generally hates the forest. To this day he has no real understanding of it and no separate words for individual trees or animals. Nor is he generally much of a hunter and his knowledge of animals is severely limited, whereas the pygmy is first and foremost a hunter, getting almost all his food from the animals he kills.

Putnam's theory was that for a period after the pygmies had been driven into the forests there was a wholesale war between the two races with the pygmies surviving only by their elusiveness and adaptability. Then slowly relations between them improved as they realised that each race possessed what the other lacked. The pygmies had meat. The negroes had salt and vegetables and iron arrow-heads; and so they began to trade them and become dependent on each other.

This arrangement works, usually much to the advantage of the negroes who always consider themselves by far the superior race and look on the pygmy as rather less than a baboon.

The pygmy on the other hand is not exactly helpless. If his village-owners treat him badly he can always say to himself—"Well, I've had enough of this," and he and his little tribe simply disappear, turning up again at another village two hundred miles away to ask if they can become this other village's pygmies. The negroes guard against this by witchcraft, telling the pygmies that if they try to escape or fail to bring in all their meat they will be killed by leopards, by falling tress, or simply by evil spirits. Belief in witchcraft is so strong that this invariably works. The pygmy in turn can of course retaliate by coming noiselessly to the negro villages at night and killing anyone he wants with his tiny poisoned arrows.

The result of all this is that in effect both races have their deterrents and live in constant distrust and fear of each other. There is one particularly unfortunate feature of this association between the two races: the negro is always on the lookout for fresh wives and not too particular where or how he gets them. To the villagers, wives are important as chattels, producers of children and general beasts of burden. Now many of the negro women are barren, despite the efforts of many suitors to prove them otherwise, and a barren woman is no use as a wife. Pygmy women on the other hand are hardly ever barren and as a result are always in danger of being taken as wives by the negro villagers. The offspring of negro father and pygmy mother is held to be negro, and never returns to the pygmy tribe, while the contempt of the negro for the pygmy is such that it would be unthinkable for a pygmy man to acquire a negro wife.

Because of this the numbers of pygmies are decreasing steadily and most of their tribes contain considerably more men than women, whilst the villagers as the result of increasing admixture of pygmy blood, are showing signs of rapid physical deterioration.

The dependence of the pygmies on their villagers always struck me as slightly pathetic. Despite the way they were treated they were always so anxious to ape the negroes, often adopting their customs and tribal markings and even taking local tribal names for their children so that in a Mohammedan district, you would even find pygmies called Youssuf or Mohammed or Hassan.

Curiously, the only people the pygmies were not interested in imitating were the white races. Perhaps this was because the white people were the only ones who made any serious attempt to interfere with their freedom. One thing I really admired in the pygmies was their completely successful resistance to every attempt the Belgian government made to settle and educate them. Certainly the government tried hard enough but never really succeeded.

Maybe it was unenlightened of me, but I just could not see the point of trying to educate and settle a people like these who enjoyed freedom and a perfectly viable way of life in the forest. If they ever did settle the most they could hope for was to become a depressed peasantry with a low standard of living, prey to the worst features of European civilisation, and dominated by the more powerful and intelligent African races around them.

Perhaps the pygmies realised this in their way, for they proved as slippery as eels. Just when you think you have got hold of them they slip through your hands and disappear. Of course there were enthusiastic Europeans who, misled by the friendliness of the pygmies, thought they would succeed in stabilising them and organising their life on approved conventional lines.

I knew well a worthy Belgian missionary priest, not far from Putnam's Camp, who had been working among them for a long time. He was a great success among them because he could play the accordion and one evening when Pat Putnam and I visited the mission we saw the strange sight of this young bearded priest sitting in the middle of the forest surrounded by forty or fifty spellbound pygmies as he played them the latest dance tunes from Paris.

It was this priest who was one of the keenest advocates of settling the pygmies. It was he who arranged to build them a village, to furnish their huts and to cut an area of forest to give them fields to plant. He was a capable man and his planning was thorough. Every male pygmy in the settlement was given farming tools, including a shovel, a hoe and a wheelbarrow, and the pygmies were delighted.

They had never had anything like this before, and had the time of their lives. They took it in turns to wheel each other around in the wheelbarrows. They ran in and out of each other's houses, shouting with delight. They slammed the doors, they jumped in and out of the windows, they sat on the roofs, they lit fires in the grates and dug holes all over the place with their shovels. Every evening the young priest would play his accordion and on Sunday they obediently went to Mass.

This went on for a week and everyone was happy. Then one night every pygmy in the place decamped and went back to the forest again.

I am sure that Pat Putnam was successful with the pygmies for the very reason that he never tried to interfere with their way of life. I asked him once about the book he was supposed to be writing about them. He looked slightly evasive.

"Oh, it's coming on," he said. "But it's not a thing you can hurry. A race like the pygmies takes years to get to know properly. I'm only at the beginning."

As far as I know, the book never was finished but Pat Putnam was an indefatigable collector of information and would use this as an excuse to his wife whenever he felt like disappearing for a week or two into the forest with his pygmies. We went off together several times into the forest when the pygmies went on their hunting expeditions.

This was not an experience I would ever recommend to anyone who depends on the normal comforts of life. For the pygmies were tough, even the women and the youngest of them. They would follow the game on foot for days on end, padding tirelessly on through the forest, and never seeming to stop to rest or eat.

In the evening they would stop in a clearing; the women would make rough shelters for the night by prodding sticks into the ground, bending them beehive-fashion and thatching them swiftly with the large shiny leaves from the forest. One of these huts would take perhaps twenty minutes to build, and although they may have been all right for pygmies, I found them decidedly cramped as they had a diameter of scarcely five feet and could have been no more than three feet high.

Putnam seemed perfectly happy in his hut, curling himself up

ON SAFARI

without a blanket and snoring hard the whole night through. But I
found it almost impossible to get any sleep at all and profoundly
envied the pygmies their ability to doze off at a moment's notice
wherever they are.

The other great drawback to hunting with the pygmies con-
cerns the way they eat. If they are very hungry and kill anything
they gorge themselves on raw meat and fat. I have seen a pygmy
who scarcely came up to my chest consume five or six pounds of
meat hacked from the body of a freshly speared antelope, go to sleep
quite comfortably, and be ready next morning to travel across another twenty or thirty miles of forest.

On the other hand if they fail to kill anything they seem perfectly resigned to go for three or four days without eating a thing,
while I seemed to be ravenous most of the time, even though
Putnam had seen to it that I carried a rucksack full of food. I remember one occasion when we had been without food for two or three
days and I had been keeping myself going on bars of chocolate. I
had been rationing myself to a couple a day and was practically down
to my last bar, so I went off on my own to eat it. Two or three
pygmy children spotted me and came running over to see what I
was up to, so I gave them each a piece of chocolate to try.

Although they were inquisitive as all pygmy children are, they
were also slightly hesitant. They smelled the chocolate. They ran
their fingers over it. They put a tentative tooth to it.

"Come on," I said, "eat it. It tastes good." And I showed
them how I was eating it and enjoying it. This encouraged them to
take a bite. Each one, without exception, pulled a face of the utmost
disgust as soon as he tasted it and could not wait to spit it out. For
some while they went on spitting to get rid of what was obviously a
horrible taste to them.

An hour later we were on the move again and I noticed the
pygmies around me sniffing the air eagerly. This went on for some
time, the pygmies all the while getting more and more excited
until they started running through the forest and we all came to a
clearing. This was where the smell was coming from. Lying there
in an advanced stage of putrefaction, was the body of a cow buffalo
that had probably died of old age. The stink was indescribable,

worse by far than the smell of the dead buffalo in Pat Putnam's museum, and the pygmies revelled in it. They attacked the body as ants swarm on the body of a tasty insect. Right in the centre of the free-for-all and eating away for all they were worth were the three children who earlier on had spat out my chocolate with such horror.

With this buffalo the pygmies followed their usual practice. They ate a lot of it raw, and then the women cut up what was left. Some of it was scorched over the fire, to make it tender enough for the old men who had no teeth. The rest was smoked and kept as supplies for the future.

It was on one of these hunting expeditions with Pat Putnam that we learned of one of the most extraordinary of all the feats of the pygmy hunter—the killing of an elephant. It was extremely cruel and must have caused the elephant untold suffering before he died. But it called for such courage and stamina on the part of the hunter that I could not honestly find it in my heart to condemn it. For once the risks the hunter ran were far greater than those of his quarry, and for the pygmy—hunting was not a sport. It was the only way he knew to feed himself and his children.

By no means all the pygmy tribes hunt elephants. The majority of them prefer to leave them strictly alone, but Pat Putnam knew of one group who did hunt them and towards the end of my stay he took me to visit them. Unlike most tribal hunting this is not a communal activity. It is strictly a one-man affair. In the elephant-hunting tribes there are usually two or at the most three men who specialise in it. These are men of great prestige in the tribe and have to be of outstanding daring and ability.

For their work they use a heavy spear with an unusually broad blade and thick shaft, and start preparing themselves for a hunt several days before it is due to start. First the hunter works on his spear, polishing it and sharpening it until the whole of the big blade gleams and is keen as a razor. Then he strips completely and getting as close to a herd of elephants as he can, rolls himself in fresh elephant dung until covered with it from head to toe. For two or three days he lives like this, trailing the herd, constantly renewing the dung until the smell of man is entirely eliminated and replaced by the smell of elephant.

Early in the hunt the hunter chooses the elephant he hopes to kill. This is usually a good-sized young animal on the edge of the herd and the hunter trails it and watches it until he knows its habits and its entire personality. And all the time he waits for the opportunity he needs.

If he is in luck, this usually comes around midday when the elephants become sleepy and start to doze on their feet. It is then that he starts to creep towards the herd. This approach is agonisingly slow and the hunter moves with the silence of all the forest people. For the last few yards the man is like a snake on the ground and like a snake he slides right between the legs of the dozing elephant.

Even when an elephant is half asleep its sense of hearing is extraordinarily acute and from now on the crack of a twig or the nearest rustle of a leaf will bring the hunter instant death. But he must be under the belly for this is the one part of an elephant where the body is soft enough for a spear to reach to any depth, and he knows that if he tried to throw the spear from any distance he would have little chance of causing a mortal wound.

Instead he lifts his spear and cautiously stands up. He braces himself with his feet firmly apart. And then with all his strength he thrusts upwards with his spear driving it home with all his force before the elephant leaps, roaring with the pain. Often the hunter is caught and trampled to death. But if he is skilful, he knows the exact moment to withdraw his spear and dodge away from the great feet.

For the man and the elephant this is not the end of the hunt but only the beginning. At this stage the wound is not mortal. The torment of the elephant will not let up until its death and this will take several days. Until peritonitis develops far enough to sap its strength the animal keeps running, and as long as it runs the hunter must follow, trailing him night and day by the undergrowth it has trampled as it passed.

For the hunter there is neither food nor sleep, and it is only by the trail of blood that he can tell that the animal he pursues is still losing strength. On the third day or possibly the fourth the elephant begins to slow down and the hunter gains on him at last. He knows by now that the beast is doomed and when the elephant finally drags to a halt and drops to its knees for the last time, the pygmy is there, waiting.

Just before it dies the man comes up to it. He watches it carefully to make sure that its strength has really gone, and then with the razor sharp spear that made the original wound, he cuts off the animal's tail as proof of his victory. Then he leaves. He has to get back to his people to tell them he has killed his elephant and to lead them back to the carcase. This could easily be another four or five days' journey through the forest, and to find his way he has to follow the trail of the elephant back to the spot where he first speared him.

Exhausted, weak with starvation he reaches the camp. " I've killed an elephant. I've killed an elephant," he shouts, brandishing the tail as proof, and the entire tribe leaves its huts and its few possessions and follows him back to his elephant. They may have to carry the hunter now, for he would be too tired to travel fast enough for the rest of the tribe and they would want to reach the dead elephant before the predators of the forest had taken too much. Even so, the elephant would probably be ten days dead by the time they reached it.

But hungry though the tribe may be the pygmies do not cut up the carcase at once. The opening of an elephant has to be performed according to a ritual that never varies. First the chief, helped by the hunters, climbs up the side of the elephant and when he is on top of the grossly swollen carcase he begins carefully cutting a flap in the skin two feet square. This is pulled back. Then the chief himself cuts thin slivers of meat from inside the elephant and presents them first to the hunter who has killed the elephant and then in strict order of precedence to his favourites. The chief puts the meat in his mouth and passes it from his own mouth to that of the hunter who chews it and then swallows it ceremoniously. The same thing happens with the next of the favourites and the next and the next.

All the time, as the chief's knife slices deeper into the body of the elephant the old man feels with his thumb for the last membrane separating the stomach of the elephant from the flesh around it. During the time the animal has lain dead the gases inside have built up a great pressure and if the knife slipped the carcase would burst like a pricked balloon.

This must not happen; the custom of the pygmies prescribes that this last membrane must be bitten through by the youngest male child in the tribe. I would have thought this a terrifying ordeal for a young boy, but he shows no sign of fear. He must have been told the pygmy belief that when the elephant explodes into his face the courage and strength of the bravest and most powerful animal in the forest passes into him. The boy I saw doing this appeared eager for his grisly task.

It took him a few minutes to chew through the tough membrane, but as he did, the elephant burst with the noise of an exploding boiler and the child was thrown to the ground.

Then there was a free-for-all. Ritual and ceremony were forgotten as the whole tribe descended on the carcase. Even the children had their knives and within half an hour the bones had been picked clean and the animal which the hunter had taken such pains to kill was nothing but a large puddle in the clearing, in which the children were fishing for titbits.

9   *The Four-Tusked Elephant*

I T was while we were still at Putnam's Camp in the middle of the
Ituri Forest that I first heard about the elephant with four tusks.
Pat Putnam mentioned it himself one evening at dinner. Five or
six tourists had arrived that afternoon, and Putnam was in the sort
of mood when you could not be sure whether he was serious or not.
The party included a Texas millionaire, a big blustering man who
refused to be impressed by anything he saw, and he had obviously
annoyed Putnam. It was not so much what he said as the way he said
it and when he started talking about the animals he had shot on a
recent safari to East Africa Putnam interrupted him.

"You'd better not speak too loudly like that round here," he
said, fingering his beard in the way he usually did when someone
had upset him.

"Why not?" said the Texan.

"The elephant king might hear," said Putnam.

"The what?" said the Texan.

"The elephant king," repeated Putnam. "He's very powerful
round here. He knows what goes on in the forest and he doesn't care
much for hunters."

"What the hell d'you mean?" said the Texan. "Who is this
elephant king of yours?"

"Oh," said Putnam in a bored voice. "He's an old bull elephant
and the pygmies say he's their leader. He's very wild and very
strong and he's supposed to know when there's any danger to the
animals in the forest. You may not believe this but all the pygmies
round here do. By the way, he's got four tusks."

Of course, that started it. "Four tusks," bellowed the Texan.

"You'll be telling me next you've a unicorn hidden away in this forest of yours."

"Perhaps I have," said Putnam, still stroking his beard. "Perhaps I have."

"But four tusks," said the Texan. "There's no such animal."

Putnam smiled and refused to be drawn. He had probably got the effect he wanted and left the table soon after with all our questions about the four-tusked elephant unanswered.

I did not see him again until late the following day. He had been away in the forest. I found him on the edge of the camp talking to four or five pygmies and when he saw me, he waved me over. The pygmies were not of our own little tribe. They came from much deeper in the forest, but as usual Putnam was at home with them, squatting on the ground just as they did and laughing and joking with them in their own tongue. I knew just enough of this to join in and we sat for a while chatting about the animals they hunted. They talked about the tiny forest antelope they caught in their long nets. The talked about the leopards that they sometimes killed with their arrows and finally they talked about elephants.

"But what about this four-tusked elephant you're supposed to have seen," I said. "D'you ever see him?"

At once there was silence. Putnam looked across at me as if I ought to have had more sense than to ask a question like that, but in the end one of the pygmies, older than the rest, answered me.

"We have seen him many times," he said. "He's very fierce and very wicked. He sees things the other elephants don't see. Many times in the forest he has come and spoiled our hunt. He has killed many of our people, and now we keep well away from him. We cannot kill with our spears an elephant with four tusks."

At this they started laughing in an embarrassed way, all except Putnam, and I did not know whether to believe them or not.

When I asked Putnam about it later the same evening he was still strangely non-committal.

"Don't ask me," he said. "You heard what the old chap said."

"But you've never seen the four-tusked elephant yourself?"

"No, but that doesn't prove much either way. There are many things in the forest I've never seen. All I know is that every pygmy in this part of the Ituri Forest believes that he exists. I also know they're scared stiff of him, and pygmies don't scare easily."

From then on all I could think of was the four-tusked elephant. Twice I dreamed about him at night and I decided that whatever the cost, whatever the risk, I was going to find him and film him. In my mind's eye I could see the excitement the film would cause if I could get it back to America. But when I asked Putnam to help he would not have anything to do with it.

"Take my advice," he said. "Leave it alone. The pygmies know what they're up to. I don't know the reason but there's something unhealthy about the whole business."

Well, I was young in those days and saw no reason for letting Putnam put me off something I had set my heart on. Whenever I saw the pygmies I asked them about the elephant and from several more of them who claimed to have seen him, I gradually pieced together a mass of legends about this mysterious animal. According to these, he was not only supposed to be the leader of the elephants, but was said to talk to them in a human voice, warning them when the hunters were approaching and killing more men than any animal they or their fathers or their fathers' fathers had ever known.

"But where is he now?" I would ask them.

"In the forest," they would reply, shaking their heads. " Many days' journey," and always I noticed they would point to the east.

It was from these talks I had with the pygmies that I finally formed some theory about where the elephant must be. All the indications pointed to one particular place, a low-lying area of swamp, eighty or ninety miles from Putnam's Camp.

None of the pygmies seemed particularly keen on accompanying me to such an ill-omened spot but in the end I found three young men, more daring than the rest, who agreed to come as my guides in return for almost all the tobacco I possessed.

I told Putnam I was going, but he said nothing and I set off hardly knowing whether to feel brave or foolish.

We travelled three and a half days, keeping up the gruelling pace the pygmies maintain in the forest. We lived on fruit, condensed milk, berries and chocolate, and at night, slept under rough shelters of leaves. By the fourth day I had had enough and I was grateful when I saw the trees beginning to thin out and felt the ground becoming wet underfoot. There was much fresh elephant dung around.

We stopped beside a narrow stream. The pygmies signalled to me to keep quiet and as I waited I could see them in action, working skilfully forward, cautiously tracking the enormous footprints of an elephant through the bush.

They went slowly as if anxious to make no mistake, and telling from the lie of the grass and the way the ferns had been broken and not yet sprung back how recently the animal had passed.

"Is it he?" I would ask them, "the one with the four tusks," and they would gesture to me to keep quiet as if I should have known better.

"We'll see," they would whisper, "we'll see."

We kept going nearly six hours more before we found our elephant. He was in a clearing with about eight others, mostly young animals and they were all placidly eating away completely unaware of us, ripping down the branches from the trees and stuffing them unconcernedly into their mouths.

The elephant we had trailed was there in the middle of them. He was a very large, very old bull. I looked at his tusks. There were only two.

The three hunters turned to me and grinned.

"It's not him," they whispered. "It's not the king. He knew you were coming and he has gone."

As far as I was concerned, that was that. I had wasted a week but at least I felt that I had proved to myself that the four-tusked king of the Ituri Forest was a myth. Even Pat Putnam looked relieved when I returned, and I left Putnam's Camp a few days later to film in other parts of the Congo.

It was several months before I was back in the pygmy country and by then I had nearly forgotten about the elephant with four tusks. I was only passing through on some other business and we had stopped our trucks for the night at a settlement called Butembo on the edge of the forest.

Putnam's Camp lay a good way to the west and Butembo itself was a sad little place at the back of beyond boasting a single lodging house with the grandiose title of the Butembo Hotel. It was kept by an elderly Belgian and the night I was there I found myself sitting alone at a table next to four local Belgian settlers who had dropped in for an evening drink.

The one thing that made me take particular notice of them was that they talked Flemish, a language I had been fairly familiar with myself as a boy and I remember thinking it strange to be sitting there in the middle of Africa listening to these four hefty, rather sombre men with their big moustaches speak the language of my childhood. For a while they talked of nothing in particular but then I began to prick up my ears, for I heard them repeating the Flemish word "olifant" time after time. I listened more closely.

"But he insisted, this elephant had four tusks," said one.

"Oh, that's an African for you," said another. "If you asked them they would tell you that all their elephants have four tusks around here" and they all started laughing and one of them called for more beer.

By now I was engrossed in what they were saying, so I went over to their table, introduced myself, and asked them what all their talk was about a four-tusked elephant.

"Oh," said the man I had heard speaking first, "it's nothing really. I was just telling my friends here how I was in the office of one of the traders down the road this afternoon when in walked an African with a couple of pairs of elephant tusks to sell. As you know they have a government tax on killing elephants round here, so the agent asked the fellow for his tax money on the two elephants he must have killed to get the ivory. D'you know what the blighter replied?"

The man paused for effect as I shook my head.

"He said, 'Bwana, I killed no elephants. I found one elephant lying dead in the forest and it had the four tusks I am selling you now.'"

As he told the story, his friends saw the funny side of it again and once more started laughing.

"So what happened then?" I asked.

"What do you think? The agent's a Greek and Greeks aren't fools. Besides, what government inspector would take any notice of this nonsense about a four-tusked elephant? No, he just deducted the tax money for two elephants from the price of the ivory, and booted the man out."

Of course, they might have been right. The African might have been trying to swindle the agent. But whether he was or he was not, the story naturally revived all my interest in the legends I heard the year before from the pygmies at Putnam's Camp and next morning, as soon as the trader opened his shutters, I was there to ask him about the tusks.

The settlers had been right about him. Like many of the traders in this part of Africa, he was a Greek, a plump genial man called Xantos, and he treated the story of the elephant with four tusks as almost as big a joke as the men had thought it the night before.

" But did you buy the ivory?" I asked.

"Sure I bought the stuff. It wasn't much good but I bought it. The four tusks must have come off a pair of really skinny old elephants. It was very discoloured ivory and although the tusks were eight feet long they were terribly thin. Not much good."

He grinned and spat on the floor, just to show what he meant.

"But can I see them?" I asked.

"Now there," he said throwing up his hands, "isn't that a nuisance. I'm sorry but you can't. Just an hour after I bought them the truck called to collect the ivory and take it down to the central warehouse at Abba where they sort it out for shipment to Belgium. If you want to see the tusks that badly, you can always write to the warehouse."

This was maddening, to have the tusks escape me just when I thought I was about to solve the whole mystery, and I wondered if there was anything else I could find out about them from Xantos while I was there. "What about their weight?" I asked, remembering that he must have weighed them when he paid the African.

"Oh yes. All about the same I think. Let me see. I've got them down in the book."

He rummaged amid a pile of books and papers that seemed to fill his roll-top desk. "Let me see," he said when he had found the book and had placed his spectacles laboriously in position. "Yes, I was right. The first was twenty-two kilos. So was the second.

The third was just over twenty-three and the fourth nearly twenty-four."

"They all seem pretty light for tusks eight feet long," I said.

Before he replied he paused just long enough to look suspiciously at me over the top of his glasses.

"You seem very interested for such bad ivory," he said. "If it's just ivory you want I'd have no difficulty getting you very much better tusks than those."

"Well," I said, "ivory's my hobby and you know how hard it is to find four old tusks so equally matched as these seem to be."

"I see," said Xantos non-committally. "It's none of my business anyhow. Is there anything else I can do for you over them?"

"Yes," I said. "You can give me the name of the African who brought them to you in the first place."

"Now how should I know that?" He spat once again on the floor. "I kicked the rogue out as soon as I'd paid him. When people try pulling a fast one over me I don't ask them to stay for a drink."

Luckily Butembo was the sort of place where everyone knew everyone else and after half an hour of discreet inquiries in the village, I knew who had sold Xantos the tusks. He was a young man called Mombeli. He was not married, and had his hut on the outskirts of the village. I found him sitting outside it rather miserably I thought, and at first he refused to answer my questions at all about the tusks as he obviously thought I had been sent to arrest him.

I gave him a cigarette, lit it for him, and then put the whole packet in his hands.

"Mombeli," I said, "I want to know the truth about this four-tusked elephant you say you found. Did you really find him, Mombeli, or were you just trying to cheat the trading company out of their tax money?"

"No, bwana, I was cheating no one."

"But you mean to say you really found an elephant with four tusks lying dead in the bush? No one's ever heard of an elephant with four tusks, Mombeli."

"I know, bwana," he said. "I would not have believed it myself, but there he was, a great elephant, bigger than I have ever seen. He had been lying dead many days and he had the four tusks I brought to the agent." He grinned sheepishly as if he realised the improbability of what he was saying.

"Where did this happen?" I asked and he pointed to the west describing a marshy area near a stream that sounded very like the place I had gone to the previous year with the pygmies in my original search for the elephant. If Mombeli really was telling the truth his discovery of the four-tusked elephant would be a fantastic coincidence. But stranger things have happened in Africa.

"Could you find the remains of the elephant again?" I asked him.

He shrugged his shoulders. "It is a long way," he said. "It might be difficult to find the place."

"Come over to my truck a minute, Mombeli," I said. He followed me without too much enthusiasm, but I opened the back and took out the first objects of value I saw—an oil lantern and a large chrome battery-operated flashlight. I also took the watch off my wrist. I knew all three objects were highly coveted among the Africans of the Congo.

"Listen, Mombeli. I want the head of that elephant and I want it badly. I have to go north but if you have that head waiting here for me when I return I will give you all these things. Do you think you will be able to find the head for me now?"

His face broke into an enraptured smile. "Sure, bwana. Now I understand. I find it. I find it all right."

I returned to my camp still not knowing quite what to think. I was certain by now that Mombeli believed what he was telling me, but that was not proof that the four-tusked elephant really had existed. I would have full and complete proof only if I succeeded in getting those tusks that had been sent on to Abba, and in fitting them, one by one, into the sockets of the skull they had originally come from. Unless I could get both the skull and the tusks, I would be wasting my time.

So the next thing was to write to the warehouse of the trading company at Abba describing the tusks in detail, offering a price well over their market value for them, and asking that they should be sent immediately to me care of the post office at Butembo. After this there was nothing to do but wait, and I set off on my journey north knowing I had done everything I could to settle the mystery. It was nearly four months before we were back again in Butembo. I went straight to Mombeli's hut. It was deserted. I asked his neighbours where he was, but nobody knew. Someone said they thought he had gone off to Stanleyville for a job five or six weeks before, but there had been no news from him, and although I searched all round his hut just in case he had left the elephant's head there, I could find nothing.

Again I asked his neighbours whether they had seen him carrying the head into the village, but they said "no," and looked at me sympathetically as if afraid I had been having a little too much sun.

Once again it looked as if the four-tusked elephant was going to escape me and keep his mystery after all. I realised then that there was one last chance of finding the head. There was a Belgian administrator living in Butembo. His name was Renaud and I knew him slightly. There was just a possibility that Mombeli, after waiting several weeks for my return, had taken the head to him for safe keeping.

Renaud was an administrator of the old school. A large, courteous old man, he was also something of a martinet and a stickler for the niceties of life. He was not a man to appreciate a story about a four-tusked elephant.

"Did an African called Mombeli leave a large package for me while I was away?" I asked him.

"No, Mr. Denis," he said sharply. "What were you expecting?"

"An important anatomical specimen," I said rather pompously. "You're sure nobody left anything like that at all?"

He shook his head. "What sort of specimen?" he said.

"Nothing important," I replied, trying to hide my disappointment. "It was just that an African from the village had promised to try and get hold of the skull of a particular elephant for me."

"An elephant skull, so that's what it was," bellowed old Renaud. "I wouldn't have recognised it. Filthy-looking thing it was when the boy brought it in. Crawling with worms. Stank the office out. Next time you go asking Africans to collect decaying elephants' heads for you, I would be obliged if you would ask them to leave them in someone else's house."

ON SAFARI

I tried to calm him down. " But what happened to it . . .
Monsieur Renaud ?" I asked.

"Happened to it? What the devil d'you think happened to it?
I told your African friend to get rid of it and pushed him out before
we all caught something from it."

Well, that was that. After so much trouble I had lost the proof I
needed. Unless I had the skull and the tusks actually fitted perfectly
into place, no one would believe the four-tusked elephant ever had
existed. The only thing to do now was to go along to the post
office and collect the tusks that I had asked the warehouse at Abba
to send me the last time I was in Butembo, but even here I was out
of luck. Instead of the tusks, there was a letter from one of the trading company's clerks.

"We have identified your tusks," he wrote. "They are in
bundles Nos. 4632 and 4639. Unfortunately, by the time we received your letter they had already been despatched to our warehouse in Belgium. If you wish to pursue the matter further, we
suggest you contact our head office in Antwerp."

As things were it hardly seemed worth taking the trouble. The
skull was lost and so the tusks proved nothing. But as I strolled,
rather despondently, back to my camp I passed Renaud's office
again, and just beyond it, in a mud ditch skirting the road, I caught
sight of something white. It looked at first like a huge ball of bone
lying half buried in the mud. I walked over and prodded it with my
stick. It was bone, and when I began pushing the earth away, I saw
that at last my luck had turned. It was the skull of a fully grown
elephant.

When I thought about it, I realised what had happened. After
old Renaud had pushed the unfortunate Mombeli out of his house,
the African had obviously looked around for somewhere to dump
the head of this elephant that had caused him so much trouble.
Understandably he had chosen the ditch.

This changed everything and I felt all my previous excitement
return. The first thing to do was to make sure of the tusks. This
was not so difficult as it might have been as my family still lives in
Antwerp. So I rushed back to the post office and sent off a telegram

to my father, asking him to go to the company's warehouse at once and buy for me tusks Nos. 4632 and 4639.

When that was done, I went back to my camp, threw a shovel into the back of one of the trucks and drove back to disinter the skull. It was hard work. The skull was even bigger than I had thought, and old Renaud had been right about it. The stench was terrible.

But finally, doing my best to hold my breath, I heaved the thing out on to the road and looked where the tusks had been. On each side of the jaw, one above the other, were two quite separate sockets. I was jubilant. All my filming was finished. We were ready to drive back to Europe at the end of my first big successful expedition, and now to crown it I had proof of the existence of an animal no one had thought to exist.

But I was still far from the end of my troubles. I still had to reunite the skull with those tusks and to do this meant carrying the skull just as it was, all the way back to Europe with us. It soon proved quite the most uncomfortable piece of luggage I have had to take anywhere.

First we tried carrying it wrapped in a tarpaulin and lashed to the roof of one of the trucks to spare us the smell but that did not work. A low branch swept it off as we drove through the forest in French Equatorial Africa, and we had a terrible time trying to rescue it from the stream where it had fallen. After this I was not taking any risks. Smell or no smell I was not letting it out of my sight. No one else in the expedition would put up with it so I drove alone in the cab with the skull in solitary state behind me.

Even then there was trouble. One evening just as we had pitched camp on the edge of the Sahara before tackling the six day drive across the desert, I had left the skull inside the truck with the rear doors open to try to let the air circulate a little. I was in my tent and just dropping off to sleep when I heard a great noise of howling and snarling outside. I peered out, and there in the moonlight I made out three hyenas fighting over something large they had just dragged from the back of the truck. It was the head, and, although we finally drove the hyenas away the bone was badly chewed and split in places. Luckily it was only the back of the head.

The jaw and the sockets were untouched, but I decided that from now on I was going to take even greater care of it, and drove the rest of the journey across the Sahara and up through Morocco, Spain and France with the truck doors locked and the skull securely roped to the floor.

By the time we reached Antwerp I had had enough; I remember driving gratefully along the Avenue Brialmont where my father had his house, and thinking to myself that in a few moments now my ordeal would be over.

We had been away altogether eighteen months and my family's welcome was wonderful but after we had greeted each other almost my first words to my father were, "You've got the tusks I cabled you about?"

As a judge my father always spoke with careful deliberation. "Ah, yes! The tusks," he said. "I received your cable from the Congo and I went to the warehouse. They showed me the tusks you had cabled about."

"Did you buy them?" I said. "Did you buy them?"

"Well, I looked at those tusks and they seemed very poor to me. They had far better tusks at the warehouse."

"Did you buy them?" I said again. "Did you buy them?"

"Well, I hesitated a long time. I don't know why you could have wanted those terrible tusks, and . . ."

My voice almost failed me, but I said once more, "Did you buy them?"

"Sure, sure. I bought them. They're quite safe. You mustn't get so excited, Armand."

"But where are they?" I almost shouted.

"They're in New York, of course."

"New York?" I said.

"Yes, New York. Didn't you ask me to send all those specimens of yours to the New York Museum of Natural History? I naturally thought you intended me to include the tusks."

When we sailed for New York a fortnight later, the elephant's head, packed in a big airtight crate, was still with us, like some grisly and cumbersome talisman. As soon as we docked I telephoned the Museum of Natural History to make sure the tusks had arrived safely. They had, so, without waiting for anything else I loaded the skull into a taxi and drove straight to the Museum.

When we arrived, Dr. James Clark, one of the directors of the Museum, met me. He had the tusks waiting in his office. They were exactly as Xantos had described them, old, heavily scarred, with the ivory pitted and discoloured. As I looked at them I could not help thinking of the first conversations I had had with the pygmies at Putnam's Camp and the way they had described the elephant king of the Ituri Forest. I wondered how many of their tribe these very tusks had accounted for.

We still had to make sure that these really were the tusks belonging to the skull. So we unwrapped the skull, placed it on the floor, and tried fitting the tusks into their original holes. There were grooves in the sockets matching slight grooves in the ends of the tusks, and the first three tusks slid home perfectly and there could be no possible doubt that they belonged.

But, try as we would we could not fit in the last tusk. Suddenly I realised the truth: the fourth tusk, instead of curving outward as normal tusks do, curved inwards. The four-tusked elephant had had three normally shaped tusks and one that pointed inwards and actually rubbed against those opposite. We turned the fourth tusk around and it slid into position as neatly as the others.

Even when the skull and the tusks were assembled, I could still hardly believe that I had finally solved the mystery of the elephant king of the Ituri Forest and that the long search for the king of the elephants who talked and who carried four tusks was over.

FOR me the real difficulties of an expedition always began when I was back in civilisation. I enjoyed life on safari because of its simplicity. I had only myself to depend on then and never had to think very far beyond the next hazard or the next decision. During the eighteen months of the Congo expedition I was probably freer from anxiety than I had ever been before in my life. Now all this changed abruptly.

Before I could get away again I had first to sell my film and persuade a new set of backers in America to put up the money I needed.

The Chrysler company were delighted with the hour-long film—"Wheels across Africa"—I made them on my journey, and promised to back me for another expedition. But their support on its own was not enough. So I set off for Hollywood, taking with me the rest of the footage I had shot in the Congo, that was later to be edited into the film "Dark Rapture." In the end "Dark Rapture" was to prove one of the most commercially successful of all my films, but this took far more time than I was prepared to give.

What I wanted was a quick deal with a film company that would give me the money I needed and the chance to escape and organise a new expedition. But speed seemed to be the one commodity Hollywood did not have to offer.

There was a lot of interest in my film, for these were the days before it had become fashionable for major film producers to spend several months and several million dollars on location in the middle of Africa. Just for a while I was something of a celebrity, and a lot of the leading directors and film stars would ask for a special showing of my film. But this seemed to be little help in getting me the sort of deal I needed and although M.G.M. gave me a contract for my film, it was on condition that I stayed on in Hollywood to supervise the editing while my material was turned into a feature film.

In the end I spent eight months there, and if there is one spot on earth where I would rather not spend another eight months, it is Hollywood. There was something about the place even then that seemed to breed inertia and frustration, and although I could have joined one of the big film companies and travelled and made films for them as an employee, I realised that my independence as a film maker was something that was worth preserving at all costs.

As a result it was over three years after my return from the Congo before I was ready to leave America again. This time my plans were really ambitious. It had taken me so long to mount this expedition that I was determined to go as far and see as much as I could. My first stop was to be Rangoon. From Rangoon I was going to drive north across Burma to the town of Lashio on the Chinese border. At Lashio I planned to take the newly constructed Burma Road into China and through to Chungking. From Chungking I then intended to travel eastwards to my final destination—Lhasa, the mountain capital of Tibet.

On paper my plans were wildly impractical. The Burma Road was barely finished, there was a civil war raging in China and there was no reliable information at all on the final stage of the journey from the Chinese border through Tibet. But I had learned in the Congo that what looks impractical on paper is often surprisingly possible when you are on the spot and I knew that the higher you set your aim, the more chance you have of finally achieving something.

My guiding principle was to travel as light as possible, for I had no idea how long we would be able to keep going by car, especially once we started travelling west from Chungking. I wanted us to be able to shift everything we had at a moment's notice from the trucks on to the backs of mules or horses. If it was really necessary we might even have to carry the equipment ourselves.

On the 4th of April, 1939, I sailed from New York to Amsterdam on the first leg of my Far Eastern expedition. From Amsterdam I picked up a Dakota that flew the seven-thousand-odd miles to Burma in just under three and a half days, and I landed at Rangoon to find the rest of my expedition waiting for me on the airfield with the trucks fuelled up and the film equipment ready for the journey.

Before we could leave, I felt I must get our Chinese visa, and visited the consulate. But although the Chinese officials were scrupulously polite, the necessary authorisation from Chungking never came. For several days I stayed on in Rangoon, sending cables and express letters to everyone I could think of who might be able to get us the authorisation we needed. I even cabled direct to Chiang himself.

Finally I decided it was pointless to stay on, getting bored in Rangoon, when there was the whole of Burma waiting to be filmed, so I arranged to keep in touch with the American consulate in Rangoon and set off north.

Burma was fascinating and the films we shot there were to be the salvation of the expedition. They included the elephants of the teak forests I have already described and the boatmen of Lake Inle who paddle their boats with their feet instead of their hands. But the strangest scenes of all concerned the priestess of the snakes.

I had first come across the cult of the snake when I was in Ceylon, and was told the ancient legend of the snake god Naga who was vanquished by a woman. At one time the cult had been common across the whole of the East, and the story of Eve and the serpent is probably a variant on the original legend. It was one of those recurrent myths that had always fascinated me, but when I inquired further I had always been told that the only place where the rites of the snake god were still practised was in some forgotten part of central Burma.

I was reminded strongly of all this on my journey, especially when we began to find the remains of several ruined temples with the elaborate carvings of the snake god still on the walls. But it was not until we reached the dead city of Pagan in northern Burma and saw the four ruined temples of Naga that I had any definite evidence that the worship of the snake god was still alive. After considerable inquiries I met an old Bhuddist priest who told me where to go if I wished to find the last priestess of this cult.

His directions led us to a mountainous area two days' journey away, and there, in the isolated village the old man had described, we found the family that kept alive the cult of the snake. There seemed to be no men in the family; there was an old grandmother, her daughter—a beautiful young woman in her early thirties—and two grandchildren of twelve and fourteen, both girls. The older women were the traditional priestesses of the snake.

They were quite open about it all and seemed to enjoy great prestige in the village, where they were regarded as women of considerable sanctity; but at first I did not believe what they told me, for they said that the snakes they worshipped were king cobras.

Now a king cobra is an enormous snake. A large one can measure fourteen or fifteen feet long. Its head is as big as a man's fist. It is extremely aggressive and treacherous and a dose of poison from a fully grown male is enough to kill twenty people.

But the women insisted that the snakes they worshipped were king cobras, and during the evening we spent with them, recounted some of the legends about the snake god. They told us how they went into the mountains to capture the snake and how the snake promised to behave and obey the priestess provided it was released at the end of a year at precisely the spot where it was first captured.

Although I found it hard to believe all this, the women were obviously sincere and ended up promising to take us next morning to visit the king cobra, the present snake god in his cave in the mountains.

We were at the house of the priestesses early next morning, but half the village seemed to be there before us, and the women were already up, the old grandmother coming out to greet us and smiling politely at us as if we were all going off to a garden party in our Sunday best.

We were given places of honour beside the priestess—the mother of the two young girls—in an ox cart at the head of the procession, while the rest of the villagers trailed behind carrying gifts to the snake god. A typical village orchestra of gongs and bells brought up the rear. The path wound its way up the side of the mountain. After about an hour the ox cart could go no further so, following the priestesses, we continued the journey on foot.

We must have walked another two or three miles, when

suddenly the orchestra stopped and the crowd fell silent. Ahead of us lay a bend in the path with a small cave just visible beyond. The procession halted. Some time passed while the gifts to the snake—I noticed rice and salt among the offerings—were laid out on the edge of the path.

The priestess of the snake then went on, beckoning me to follow. Calmly, gracefully, she walked towards the mouth of the cave, then paused. Everyone was waiting and in the silence I heard her call softly. For several minutes nothing happened. Then suddenly, out of the cave, slid a fourteen foot king cobra. It came swiftly, as if it had been expecting her, coiled itself almost at her feet, and reared up its head to strike.

The priestess watched this without the slightest movement. She was perhaps four feet away from the snake—certainly no more—and she bowed to the snake once, solemnly inclining her head.

She must have known by instinct when the snake would strike for she moved her knees so as to deflect the blow and the cobra buried its fangs into the folds of her skirt. This happened again and again, almost as if the girl was dancing with the snake. Her motions were unhurried and as graceful as those of a dancer. Each time she would move her knees a fraction and each time the snake would strike harmlessly at her skirt until the white of the material was yellow with venom.

But now the girl moved forward, closer to the snake; she waited until it was quite motionless. Then, slowly she put her hands behind her back and leant forward to kiss the snake lightly on the top of its head, drawing back just before it struck again. Three times she did this, then turned away and began her unhurried walk back towards us. For a moment I thought the snake might follow her and strike from behind. Instead it lowered its head and slid back into its cave.

The girl seemed completely unaffected by what she had been through and smiled cheerfully at me as she took her place beside me in the bullock cart. We returned to the village as we had come, with the procession trailing behind us and the orchestra bringing up the rear.

We left the village that afternoon. Throughout our journey

across Burma I had kept in touch with the American consulate in Rangoon, but as they had no news for me about the permits needed to drive to Chungking, I finally decided to continue into China, visa or no visa. To start with this presented no difficulty. The border town of Lashio that marked the beginning of the Burma Road was in chaos. It was choked with war supplies waiting to be driven the seventeen hundred miles to Chiang Kai-Shek and his armies in Chungking, and everything seemed to have broken down. The monsoon had started, turning Lashio into a wilderness of mud and corrugated iron; left in the middle of it all were great dumps of forgotten stores and acres of abandoned lorries.

The authorities there had other things than us to worry about. We would watch convoys of a hundred or two hundred brand new lorries arriving on the road from Rangoon. They would be parked for the night, and then next morning we would see that half of them had had their tyres stolen. They would be left where they were and a few hours later fresh lorries would arrive to add to the chaos.

As soon as we saw this, our one ambition was to drive on and away from it all; so we left Lashio less than forty-eight hours after we arrived, and took the spectacular Burma Road to the north. The landscape was overwhelming—a succession of gorges and mountains, most of them covered with thick forest, with the road like a thin ribbon looping its way along the sides of ravines and across mountain ranges where no one would ever have thought a road could be built.

The Chinese had built the road before the rains and it must have looked very beautiful when they had finished it, with the surface as smooth and level as a tennis court. But there was no real foundation to it, and with the monsoons, as truck after truck ground its way north, the road began to collapse. Mile after mile of the Burma Road was simply washing away.

All this made the journey quite hair-raising. Every ravine we crossed would have its litter of smashed trucks lying at the bottom, many of them with the bodies of the drivers still inside since there was nobody to bother to get them out. The drivers of the endless convoys would be worn out with fatigue or drugged with opium and quite unfit to drive. But the convoys would grind and skid their way forward through the blinding rain—the windscreen wipers would have been stolen before ever the trucks left the docks in Rangoon—and often when one truck was forced to stop the one behind would crash into it, blocking the road again.

During these stops we often met the convoy drivers. Few of them seemed to care whether they reached Chungking or not, and we never had much difficulty buying extra stocks of petrol from them for our own trucks.

For nearly a week I still believed we would get to our destination. Then we reached a spot where the road was completely impassable. Two entire convoys were jammed ahead of us, and the only place where we could camp was in a Chinese cemetery overlooking the road.

Four days we stayed there and it rained steadily the whole time. The convoys ahead of us showed no sign of moving. The drivers, desperate with hunger, started raiding the farms, and the local farmers, in retaliation, started attacking the convoys at night with pitchforks. Then rumours reached us that bandits were further along the road and would attack any crippled truck.

What finally decided me to turn back was the sight of the first refugees straggling back along the road. A woman passed, carrying the body of her dead husband and holding a child by the hand. An epidemic of cerebral malaria broke out in the villages ahead, and I realised that if we did not get out now, and fast, we would stay in that cemetery until we were buried in it.

This was the nearest my Far Eastern expedition ever got to its destination. We managed to turn our trucks and however bitter my disappointment, I was profoundly relieved when we finally got back to the welcoming chaos of Lashio. The expedition I had worked four years to achieve had failed, and I had no idea what we were going to do next.

In situations like this, the one thing to avoid is to stand still. So the morning we arrived at Lashio I insisted on refuelling our trucks and driving as steadily as we could back to Rangoon. Three days later we were on board a tramp steamer, headed for Calcutta. I had another idea, doomed to failure, that if we could get to Calcutta, we might be able to strike north again and to reach Tibet by the back door across the Himalayas.

But as soon as we reached Calcutta we found that the rains were worse than ever; the flat lands to the north were so badly flooded that there was no question of driving that way for several weeks. Worse still, I was told that because of the prevailing political tension and the serious threat of war, the northern borders of India had been closed.

This time there was nothing for it but to stop. Reluctantly I booked my whole party in at the Great Eastern Hotel and prepared to wait out the rains. There was no point in being miserable. We had enough money. It was a good hotel, and there was all the time in the world. So I started giving parties. These would begin every day after lunch and go on as long as anyone cared to stay. We invited anyone who looked interesting, and within a few days our parties at the Great Eastern Hotel had become quite a feature of life in Calcutta. More and more people turned up. There would be high caste Brahmins, and Saddhus clad only in loin-cloths. Local politicians came and philosophers and holy men. Journalists arrived and lots of pretty girls in saris, and however many gatecrashers there were we never really minded as long as the parties went with a swing.

It was one of these parties that was to save the expedition. For one afternoon, when most of us were beginning to feel the effects of nearly a fortnight of non-stop party giving, I found myself talking to a very beautiful Indian girl. I suppose I was feeling sorry for myself and as she was the sort of pretty girl you could tell your troubles to, I proceeded to tell her all the difficulties we had encountered.

This went on for some time, and she kept interrupting me, saying, "But Mr. Denis, why don't you go to Nepal?"

For a while I ignored these remarks, for I knew as well as anyone that it was impossible to go to Nepal. Nepal was a sort of modern Shangri-La. It was inaccessible. It was carefully protected by the British Government, and to enter it you needed a special invitation from the Maharajah of Nepal, an invitation that I knew was very rarely given.

Finally I said to her, "But don't be ridiculous. It's impossible to get to Nepal."

"Not really," she replied. "My father is the Maharajah. I think it would be easy enough to arrange."

11   *Nepal*

THAT was the last party we held at the Great Eastern Hotel. Without wasting a moment I grabbed the girl by the hand, called a taxi, and drove at full speed to the General Post Office where we sent a long telegram to the Maharajah of Nepal. The reply inviting us to visit him, arrived the next morning.

Nepal is a mountain kingdom rather larger than Britain, lying to the north-east of India and containing within its borders a very substantial portion of the Himalayas, including Mount Everest. At this time, after Tibet, it was probably the most difficult place in the world to reach, since there was no road from India and everything had to enter on foot or be carried on the backs of porters through a succession of mountain passes.

It was a bizarre journey. Somehow we managed to negotiate the floods and get as far north as the town of Patna where we had to leave our trucks and load our equipment aboard the tiny train that puffed its way twice a week to a town called Raxaul at the foot of the Himalayas. From Raxaul the Maharajah had arranged for an ancient Buick of his to meet us and jolt us a few miles further on. It left us at a village where the track ended. From there we either travelled in an open carrying-chair borne by porters or we walked. I walked!

This journey across the mountains I found agreeably relaxing after the nerve-racking splendours of the Burma Road. It took us four days of leisurely travel, and each evening we would reach a rest-house where a meal would usually be waiting for us. These rest-houses were extremely primitive, and at our first stop I was surprised to find a large gleaming white enamel bath full of hot water waiting for me in my room. This happened again on the

131

second night in the second rest-house, and again on the third night when I found the identical tub waiting for me in the third rest-house.

It was then that I realised that every morning, just before we left, my magnificent bath was being disconnected, rushed on ahead by a special gang of porters, and then installed and filled in the next rest-house along the route, to await my arrival.

The skill and staying power of these porters of the Himalayas never ceased to astonish us. At one point on the journey we passed a large Dodge car being carried across the mountains to Nepal by a gang of them. Just after this point we found ourselves picking our way over boulders up an almost vertical incline. But a few days later we saw this very Dodge car on the streets of Katmandu, so somehow or other these porters must have manhandled it up. We saw a steamroller in Katmandu, and a huge bronze equestrian statue of the reigning Maharajah. They too could only have reached Nepal by being carried on men's backs across the mountains.

Several times we passed individual porters, tough wiry little men who could not have weighed much more than 140 lbs., climbing up a steep slope with a basket-work affair on their backs in which sat a large Indian lady with a couple of children squatting calmly on her lap.

Just to try out one of the porters we met, I asked him how much he would charge to carry me to Katmandu, at that time still two days' journey distant. This porter was particularly small and I weighed well over 15 stone at the time. Without bothering to look at me he said two rupees and motioned me to climb up on his back. In those days two rupees were worth about ten shillings, so I paid him in advance, climbed aboard the chair, let him carry me about fifty yards just to see what it felt like, and then told him I had had enough. To this day he is still probably wondering about the mad foreigner who gave him two rupees for nothing.

On the fourth day we had finished the worst part of the journey, and reached a village to find that the Maharajah had sent us a horse. This was considered a great honour, and I felt I ought to try to live up to it. But this was difficult as the horse could barely stand. As soon as he felt my weight across his back he would immediately sit down. The man who had brought him would then pull the poor creature to his feet again, but as soon as he let go, my mount would sink to his knees like a rubber horse someone had let the air out of.

After two or three attempts I felt it would be kindlier and more dignified to enter Katmandu on foot and left the horse with a relieved expression on its face, still lying in the main street of the village. In the end, however, we had to pay for the horse. We also paid for the bath-tub, for the guides, and for the ancient Buick. We paid for everything at an extremely unfavourable rate of exchange, and the recipient was the Maharajah.

For when we arrived in Katmandu next day we found that this enigmatic gentleman controlled everything in Nepal and made a very good thing out of it. Officially of course we were the Maharajah's guests, but that merely made us more vulnerable. We were assigned an old and irascible court official whose visiting card carried the printed legend, "Official in charge of Hospitality," and whose sole purpose seemed to be to stop us going where we wanted or filming what we liked. We would try to film the whole great chain of the Himalayas, sometimes visible from Katmandu, but every time we climbed to a second story window to shoot our film over the roofs of the city, "Old Hospitality" as we called him, would be there before us and would officiously inform us that what we planned to do was impossible without the Maharajah's permission. This seemed to apply to almost everything in Katmandu and I realised that the only way we would ever get a chance of any worthwhile films was to see the Maharajah in person.

For several days we were unlucky and we became thoroughly sick of Katmandu. Despite all its romantic associations, I found it a thoroughly dreary, decaying place without a scrap of charm or interest in it. But after nearly a week of waiting, "Old Hospitality" appeared, looking more bad-tempered than ever, to inform us that the Maharajah was graciously pleased to grant our request and would see us at two-thirty the following afternoon.

So the next day, just after lunch, we duly presented ourselves at the royal palace in Katmandu in our best khaki suits and our cleanest brown shoes, and were escorted in to meet His Highness. The palace was quite awful. It was built of a ginger-coloured stone and looked like a large piece of overcooked pastry. Everywhere we looked there

133

seemed to be ponds and staircases and marble fountains and stained-glass windows. After a considerable walk through reception room after reception room we finally reached the great state staircase. There to my horror I realised that this was not going to be the sort of informal interview with the Maharajah I had hoped for. Instead, visitors of any sort were presumably so rare in Katmandu in those days that our arrival—which had automatically doubled the European population of Nepal—was being made an excuse for a complete state occasion.

Solemnly marshalled in order of precedence along the top of the staircase and waiting to greet us, was the entire cabinet of Nepal. Every minister was there complete with morning coat, wing collar and decorations. Each wore a fez, each had small spectacles with old-fashioned steel frames and, as we came up the stairs, they all bowed in unison.

Now, along the wall behind the row of bobbing dignitaries, and occupying the full width of the landing, was a complete set of distorting mirrors. I suppose some earlier maharajah of Nepal had seen them on his travels in Europe, fallen in love with them, and had them shipped back to Katmandu. But as the ministers bowed so gravely before us, I caught sight of their backs in the mirrors, popping up and down in grotesque distortion like something in the Fun House at Coney Island.

The Maharajah himself was most cordial. He received us in a room crammed with a strange mixture of junk and genuine treasure. There was a stuffed racehorse in one corner, whilst a huge German clock, in which all the gears were made of glass, stood on one side of the room with a cabinet of priceless Ming porcelain on the other.

We talked polite generalities for a while; I had some difficulty in reminding him why we were there. I told him about his daughter in Calcutta. "Daughter, daughter," he kept repeating, "which daughter?" And although he finally grasped who I was talking about, one of the ministers later explained that the Maharajah often had this sort of difficulty keeping track of his children; he had over forty legitimate sons alone, all full generals in the Nepalese army, not to mention the countless colonels and brigadiers that nobody mentioned in his presence.

After a while I managed to explain that if it was possible I wanted to shoot scenes of animals in Nepal. At once the Maharajah's face lit up.

"You shoot?" he said.

I tried to explain that the sort of shooting we did was with cameras but he did not seem to understand the distinction I was making between this and big game hunting, and led me off to another room. It was really a hall, some forty feet long, and I realised it was the Maharajah's own trophy room. An artist had been brought all the way from Paris to cover one whole wall with an immense mural depicting, in heroic proportions, the Maharajah hunting rhinoceroses in the Himalayas. Along the length of the hall ran a series of low marble pillars. There must have been at least twenty on each side of the room. On each, expertly mounted, rested the stuffed head of a rhino.

That great room itself with its unspeakable mural was unpleasant enough, but those forty heads sent shudders down my spine. For they were the heads of East Indian rhinoceroses and as far as I knew there were hardly forty still in existence.

These huge animals are quite distinct from the African rhino, and first reached Europe in Roman times. Albrecht Dürer used one as a model for his famous engraving of a rhinoceros. They are covered with a set of leathery plates like armour and occur in the forest belt below the Himalayas near the border of India from Nepal.

While the Maharajah was talking to me about his hunting, I peered at the back of one of these heads and was fascinated to see that the plaster at the back of the neck, where the head had been severed, had been carefully painted to show every blood vessel and air tube, as if the head had been freshly cut off.

Suddenly this macabre collection seemed to expose the whole cult of big game hunting for the gruesome, useless business it is. As politely as I could I said to the Maharajah, "You are aware, of course, Your Highness, that there are very, very few of these animals left and that when you have shot the last of them the whole species will then be extinct."

He took his time to reply and then turned to me and winked.

"I think you will find," he said, "that there will be just enough to last me my lifetime."

That was not the only occasion on which we met the Maharajah. He seemed to like the idea of being filmed and sent a message to me a few days later through "Old Hospitality" saying that if we would like to come to the palace with our camera, he would be delighted to pose for us. Up to now we had had little enough to film as wild life was scarce around Katmandu and we soon got tired of filming the holy cows that wandered where they wanted to along the streets —(one of the few amusing things I found in Katmandu, incidentally, was an alms-house for elderly cows, for the cow, of course, could not be killed, and the aged but still sacred beasts presented something of a problem).

We sent a message back, thanking the Maharajah, and duly presented ourselves once more at the palace the following afternoon. This time there was no sign of the courtiers we had met on our first visit, and "Old Hospitality" handed us over to a sort of vizier who conducted us to the throne room where the Maharajah was waiting for us.

This time he was looking quite splendid, covered in medals, orders and gold braid and wearing the uniform of a field-marshal of the Nepalese army. We set up the camera, and were just about to start filming him when the Maharajah clapped his hands.

"One moment," he said. "Before you start. You would prefer to film me with my crown, I think."

I had never heard of anyone in a field-marshal's uniform wearing a crown before, but I thanked him and said, yes, I thought he would look very nice in his crown if he could get it without too much trouble. He immediately spoke a few words to the vizier who scurried away, returning a few minutes later with a large Huntley and Palmers biscuit tin. This was placed carefully on the floor in front of the throne, and the Maharajah took off the lid and drew out the most elaborate crown I have ever seen. It was covered with diamonds, and emeralds as large as grapes. Quite casually the Maharajah took off his field-marshal's cap and put the crown in its place.

136

But even then he was clearly not happy with his appearance, and started a worried conversation with the vizier. This went on for some minutes, and at the end of it the vizier came over to where we were standing.

"The Maharajah wants to know," he said solemnly, "will you take his picture with specs or without specs?"

I looked towards the throne and saw the Maharajah beneath his enormous crown blinking owlishly at us through completely round gold-rimmed spectacles.

"Your Royal Highness looks splendid in specs," I said. He beamed and we took our film.

The Maharajah was clearly in an affable mood for when we had finished, he put his crown back in the biscuit tin and spent some time asking us how our filming was going. I replied that much as we liked Katmandu we would be grateful for permission to visit other parts of Nepal and in particular to see the dense jungle area of Terai, where the survivors of Nepal's rhino and tigers still lived.

"But of course," he said "that would be easy to arrange. In a fortnight's time I will be going on a tiger shoot in the Northern Terai. You must bring your camera and come as my guest."

I could not refuse, but this was the very last thing I ever wanted to do for I had already heard quite enough about the Maharajah's tiger hunts. He pursued these animals almost as enthusiastically as he did the East Indian rhino, from the safety of a howdah on the back of an elephant. There might be as many as sixty or seventy elephants in his party, and the tiger would be driven until he was totally surrounded by a wall of elephants. Then the Maharajah would shoot. When the day's bag of tigers was complete he would drive back to Katmandu in his Rolls Royce, and the stuffed heads of the tigers would duly appear beside the rhinos in the Maharajah's trophy room.

I had already seen several pictures of the Maharajah at the end of a good day's shooting, for Katmandu's official photographer was a businesslike Japanese gentleman with a shop just behind the royal palace, and his window was full of photographs of the Maharajah, in jodhpurs, tweed Norfolk jacket and bowler hat, standing proudly over several very dead tigers. The photographs were bad enough.

The reality would be very much worse, and I was dreading the hunt and trying my hardest to think of some way of getting out of it.

In fact I was given a much better excuse than I wanted. Two days before the hunt was due to take place a servant arrived from the official British Resident in Katmandu with a message that had just been received over the radio. War had broken out between Britain and Germany and I was advised to leave Nepal as soon as possible. So the following day we went to say good-bye to the Maharajah and excused ourselves for not turning up for the tiger hunt. It was then, almost as an afterthought, that "Old Hospitality" presented us with his Royal Highness's extortionate bill. Everything was on it, from the bath-tub that had been carried across the mountains to a special fee for the Maharajah's personal appearance, crowned for our film. But there was no question of querying it if we wanted to get away from Nepal. I paid the Maharajah himself in American dollars. That afternoon we started the long walk back through the Himalayas to India.

I was now in a serious predicament. As an American citizen there was nothing I could do immediately, but as a Belgian by birth I hated the idea of being isolated and helpless on the other side of the world while my parents in Antwerp were so close to the war. But because of this very war we had no idea where we could get to next. For several weeks it was impossible to get aboard a ship leaving India and when we finally found an old freighter sailing from Bombay, she was under sealed orders. Not even the captain knew her destination until he was far out of port. But by then we hardly cared where we went.

When we had been at sea two days the captain came to tell us what the orders had contained. We were bound for Mombasa. At least this was half way home and since I still needed a considerable amount of footage to complete my film, I decided to make the most of the legendary game area of East Africa while there was still a chance.

12 *Close up of Lions*

HE was a small, dapper man with a neatly pressed linen suit and a face the colour of ancient teak. I spotted him the first afternoon we arrived sitting in the lounge of our hotel in Mombasa. He was puffing at a cheroot and leafing through an old copy of the *New York Times* with the air of a man whose mind is not really on what he is reading.

"Hullo, Al," I said.

"Hi," he replied, eyeing me carefully over the top of his paper. "Business good?"

"So-so." He puffed non-committally at the cheroot. "So-so."

"What are you doing in Mombasa then? Vacation?"

"Well, you could call it a vacation. Because of this goddam war every client I had is back in the States by now."

"How's about a trip with me?" I said. "No shooting of course. Just filming."

"Sounds all right, but depends on the price," he replied, still puffing smoke towards me. "If you're interested, I could show you the finest game in Africa—something you've never seen before and will never see again."

It was a chance too good to miss and that was how I came to engage Al Klein.

I had known him on and off for years and now, in his middle sixties, this unlikely little American had become something of a legend. As a very young man he had worked in the Natural History Museum in New York but for the last thirty years he had lived in Africa as a professional white hunter, accompanying the rich visitors to East Africa who had come in search of game. But Klein was more than just a hunter. He was a born naturalist and his knowledge of animals was prodigious. He was far more interested in studying animals than in killing them and for my purpose was the best guide I could have wished for.

It was that afternoon that we fixed our destination. It was a place I had heard of many times. It was called the Ngorongoro Crater, a huge natural depression twelve miles across on the edge of the Serengeti Plains in Tanganyika, and according to Al it was the one place above all others in the whole of Africa to see animals in the wild.

Despite its name, Ngorongoro is not really the crater of a volcano. I have seen some large craters of extinct volcanoes in Hawaii but they could never reach the immense proportions of Ngorongoro. Ngorongoro is what the geologists call a caldera, a large area of land that millions of years before had been blown up by volcanic pressure from beneath and that then collapsed inwards, leaving this huge, plate-shaped depression. With its steep sides and abundant water it formed a natural sanctuary for wild life of almost every kind. It teemed with game. During the dry season great herds of zebra, wildebeest, and antelope migrated into the crater in search of water. There were rhinos in great numbers and above all there were lions in their hundreds and particularly handsome ones at that.

But the most remarkable thing of all about Ngorongoro was that in those days it still remained virtually untouched. The roads leading to it were bad. Only a few Masai, a nomadic tribe who are not hunters and respect game, used the crater, and no tribesmen settled there permanently. As for the white hunters, they knew of easier places to take their clients to.

I had already had so many disappointments on this trip that as soon as we had settled our destination I was anxious to be off, but Al was not a man to be hurried, and we took our time. Of course, some safaris in this part of Africa have been absurdly opulent affairs. I have known of safaris for rich Americans where a private plane was chartered to bring fresh fish from the coast to the safari every day, and others where wives on safari with their husbands would say good night to their children in the States every evening by radio telephone.

Ours was not a safari on this scale, but Al was a man with definite standards and he insisted on driving first to Nairobi where we spent several days methodically stocking up for some months in the bush. As I went with him to the stores along Delamere Avenue that had specialised in fitting out the big pre-war safaris I could see that Al had no intention of roughing it. In India and Burma we had got used to sleeping rough and using sleeping-bags that we unrolled beside the trucks, but Al insisted on buying proper mattresses for the trip. Instead of the coffee essence we had always made do with, he made us get a proper coffee mill and several sacks of coffee beans. He also bought a small portable refrigerator that ran on paraffin. " Once you've got used to having ice with your martini," he said, "it's something you just can't do without."

To Klein we must have been a very different proposition from the millionaire clients he had grown used to before the war, but during the following weeks I spent with him I got just enough of a taste of the old safari life to understand something of the luxury and comfort the big safari could offer.

But at that time I was not particularly interested in comfort. I wanted to see some animals that we could film and during these days of leisurely preparation I was getting more and more impatient. Al was a man it was impossible to hurry and even when we had set out from Nairobi I remember sitting beside him in the leading truck as he drove down the Great Rift Valley at a steady twenty miles an hour.

We seemed to be taking the journey in such easy stages that by the third day I was almost beside myself with impatience and decided to complain. Al listened carefully to what I had to say and paused to puff once more at his cigar before replying.

He pointed to the binoculars hanging round his neck. "You see those," he said. " By four o'clock this afternoon you'll be looking through them at ten thousand head of big game."

"And if we don't?" I said.

"If we don't, I'll eat the binoculars for you."

Klein must have known that his digestion was safe, for just after three he slowed down and signalled to the rest of the trucks to stop. He jumped down from the cab and I followed him for a few hundred yards through the bush. Suddenly the bush ceased. A few yards ahead the ground dropped abruptly and below us, stretching as far as I could see, lay the great arena of Ngorongoro. Never before or since have I seen so many animals in one place. Herd after herd of zebra and gazelle, wildebeest and buffalo dotted the immense landscape, grazing peacefully in this extraordinary wild life sanctuary.

To start with all I wanted to do was to stay where we were and watch, but once I had got over the first excitement of Ngorongoro, I had to settle the problem of exactly what we were going to film. Almost inevitably I decided to begin with lions, for at this time the lions of Ngorongoro and the surrounding parts of the Serengeti really were unique. Despite their numbers they had very rarely been hunted, and unlike the lions I had seen in the Congo and West Africa, these had no particular fear of man. Here there was a chance of finding a pride of lions—of staying with it, filming it, and discovering everything we could about the family life of a group of lions living freely and naturally in the wild.

But first we had to find our pride and I soon realised that it was going to be difficult to get a family of the size I wanted. We kept seeing lions in twos and threes but they were no use and we had to spend several days before we were lucky.

The usual way you spot a pride of lions from a distance is to watch for a column of vultures in the sky. Vultures act as a signpost of the wild. Several of these birds circling above one spot almost always indicate a kill and where there has been a kill the chances are that you will find your lions.

But on this occasion even the vultures let us down. Once they led us to a buck that had been killed by a leopard. Another time they were circling above the carcase of an old buffalo that had probably died of age and had nearly been devoured already by the hyenas and the jackals. For vultures are patient birds. If you abandon a car for a day or two in the bush, the chances are that when you come back you will find the vultures circling overhead waiting for it to die.

In the end we gave up watching the vultures and decided to rely on the sharp eyes of the African boys who were with us to spot our lions for us. The sight of these boys is extraordinarily acute and it was on the third afternoon after we reached Ngorongoro that I heard one of them whispering "simba, simba" and saw him pointing to a spot amid the long grass about a quarter of a mile away. At first I could not see what it was that was exciting him. But he kept whispering, "minghi, minghi," which means "many, many" and at last I did make out the two rounded ears of a young lion sticking up above the grass. Then I saw another pair, and another, until I realised that I was looking at a pride of twenty-five lions.

Even in those days this was out of the ordinary. To-day a group of this size would be very remarkable indeed. To my delight the whole family seemed quite unconcerned about us. We were actually able to stay with them and film them day after day, to our heart's content, for nearly three weeks.

My first surprise about this particular pride was that it contained two fully grown male lions and that far from fighting over the females they all behaved quite sensibly and seemed to get along quite amicably. I discovered that lions live rather freely. They are not monogamous, and they are not particularly dog-in-the-manger about their wives.

On the other hand, all of us were soon struck by the obvious affection existing between the different members of the family; there was nothing more touching than the sight of the cubs welcoming back one of the females when she returned from the hunt. They would run up to her and rub her face with theirs and lick her and make no end of a fuss.

We soon saw that on these occasions, the least demonstrative members of the family were the two big males. It was as if they felt any show of affection to be below their dignity. They would pretend to behave like a couple of touchy old martinets, and I am quite sure that their cantankerous behaviour was strictly deliberate.

Much as I admire lions, and I do admire them tremendously, I have to admit that the male lion possesses nothing like the qualities of the female. He is selfish. He is usually very much on his dignity. And he is incurably lazy.

The one time when the male lion's personality really changes is when he falls in love. This happens rather more often than is usually imagined and when it does the wretched animal can become completely bemused by the female.

Nothing looks sillier than a lion in love. One of the lions we were watching was in love with a very handsome, full-grown lioness; he followed her everywhere she went, panting away, his mouth wide open, his tongue hanging out, and a most stupid, infatuated expression on his face.

On the other hand, being courted by a lion always seems to bring out the liveliest side of a lioness. This particular one thoroughly enjoyed all the attention she was getting. She became very skittish, rolling over on her back and teasing and tormenting her unhappy suitor in the most outrageous way.

But even she had to mind her manners occasionally: I soon noticed that her lion could not bear to be left. If she went so much as a hundred yards away, the lion would become jealous and bound after her, sometimes even lashing out at her quite hard just to show that he would not stand for that kind of behaviour.

Lions do not even need to be in love to look decidedly silly. They loathe heat and feel comfortable only in the early morning and late afternoon. During the heat of the day they lie helpless, panting, eyes half shut, and looking not at all like the majestic beasts I had always pictured to myself. This was a serious handicap to us in our film making. It used to get very hot, especially in the afternoon, and it was then impossible to get any expression on their faces, other than one of suffering and extreme unhappiness. I am sure that if lions had their way they would live in far cooler climates than the tropical areas where they usually occur, for by nine o'clock in the morning our lions would all have scampered for the shade and there they would stay until late afternoon with their eyes half shut and their tongues hanging out.

It was only then in the comparative coolness of late afternoon that the hunting would start. The routine was almost always the same. The males would have nothing at all to do with it. Hunting was woman's work and it was extraordinarily interesting to watch.

One of the lionesses would be left behind as a nurse to look after the cubs and the rest of them would trot off together in search of

"*Much as I admire lions, I have to admit that the male lion possesses nothing like the qualities of the female. He is selfish. And he is incurably lazy*"

The male above has a fine mane, but the young lion below has still to grow his

"All of us were struck by the obvious affection existing between different members of our family of lions." A lion and lioness and, above, a young cub

"*Ever since my surreptitious visit as a child to the primate house at Antwerp Zoo I had been fascinated by chimpanzees*"

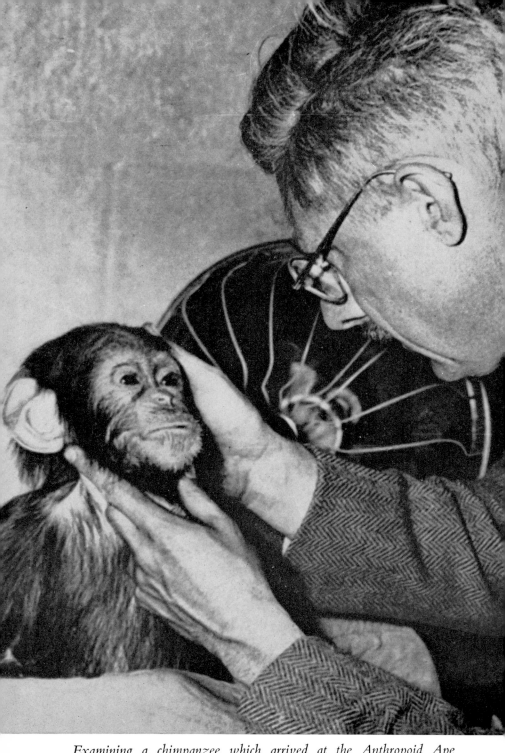

Examining a chimpanzee which arrived at the Anthropoid Ape Research Foundation in Florida with pneumonia

*Life on the chimpanzee farm in Florida. Below, Mugwump and friend
(the only surviving photographs have faded)*

"Mugwump was a splendid looking animal and knew it"

their evening meal. The great mystery I never really settled was how the lionesses managed to work together as a team when they hunted. Each one knew so exactly what to do that it was almost as if they had been in radio contact with each other and it looked just as though they had been able to plan the hunt in advance.

They would pick out a buck or a zebra and plan their approach one lioness running far out ahead to head the animal back, the others carrying out a flanking movement on each side. Whatever movement their quarry made they would know instinctively what to do, working together as if in one concerted action, although they were often completely out of sight of each other in the long grass.

The only possible explanation is some sort of animal telepathy of which the scientists have so far very little understanding. Cheetahs show the same phenomenon when they are hunting; and the elephants seem to have this particular ability of communication at a distance in its most highly developed form. Many times I have watched the big herds of elephant in Central Africa eating peacefully over several miles of country and seen how one isolated elephant can become alarmed and instantly communicate this sense of danger to the whole herd.

Whatever form of telepathy these lionesses used was not as complex as this, but it had a deadly efficiency about it all the same and I never saw them miss their quarry. Their aim would always be to work close enough to the animal to panic it. Then, when it had no hope of evading them, one of the lionesses would get beside it and knock it down with a swift blow of the paw. The other lionesses would all jump on the animal together and the actual killing would be surprisingly swift. When lionesses hunt, the hunt always ends with a businesslike death. Unlike human beings they do not hunt for pleasure.

During the hunt the cubs would never be far away, and immediately after the kill the lionesses would start grunting and calling to tell the rest of the family that supper was ready. The way they used to eat always amused me. It generally followed the same pattern: the cubs would be the first to arrive, scampering up to their mothers who would already be eating but who would immediately make room for them. For a few minutes they would all be there, munching away contentedly. The males all this time would put on a great show of indifference, pretending to ignore what was going on. But one could see them smelling the air and watching out of the corner of their eyes and all the time growing more and more restless until suddenly they would decide that, dignity or no dignity, they would have to hurry if they were going to get anything to eat that night. Then, with a great roar, they would get up and charge, scattering everyone else away from the meal.

It was always quite a sight to see the females and the cubs waiting in a ring at a respectful distance while the two males began to eat. They would do this with a great show of importance and dignity; any cub who came too close would be cuffed and made to mind his manners.

Meanwhile the females, who after all had done all the work, would be getting restless in their turn, and it would be one of them—usually the current favourite of one of the infatuated lions—who would at last make a move. Her tactics could be most amusing. She would move closer and closer to her lion, her ears back, her belly touching the ground. She would come directly behind him, creeping, with her head against his hind-quarters so as to keep out of danger of too vicious a swipe of his front paws.

Then she would work her way along the side of his body until her nose was tightly in the crook of his shoulder. She knew she was safe there and for a while she sniffed at the meat and the lion growled back at her. But gradually his growling grew less angry. He had had enough to eat and was beginning to feel almost mellow. Then the lioness would decide to take a chance.

With the tip of her teeth she would try to grab at a tiny piece of meat. The first time she got a hearty cuff on her paws and drew back. But the growling subsided and, eyes tightly shut, ears back against her head, she tried once more. This time it would work. She would get a mouthful, the lion would let her eat it, and then in no time at all, the whole family would move back again to finish off its meal.

Lions are really kindly, generous creatures, even where food is concerned. Several times I have seen a hungry lion turn up at the scene of a kill when another pride was in possession. For a while the atmosphere is strained. The intruder prowls around trying hard not to look interested and the rest of the lions growl threateningly enough for some minutes, but it always seems to end up with the outsider pushing his way in with the rest and joining the party.

13　*The Pride Departs*

THE days we spent virtually living with our pride of lions were exciting in a way I had never quite known before, and even old Al Klein who had been concerned with lions most of his adult life seemed impressed. I had never felt so totally accepted before by a group of large animals living in the wild.

Each morning the first thing Al and I would do when we had rolled out of our tents was to make sure our lions had not moved on during the night. But although we thought we had lost them on several occasions one of us would always end up spotting a pair of those cubs' ears poking up at us over the grass and we would know the pride was still there.

"Can't think what you're so worried about," Al would say then, pulling a face and spitting on the ground. "After all, lions are only lions. Who cares what happens to them?"

But I always noticed that when we set off to film them, Al would be careful to get into the first truck and in the afternoons when most of us were grateful enough to get some sleep, he would lie for hours on end in the long grass watching these animals he made such a show of despising.

He had a feeling for animals that was instinctive and quite unerring. He knew how they would behave, how they would react, where they would go, and with these lions he was so completely unafraid that all of us soon became casual to a degree. At night after supper we used to sit outside the tent round the table. Sometimes we would play cards. Sometimes we would set a couple of bottles of beer before Al Klein and let him talk. He had the biggest fund of stories about animals I have ever heard and we would sit there hour after hour listening to his nutmeg-grater voice and the faint hiss of the big petrol lamp on the table.

It was on these nights we used to spot the lions. The lamp was so brilliant that it completely blinded you to the surrounding darkness and at first we would not notice them. Then we would see their eyes gleaming out of the darkness like amber torch bulbs and if we looked very carefully we could make out the shape of lion after lion sitting patiently, silently in a circle round our camp, all listening with the utmost politeness to Al Klein's unrepeatable stories.

At first I used to find this exhilarating. You really felt you were back in the Garden of Eden and on a footing of trust and friendship with these animals.

But a little later when you retired to your tent for the night you were not quite so sure. For a while it was all right and you remembered that the petrol lamp was still burning outside. But then, when you were sure everyone else was asleep, you caught the noise of lions hunting in the distance and this was something very different from the way you remembered the lions before.

It is an unmistakable noise that carries for miles across the bush. At first it is a long way off. Then, about forty seconds later, you hear it again and it is closer. Another forty seconds and it is closer still, and you lie there sweating, certain that the next forty seconds will bring the lion right to the edge of this tent where you are lying alone.

And of course, in a sense, it was ridiculous of us to be taken in too much by the apparent amiability of these lions. For accidents do happen with wild lions when you are least expecting them; only last year a tourist was taken out of his tent one night by a lion in the Serengeti Park and mauled so badly that he died within a few hours.

One must remember that lions, for all their good qualities, are really highly unpredictable animals. Several times Michaela and I have filmed lions on foot and provided you know what you are up to this is usually all right. But whenever we have to do this, I always make sure first that I can get close enough to the lions in our Land Rover to be able to get a good look at them all, and I examine each one very carefully indeed.

By now I think I can tell if a lion is dangerous or not. Not that there is anything particularly mysterious about it. You hardly have to be an expert on dogs to be able to tell which are friendly and which are not; it is much the same with lions. Quite often, after I have looked some lions over I say to Michaela, "Let's get out of here. I don't like the expression on that second lioness's face."

I do not know exactly what it is about the animal. Perhaps she is twitching her tail or putting her ears back or perhaps she just looks nervous. But in a life like ours you have to get in the habit of making this sort of judgment on the spur of the moment if you really hope to last.

Of course luck comes into it as well. We have been charged by animals several times, but the fact that an animal charges you does not mean that he is going to go through with the charge. I was stupid enough to get charged by a lion on this trip with Klein just after we had left Ngorongoro, but although it scared me to death the animal did not go through with the charge, but at the last minute swerved away and went off growling. Klein told me afterwards that nineteen times out of twenty a charging lion fails to complete his charge just as mine had. He just wants you out of the way and provided you are not unlucky enough to be there on the twentieth time, you escape unhurt.

As a rule the only time an animal is really dangerous is when he is cornered or thinks he is. For the rest of the time wild animals have really very little interest in men, and certainly not as food. The smell of man does not even seem to make a lion hungry.

The exception to this of course is the man-eating lion, but man-eaters are very rare and there is usually a very definite reason to account for them when they do occur. The most common cause of man-eating is simply old age. A lion normally hunts its customary food as long as it can, but when it becomes too old or arthritic to hunt with the pride the wretched animal goes around perpetually famished. Soon it begins hanging around the villages. To start with it kills a chicken. Then a goat. One fine day it kills a child, and when he has discovered how easy a man is to kill, and that man, despite his strange smell, is meat after all, he becomes a man-eater. It is as simple as that.

Occasionally epidemics of man-eating occur among carnivorous animals in the wild, but again there is usually some reasonable explanation for them. The most notorious man-eaters of all, for instance, were the man-eaters of Tsavo in East Africa, and their history is all too easy to understand. They picked up the habit at the beginning of this century when the railway was being built between Nairobi and Entebbe. The local Africans were not interested in working on the line so the construction company imported Indian labourers in their hundreds. In those days the country around Tsavo was extremely wild. The Indians were not used to these conditions and had no idea how to take care of themselves and the death rate from malaria and dysentery was abnormally high. It became so high that the Indians gave up burying the corpses and simply carried them out of the camp and left them in the open for the vultures and the hyenas.

Lions are often found close to hyenas. One theory is that they saw the hyenas gorging on the human corpses and learned to relish the unfamiliar meat. Soon the lions turned from dead Indians to live ones and the man-eating epidemic became so serious that for some time work on the line ceased completely.

But the lions we were watching at Ngorongoro were safe as far as deliberate man-eating was concerned and the only real danger from them would have resulted from some misstep on our part. Still, accidents happen easily on this sort of trip, so easily that three days after we arrived at Ngorongoro we nearly lost two members of our party to the very lions we were trying to film.

It all happened quite suddenly in the early afternoon. By now Al was as enthusiastic about filming lions as I was. We had found a tall outcrop of rock, which had given me an idea. The plan was to plant a carcase at the highest point of the outcrop, entice the lions there, and so to get unique scenes of the lions tearing at the carcase dramatically outlined against the sky.

There should have been no difficulty about carrying out this plan. Al and I drove with two of our trucks to the foot of the outcrop, we climbed the rock on foot, dragging on the end of a chain the leg of a zebra which we had stolen from some hyenas earlier in the day, and thus laying a trail from the ground to the top of the rocks, which the keen-nosed lions would follow with ease. At the top of the outcrop we fastened the leg of zebra securely, knotting the chain around a stump, so that the lions could not drag the zebra leg out of the field of the camera.

Back on level ground, we got cameras and reflectors ready in one of the trucks and aimed them at the top of the rocks. While we installed this equipment, I sent the other truck off to fetch some lions. "To fetch some lions" probably sounds odd but again there was a perfectly easy way to do this, and one we used almost daily.

The driver of the truck would scout around until he found a fair group of lions. In full sight of the lions but at a safe distance from them he would drop the remainder of the zebra carcase, securely tied to the truck with a heavy rope; he would then drive back to where we were waiting with the cameras, dragging the carcase and thus laying a trail of scent from the lions to the trail already laid by us. Arriving back well ahead of the lions, he would have plenty of time to pick up the zebra carcase, place it again in his truck and take it back to camp. The lions would soon arrive, follow the trail to the top of the rocks, find the zebra leg, and give us the pictures we wanted.

But things did not happen according to plan.

Lions were plentiful in the area, and when I sent off the truck—containing the zebra carcase—to fetch some lions, I expected the truck to be back in one hour, at most two. Al lit one of his cigars and we sat back to wait. After fifteen or twenty minutes Al was asleep, his dead cigar between his lips. I was feeling very sleepy myself and decided to stretch out in the back of the truck. It was then that I heard a faint sound in the distance—a car's horn. It was repeated insistently and finally I woke Al and told him to listen.

"My God," he said. "It's an S.O.S. Your truck's in trouble." We left the cameras where they were and raced off in the direction of the sound. We drove about half a mile through bush and long grass before we reached the truck. In front of us lay a stretch of marshy ground and there, two hundred yards away, with mud well up past its axles rested our truck. The driver and mechanic who had come with us out to the rock were sitting bolt upright in the cab and outside, stalking backwards and forwards with understandable impatience, were eight large lions.

Obviously the driver had not realised the treacherous character of the ground he was crossing, and had become bogged down. Then these lions had caught wind of the dead zebra he had in the back, and they wanted to get to the meat. What terrified me was that one of the windows in the door at the back of the truck was broken, and that the lions were already attempting to leap at it. Awkward as it would be for a lion to get his heavy body through the window, it could have been done. There was no partition between the back of the truck where the zebra lay and the cab where the two men were sitting—so if the lions got inside, the lions, the dead zebra and the men would find themselves all together. And eight lions would make short work of a dead zebra. I could see the two men looking anxiously in our direction. How were we to get them out? Whatever we did we would have to be quick about it.

"Shall I try to get back to camp for a gun?" asked Al. "I might at least be able to scare them off."

"The camp's too far," I said. "By the time you got back the lions would be inside and there would be nothing you could do with a gun then."

"But hell, what are we going to do? Sit and watch eight lions make a meal off a couple of our own guys in the back of our own truck?"

For a while it looked as if this was just what we would have to do; we both knew that if the lions got inside the truck it would be only a matter of seconds before the two men were attacked. By this time one of the lions had actually got its head and front paws through the broken back window. He had hung there for a while, half in and half out, and then fallen back; but obviously he would try again, and obviously if he tried again he would finally succeed in getting in.

As far as I could see there was only one thing to do. It was risky and there was no certainty it would work. But when I was in the Congo five years earlier I had had some experience of driving over marshy ground. The secret is to deflate your tyres almost completely so that they act as cushions and it is surprising just how much weight they will carry. It all depended on how soft this ground really was.

We let the tyres down on our truck and slowly drove out to the

153

other car. By this time the lions were so excited by the smell of the zebra that they took hardly any notice of us. We were in bottom gear and actually had to push our way through them to draw alongside the other car.

Somehow we managed it. I never thought we would, but we finally got close enough to be able to open our door and let the two men leap across from the truck. Then of course, with the extra load, we got stuck. The wheels spun, the engine raced, and we took half an hour backing our way out. By the time we made it four of the lions were already inside the other truck, and next morning when we came back to salvage it I had never seen such a mess in my life.

They must have fought over the remains of the zebra actually in the truck. There was blood everywhere, bloody paw prints actually on the ceiling. The seats had been ripped, the instrument panel smashed and in the end the only way we could get the truck clean was to tow it into the nearest river and practically submerge it while we scrubbed it out with soap and disinfectant.

The evening after this happened, all of us, even Al Klein himself, went off to bed early without waiting for the night's audience of lions to arrive around our petrol lamp.

One of the things I was to learn during the days to come, as we went on observing our lions, was that they were by no means as all-powerful in the wild as most people think. Of course, the general idea that all animals living free are naturally healthy simply is not true. Life is at best an uneasy battle between disease and survival for almost every animal and I realised that this was true for lions as well. All the lions we filmed, even the proud old male with the silvery mane, were tormented by flies. I used to lie there watching the lions, and feeling sorry for them, plagued as they were by these unrelenting insects that attacked their eyes and their noses and the chewed up edges of their ears.

I have carried out many post-mortems on wild lions and other wild animals and have always been surprised by the parasites and worms you find in their stomachs and intestines and even in their lungs.

Obviously disease keeps the numbers of lions down all the time.

Also, while there are not many animals that will attack a fully grown lion, they tend to be surprisingly accident-prone.

I have seen a giraffe break a lioness's jaw beyond repair, so that she must inevitably have died soon after of starvation. She tried leaping on to the animal's back while it was running, but missed her hold and slipped back to be caught by the rear hoofs which can strike with ferocious power. Al Klein used to claim that he had seen a zebra kill a young lioness outright with a well-aimed blow of its hoofs. It could certainly have happened, and I have seen several zebras with the claw marks of a lion on their backs, proving that, even after a lion has struck, it does not have things all its own way.

For lions live dangerously. A rhino could theoretically kill a lion and I am sure it sometimes does. Again, I know an area in the Congo where lions and gorillas occur together. I have no doubt that from time to time a lion must make a grab at a baby gorilla and if the parents came to its aid there would be an unimaginable fight between full-grown lion and full-grown gorilla. I am by no means sure that the lion would have the advantage.

In spite of all this, lions, even when completely unmolested as they were at Ngorongoro when we were there, never seem to increase at the rate that might be expected. With so much game around, it would seem that they should almost have been the most numerous animals there, and my own theory of why they were not, is that lions have a remarkably high incidence of infant mortality.

At Ngorongoro we saw several examples of how this comes about. For one thing, lionesses, although the most affectionate of mothers, are also rather vague and often extremely stupid where their cubs are concerned. In the particularly large pride which we came to call "our" lions it was obvious that the individual lionesses half the time were not sure which cubs belonged to them and which to someone else and the cubs themselves seemed quite cheerfully to suckle first at one lioness and then at another. As a result we would often see individual cubs mislaid, especially when the mothers left in the evening on their hunting expeditions; and the hyenas that are never far from the lions would make short work of a tasty young lion cub.

But although Al and I felt anxious on several occasions when we saw hyenas following cubs loitering a long way behind their mothers, we never actually witnessed any real harm come to them. For nearly three weeks we followed this remarkable family and by this time I was feeling a respect and admiration for lions that I have kept ever since. Their virtues seem so outstanding, and their faults are understandable and easy to forgive.

One night, there was a thunderstorm and the rain kept on all the next morning.

"This'll drive 'em off," said Al. "Lions hate rain and they'll scatter for miles to escape it. They'll take to the hills. We'd better pack and be ready to move on."

Of course he was right. We spent most of the afternoon searching for them but they had disappeared and although we stayed on in Ngorongoro and Serengeti and saw many wonderful things I have never to this day seen another pride of lions quite like the one we called ours in 1940 before the terrible devastation of war reached even the wilds of Africa.

14   *A Farm for Chimpanzees*

WHEN I returned from the Serengeti to the United States, I found that the threat of war was affecting my life as well as millions of others. The world was closing up and I could no longer travel as I used to or make the films I wanted. At the same time I found that I was missing Africa as I had never missed anywhere before. I longed for its people, its landscape, its smell, but above all I longed for its animals. I knew now that I would never be really happy unless I could work with them and live close to them.

This was the frame of mind I was in when I heard that a record shipment of twenty-five chimpanzees had just arrived at New York from Sierra Leone. As soon as I heard, I decided that the time had come for me to change my profession once again.

Ever since my surreptitious visits as a child to the monkey house at the Antwerp Zoo, I had been fascinated by chimpanzees. What interested me in all the anthropoid apes was their similarity to man. When I watched them I got the same pleasure as if I had been observing totally uninhibited human beings; I had also been greatly impressed by the research work into human mental disease and immunology that had already been carried on in the United States with chimpanzees.

At the same time I was afraid that as this research work grew the chimpanzees would be bought haphazardly from animal dealers and looked after by people who were scientists rather than animal experts. The arrival of these twenty-five chimpanzees gave me the idea of starting a really large anthropoid ape research station where the animals could be properly looked after and where every aspect of their make-up could be studied humanely and under ideal conditions. The chimpanzees, of course, would not be used for any experiments involving cruelty; there was a whole range of research involving their behaviour, their psychology, and their resistance to a large number of human diseases, where they would be invaluable to scientists.

At the same time I saw no reason why the research station should not be made to pay its way by allowing the public in and charging for admission. I remember the way that the chimpanzees always managed to be the centre of attraction in every zoo and felt sure that I could combine a valuable scientific project with a profitable public exhibit.

Before the station could become self-supporting I needed backers and began campaigning hard for support among the doctors and scientists I knew. To this day I am convinced that scientists have still a lot to learn from the relative immunity of the chimpanzee and the other anthropoid apes to certain diseases like cancer, malaria and yellow fever, and I remember one evening discussing my project with a group of doctors in Chicago. I mentioned the possible value of chimpanzees for cancer research and for some reason this seemed to annoy an elderly doctor at the back of the room.

"You must know that a chimpanzee would be totally useless for this sort of research," he said irritably.

"Why?" I asked.

"Why, everybody knows that the chimpanzee is immune to cancer; so what use is an animal like that for cancer research?"

"I do not take it as proved," I replied, "that the chimpanzee is immune to cancer, but if it really is, wouldn't you like to know why?"

This sort of argument proved effective. Before long I had enough support to buy the whole shipment of chimpanzees outright, along with ten acres of land along Federal Highway No. 1, a few miles north of Miami.

It was then that my work started in earnest. We had the chimpanzees, but we had little else, and all that summer we worked desperately, building cages, offices, and enclosures and getting the place under way. Before long I discovered that twenty-five chimpanzees are infinitely more trouble to look after than twenty-five of the most demanding and unpredictable human beings.

My original plan was to give the chimpanzees as much freedom as possible. I soon found though that this was difficult to reconcile with my plan to admit the public at a dollar a time and I was never really satisfied that it was possible to compromise between the two aims.

The first problem was not so much to protect the public from the chimpanzees as to protect the chimpanzees from the public. To do this the only completely effective way was to use cages, but if cages are to be at all impressive to look at they have to be big enough for several animals, and the chimpanzees simply hated this. It was not the cages they objected to. If you can find a pair of chimpanzees that get on well together they will be perfectly happy inside a fairly small cage. But once you put three or more chimpanzees together you have trouble. Almost at once one of the animals emerges as a tyrant and another becomes a scapegoat for the entire group. As long as they are together, the persecution goes on. There are fights. The animals tend to sulk and look unhappy, while the weakest one becomes too terrified to eat and can actually die of starvation.

It was because of this that I decided that cages were not entirely satisfactory and finally devised a special system of my own for my star animals. This consisted of setting a long, sturdy table out in the open and giving it to a pair of chimpanzees that I knew got on well together. During the day they would wear a collar with a long thin chain so attached as to give each the freedom of one half of the table —enabling them to meet and play together in the middle of the table, but only if both desired to do so; and enabling each one to retire to his end of the table in complete privacy. The animals very obviously enjoyed this far more than living in a cage and whenever they had an audience would use their chains for an extraordinary variety of acrobatic tricks. Any attendant passing by their table could stop and let them indulge in a brief hug and cuddle such as chimpanzees love.

That summer as the research station became established, the number of my chimpanzees grew, and by the autumn of 1941 I had bought over forty of all ages. Coping with this family I soon learned more about chimpanzees than I ever picked up about any animal living in the wild.

The first thing I learned is that chimpanzees are by no means always the harmless cheerful clowns most people think of when they see them having their tea-parties at the zoo. In fact the great majority of people have got chimpanzees all wrong. For just as with human beings so with chimpanzees I found enormous differences between the character of one individual and another. One would have a calm, easy-going temperament. Another would always be nervous and agitated. Some would be kind and reliable, and some would have such vicious tempers that it seemed as if they were always having a struggle to control themselves.

Then on top of this, chimpanzees undergo a profound mental and physical change as they reach maturity around the age of seven or so. Most of them are cheerful, affectionate and reasonably docile until then, but once they approach their full growth chimpanzees change into powerful and often extremely dangerous animals. A male chimpanzee in his prime can weigh upwards of 160 lbs. and as most of this weight is concentrated in the arms and chest he is more powerful than two or three men of the same weight.

With some of my chimpanzees this strength and uncertain temper became quite a problem, especially as the only thing the visitors seemed aware of was their outrageous capacity for showing off. The biggest exhibitionist I have ever known, humans included, was a chimpanzee I owned called Mugwump. I have no idea incidentally where he got his name from. His previous owner, a rich and idealistic Miami widow had named him Mahatma Gandhi, but I never felt this name fitted his riotous personality and quietly suppressed it. The name of Mugwump grew mysteriously in its place.

Mugwump, or to be precise the ex-Mahatma Gandhi, was about three years old when I bought him; he grew into a large and powerful animal, but he was such a good-natured individual that I never worried about him as I did with the other large males and I think he was easily the best chimpanzee I ever had. Of course he was mischievous and troublesome and a continual problem, but he was resourceful and affectionate as well and knew that I would forgive

him almost anything. This was an advantage he exploited unmercifully.

His greatest vice was vanity. He was a splendid-looking animal
and knew it. He was tall for a chimpanzee and a wonderful athlete;
as soon as he had an audience he would also reveal himself as the
great showman he was. It was then that he would really come to
life, showing the most remarkable inventiveness and performing
acrobatic exploits he would never bother to get up to when he was
on his own. He would swing and jump and do double somersaults
and when he felt his audience was tiring of them, he would change
his programme and suddenly put on a really terrifying show of
strength and ferocity, standing on his hands and pounding his
table with his feet whilst the hair on his shoulders stood right out
making him look as shaggy and powerful as a gorilla.

Despite this, Mugwump was really a sentimentalist and always
put on his best show when Katie was with him. Katie was an extremely beautiful female chimpanzee I had bought from an eccentric
Texas oil man who thought she was growing too big to continue
playing with his children; but she remained a remarkably gentle
soul and Mugwump discreetly adored her.

At week-ends we used to keep the pair of them by the entrance to
the station with a very large and massive table as a stage. The show
they put on for the passing motorists was the best advertisement we
could have had. The only trouble with them was that their intelligence was always getting them into mischief. All chimpanzees are
accident prone, but Mugwump and Katie seemed to make a special
profession of it and half my time seemed to be spent getting them
out of one scrape or another. They would try eating nails—or
they would discover a manhole and disappear down it; or they
would try winding their thin chains a couple of times around
their necks before leaping into space just to see what would
happen.

Mugwump's great failing was a passion for visitors' babies. Any
baby would do. He was such an easy-going animal that some of our
visitors, unused to his ways and unaware of his strange passion,
would naïvely let him peer into the pram. Several times he was able
to grab somebody's baby and run off with it. That would cause a

frightful to-do. The parents would come with tears in their eyes and start hammering on my office door.

"One of your monkeys has got our baby," they would shout. "For God's sake bring a gun and shoot him before he kills our baby."

"It's all right," I would reply as calmly as I could. "It's only Mugwump. He just loves babies. As long as you leave him alone it will be quite safe, and you'll have it back sooner than you think."

"But you must bring a gun, just in case," they would say, and to set their minds at rest I would pick up the old empty .45 revolver I kept on the top of the safe in case of burglars and follow them out to see what Mugwump had got up to.

It would always be the same. There would be Mugwump sitting peacefully on the edge of his table hugging the baby for all the world as if he was its mother and someone else had just tried to steal it. He would always be surprisingly gentle, stroking the baby and kissing it and I never really worried much about him on these occasions. The only thing I did not like was if he ever tried taking a baby up a tree with him. There was always a chance then that he might put it in a fork somewhere for safety and forget about it.

Provided everyone was patient and refrained from making any loud and upsetting noise, no crisis developed, and after an hour or so Mugwump grew tired of the baby and came and handed it back to its parents or to me with an enormous air of relief at being rid of it.

If baby stealing was Mugwump's great failing, Katie was really more of a problem. She loved picking locks. In time she grew into such an accomplished escapologist that at night she would have to be kept in a sleeping cage of her own with a padlock and chain around her neck and another padlock on the door. Even then, on more than one occasion, she opened her two padlocks and got out.

This skill at picking locks is fairly common among chimpanzees and as several of the animals learnt the knack, keeping them safe became increasingly complicated. They would find or break off a piece of wire, bend it, and then, with endless patience set to work on the lock until sooner or later they clicked it open and got out. Katie was a virtuoso at this sort of thing. The other chimpanzees would work away at their lock for a while and then suddenly lose their tempers, hurl the wire to the far side of the cage and roll on their backs, tearing their hair and screaming with rage. Then the next minute they would calm down, pick up their piece of wire, and go so patiently to work again that you would never have thought this was the same animal as the one whose outburst you had just witnessed.

But Katie never seemed to indulge in these rages. Instead she would be methodical and businesslike, probing, twisting and trying every possible way of holding the wire until the padlock finally clicked open. Because of this, we had to be careful never to allow anything like a piece of wire or a hairpin near her, whilst she on her part would go to extreme lengths of ingenuity to get the raw material for her lock-picking.

One trick she had was suggested to her, I believe, by the method we used ourselves to get the sleeping cages cleaned out in the morning. We encouraged the chimpanzees to clean them out for themselves, rewarding them with a banana when everything had been thrown out. This worked wonderfully well. I simply had to walk along the cages in the morning with a bunch of bananas and all the chimpanzees would start clearing away like mad, throwing out all that didn't belong in the cage. If there was anything at all left I would only have to say, "Over there, Fifi. Clean up." And Fifi would finish cleaning her cage and get her banana.

I suppose it was this practice of offering bananas in return for services rendered which gave Katie the basic idea of exchange and barter. She was an extremely intelligent animal and this was the sort of thing she could understand. You threw something out of the cage and then in return you got something that you wanted. It was not long before she put this principle into practice.

One morning, on my rounds, I saw Katie in the middle of a large crowd of visitors all of whom were in fits of laughter. There was nothing unusual in this, but when I went over I saw that she was holding out towards the crowd the banana I had given her earlier. At the same time she was pointing insistently to a piece of wire just out of reach in front of her cage. She wanted it and quite logically was offering the banana in return. For a while nobody seemed to understand, but finally somebody did and pushed the piece of wire to her on the end of his umbrella. She grabbed it immediately and

163

then in the best female manner turned her back on him and started eating the banana.

As soon as the banana was gone she turned her attention back to the wire and padlock; she went about it in so methodical a manner that as I continued to watch her, it was as if she had been picking locks all her life. She realised that the wire was straight and straight wire, as every good chimpanzee knows, is no use for opening locks. So she bunched up one end of her chain and held it on the ground, put the wire across it, and then used another section of the chain as a hammer to beat at it until the wire was bent at the right angle. From then on it took her exactly twelve minutes to open the padlock on her collar.

It was from watching Katie that I was finally convinced that the usual idea that chimpanzees get their skill through painstaking imitation of human actions is quite wrong. It was completely useless trying to teach her a trick by repeating it and repeating it in front of her. She would just get bored. I tried once to teach her to put some of her possessions away in a small cupboard in her cage. I spent the whole afternoon at it, showing her time after time how it should be done, but even when I tried rewarding her she was still not remotely interested.

On the other hand, although she was no good as an imitator, she seemed to have a highly developed instinct for finding things out for herself. I know that the first time I gave her a bowl of water and some soap she had never seen anyone using this sort of thing before and had no real idea of washing, yet within half an hour she was scrubbing away at her face and washing down her table and chairs with almost obsessional care.

It was the same with Mugwump. I never seemed to be able to teach him anything, yet when I gave him a hammer, some nails and a piece of wood, he soon discovered how to use them. True, he insisted at first on placing the nails point upwards on the wood, but when the hammer bounced off and hit his thumb he responded in an extremely human way and afterwards always used nails the right way up.

Another common misconception about chimpanzees that Katie and Mugwump finally dispelled for me was the idea that chimpanzees have some sort of conscious language by which they can communicate with each other. This pair got on so well together that if they had had any sort of language they would certainly have used it; but although they made a variety of sounds when they were together I soon realised that these noises were made quite unconsciously, and were not a means of intentional communication. They were simply part of the animals' automatic reaction to whatever was occurring. As far as I could see the chimpanzee was not even aware that he had made any sound at all.

At the same time these unconscious sounds did differ considerably and were quite characteristic. For instance, the noises made by Mugwump when he was annoyed were very different from those he made when he knew food was coming. Just as I could tell the difference so could Katie. Without knowing he was doing it, Mugwump would always make the same excited sound when his keeper was coming with food and Katie would instantly pick the information up from him. In this way the sounds the chimpanzees made provided, not a language, but an instinctive means of communication between them.

Perhaps the most unusual thing of all about Mugwump and Katie was that they seemed to be perfectly happy to remain together. They were almost the only pair that did not quarrel, for most of my chimpanzees seemed to have a casual and at times even a hostile attitude to the opposite sex.

Naturally we tried breeding chimpanzees but we found this far more difficult than one would have imagined. Out of ten females four or five would have a deep-seated aversion to the opposite sex from the start. With the males this intolerance was even higher. Some were dangerous and if placed in a cage with a female would attack her instantly. Other males would mate perfectly and then, immediately after, become violent and attack the unfortunate female.

Then there would be other difficulties. Cases of miscarriage were frequent among the females and even once the baby was born the mother chimpanzee often made the most haphazard of mothers. Sometimes she hardly seemed to know what to do with her baby, or did not have enough milk to feed it, or generally neglected it in the most reprehensible manner. Because of all these difficulties I decided that chimpanzee breeding was hardly a practical proposition. I calculated that a young chimpanzee that would cost us 500 dollars to import from West Africa would cost us 3,000 dollars to raise ourselves to the same age.

Despite this there was another pair—Magnolia and Gussie—who made a shining exception to the normal run of chimpanzee family life. They lived together. They mated happily and finally Magnolia performed one of the most outstanding feats of motherhood that an anthropoid ape is capable of. She had twins. This was very rare—only one other instance was known of the birth of chimpanzee twins in captivity—and for several days Magnolia looked as if she was going to be as devoted a mother as she was a wife. All her attention went on her twins. She would pick one up and hold it to her breast and make the most desperate fuss of it. But she never seemed to understand that she had two babies instead of the usual one and while she had one chimpanzee in her arms she would pay not the slightest attention to the other one lying on the ground.

Then suddenly she would hear the poor thing making the most pitiful cries as it lay on the concrete floor of her cage, and immediately she would become the very picture of anxious motherhood.

"My God," she would obviously say to herself, "that's my baby lying there. What am I thinking of?" And she would drop the unfortunate baby she was holding, letting it fall on its head, and grasp the other one, anxiously picking it up and fondling it and nursing it as eagerly as she had the first one until she heard that one's cries and repeated the process all over again.

I soon realised that this just could not go on. Gussie was being neglected. Magnolia was becoming a nervous wreck, and clearly if no action was taken the twins would not survive. Reluctantly I decided that for everybody's sake we would have to bring up the babies ourselves.

This was all right in theory. In practice it took us nearly a week to take the twins away from her and by then the poor things were almost dead. For although Magnolia seemed so absent-minded with her twins when she was on her own, she guarded them with her life when anyone came near.

First I had a cage specially fitted with sliding doors and special compartments, hoping that we could entice Magnolia into one side and then slide the door across to catch the twins on the other. But this plan was defeated. She seemed to know instinctively what we were up to and never once would she let go of one of her babies without first putting a foot or hand on the sliding door to stop us pushing it across.

We thought of sleeping powders, but the attempt to feed a sleeping pill or sleeping powder to a wary chimpanzee is doomed to failure. We would carefully mix the powder with crushed banana, hollow out a fresh banana with an apple corer, stuff the medicated paste inside, plug up the hole with a bit of the banana core, and offer the tempting tit-bit to Magnolia. Without even putting it to her mouth she would break the banana in two. With one finger she would carefully scrape out every bit of the paste, and then eat the banana, with an infuriatingly smug expression on her face.

We tried every sort of sleeping-draught on her. The doctors said that Nembutal was the safest thing to use; to mask the bitterness of the drug I tried giving it her in grape juice which she loved. She refused it. I had the idea of putting quinine in with the grape juice to start with, as quinine had exactly the same taste and bitterness as Nembutal. We would gradually increase the dose of quinine; then when she had got used to it we would suddenly shift from quinine to Nembutal.

That was the idea, and to start with it seemed to work. Magnolia would drink down her grape juice laced with quinine and show every sign of relish, but just as soon as I put the slightest drop of Nembutal in it—an amount so small that she could not possibly have detected it by taste—she would know and refuse to drink. This puzzled me and I came to the conclusion that she was learning about the Nembutal from her attendant. For chimpanzees have an uncanny intuition about people and whatever the keeper knew she knew as well.

In the end, with the twins' condition becoming more precarious every day, things got so desperate that I had to resort to the one method I did not want to use. I waited until she was close to one of the sliding doors and then, very quickly, fired a blank cartridge. Chimpanzees hate sudden noises and she moved so quickly that we were just able to pull the sliding door between her and the twins before she realised what had happened.

Once she was away from her twins, Magnolia no longer seemed to mind about them and relations between her and Gussie were soon back to normal. As for the babies, they were soon getting far more care from us than the majority of human babies get. For me they really were more important than human babies. There always seemed to be so many ordinary babies around and so few chimpanzee ones. Also, so much more would be learned from them. I hired the best children's nurses I could find in Miami, and spent day after day studying diet sheets and balancing their calories, proteins and carbo-hydrates. The whole regime of baby-care was followed with a precision to gladden the heart of Dr. Spock himself, and for some reason the nursery was always one of the most popular places in the whole station for visitors.

The twins soon responded to their treatment, and really made the most ideal babies. Certainly I would always advise anyone who has the choice of looking after a human baby or a chimpanzee one to pick the chimpanzee! For up to a certain age the intelligence of very young chimpanzees develops faster than that of comparable human children and this makes them perfect babies to look after. They are trustful and affectionate and seem altogether much better adapted to the processes of cuddling, nursing, feeding and diaper-changing than the human babies I have known.

Curiously the twins never seemed to miss their mother, and when they were a little older, neither Gussie nor Magnolia took the faintest interest in them either. It was as if these two sedate chimpanzees had no wish to be reminded of their brief and unfortunate excursion into parenthood. They continued to live together very happily but Magnolia never again showed the slightest inclination towards motherhood.

It was not long after Pearl Harbour, late in 1941 that the research station was first hit by the restrictions of war. Almost everything we neeeded was soon in short supply. We could not get steel for the cages or building materials for living quarters for the staff. It was practically impossible to buy any more chimpanzees and the entrance money never began to cover the running costs.

Worse still, because of the war, many of the research projects I had been expecting to make use of my chimpanzees were discontinued and almost all the research that scientists were now interested in doing with anthropoid apes would have involved cruelty of some sort. The only work I would permit was the regular taking of blood samples from several groups of my chimpanzees. As I had foreseen, several universities were interested in the chimpanzee's relative immunity to tropical diseases and this sample-taking soon became highly popular among the chimpanzees themselves. They always liked being the centre of attention and when they saw the doctor with his hypodermic they soon got the idea and became enthusiastic blood donors. They would offer him their arms, wait patiently while he found the vein, and show considerable interest in the blood as it mounted in the tube.

But the full potentialities of the research station were not really being used, and I realised that we were going to have to hold on until the war was over if this particular dream of mine was to come true.

15   *A Rumour of Gorillas*

IT was the purest chance that my journey to New York in the autumn of 1941 should have involved me in what was to be the most harrowing adventure in my life. I had flown up from Florida to take delivery of a fresh shipment of chimpanzees that had just arrived from West Africa. There were eight of them—five males and three females—and as they were all in excellent condition, I had paid for them and sent them on ahead by plane. I was due to follow in a couple of days and was staying at my usual hotel on Central Park.

I never sleep well in cities and the night before I had arranged to return I found it so hot inside the hotel that just before midnight I decided to go for a stroll and wandered down Sixth Avenue. There was a bar just beyond 42nd Street. I stopped there for a drink and the first man I saw inside was Rainez. I had not seen him for six years but I recognised him at once from the long scar that ran from his left cheek-bone down the side of his face. It had been inflicted by a leopard in French Equatorial Africa and it was there that I had met him originally. Rainez was an Argentinian. He called himself a prospector and had come to Equatorial Africa looking for gold, but when the gold had failed to turn up he had tried to make a living collecting wild animals for zoos.

When I had first known him he was not doing particularly well, but clearly his fortune had changed from those days and he offered me a drink as soon as he saw me.

"What are you doing in New York?" I said. "Have you found gold at last?"

He nodded. "Yes, I've struck it rich."

"Congratulations," I said. "Where?"

"French Equatorial," he replied. "It was there all the time, only it wasn't in the form I expected."

"What form was it in then?" I asked.

"Gorillas," he said. "I'm in partnership with a man in Brazzaville who has three on his hands at the moment. We're shipping them over to America in a few weeks' time. If you want one I'll let you have it cheap. Five thousand dollars and no questions asked."

"Not interested," I replied. "I don't buy smuggled animals. Anyhow, I couldn't afford your price even if I did."

"Pity," he said, smiling. "I'll have no difficulty raising fifteen thousand on the three of them. If I don't sell them here they'll go easily enough in South America. You know, they're getting scarce. Once I've brought this batch over I'm not risking any more. This smuggling as you call it is getting too damned risky."

We had another drink and chatted a while, but the truth was that I simply did not believe a word Rainez was saying. I remembered that he could be a boastful man, especially when he had had a drink or two, and I knew that according to all the experts, there were very few gorillas left in Africa. These were in the Virunga range of the Congo, and on my own Congo expedition, I had already experienced how jealously the Belgian authorities guarded them.

"You know, Rainez," I said, "you've not got these gorillas. Even if you could have got into the Congo to catch them you'd never bring them out alive."

"Who's talking about the Congo?" he replied. "It's not the only place you can get gorillas. Haven't you heard of French Equatorial itself? There's more gorillas there to-day than in the whole of the Belgian Congo put together. Why, there's one place I know where they're so common the local tribe actually hunts them for food."

At this I started laughing. "Really, Rainez," I said. "You know perfectly well the gorilla's the one animal that every African steers clear of. They're so dangerous that you'd never find a tribe mad enough to hunt them."

"Very well," he said, getting up to go, "there's only one way to convince you," and pulling his wallet out, he showed me a dog-eared snapshot. It was of three young gorillas playing in what looked like a heap of straw. There could be no mistake about them and I estimated that each gorilla weighed about forty pounds.

As he put the picture back in his wallet, I told him to wait and have another drink but he shook his head, buttoned up his jacket and left.

I went back to Florida two days later as arranged, but during the next few weeks I could not keep that conversation with Rainez out of my mind. The snapshot he had shown me was certainly of gorillas, but I could not believe that they could have come from French Equatorial Africa. If a few gorillas did occur in that vast, little-known area, I could not believe that they were any commoner there than in the Congo and nothing was going to convince me that there was actually a tribe mad enough to hunt them.

I was particularly concerned about all this because of the lifelong fascination gorillas had always held for me. As a child in Antwerp I remembered marvelling at the pictures of gorillas in du Chaillu's account of his travels in West Africa which were my favourite reading in the whole of my father's library. If anything, my interest in them had grown over the years. It was partly the closeness of gorillas to man in the pattern of evolution that caught my imagination. I was intrigued when I learned that they were so near to extinction, but what fascinated me more than anything else was that so little was really known about them. With their size, their ferocity and their phenomenal strength, they had attracted the most far-fetched stories and legends ever since they had been rediscovered by a German naturalist in the Congo in the 1890's. But in 1941 they were still among the least known animals in the world and the policy of the Belgian government in virtually sealing them off from all outside contact inside the Albert Park had only heightened the mystery.

The nearest I had ever been to wild gorillas myself was on my Congo expedition when, in spite of the ban the Belgians put on my approaching them, I did actually see a family of five in the distance in a patch of wild celery when we were working high in the mountains in the Albert Park. Several times since then I had tried to get permission to go back and film them properly but permission was always refused, and once I had started the chimpanzee farm I often thought what an achievement it would be if I could only have established a similar breeding colony of gorillas in Florida itself.

I heard nothing more from Rainez and cursed myself for not asking him for his address. I wrote to the bar on Sixth Avenue, but the bartender wrote back that he had never seen the man with the scar before or since. So I finally decided there was only one thing to do. I would start an inquiry of my own to find out whether Rainez could be right and whether there actually was an area I had never suspected somewhere in French Equatorial Africa where gorillas were abundant and where the people were bold enough to hunt them.

I spent many weeks reading all the reports of Equatorial Africa that I could lay my hands on, and the only information I could find about gorillas outside the Belgian Congo pointed to an area which began some two or three hundred miles north of Brazzaville, the capital of French Equatorial Africa. There was no reliable information about their numbers but this was hardly surprising since the whole area was huge, difficult of access, largely uninhabited and virtually unexplored. It was little more than a blank on the map and no one could even tell me what the terrain was like. But by the time I had finished my work, I was convinced that at least part of Rainez's story was correct. The gorillas were there and there was a chance that they really were more plentiful than in the Congo mountains.

From then on these gorillas became something of an obsession and I began working out ways of getting to Brazzaville to solve the mystery and if possible to bring back enough young gorillas to start the first breeding colony of them outside Africa.

There was some urgency in this, for in 1942 it looked as if Germany was about to sweep across the whole of Africa, cutting us off from this entire area. If I did not hurry, I felt I might never get a chance like this again. Also if gorillas really were as seriously threatened as some people said, a breeding colony somewhere like Florida might be one way of ensuring the survival of the species.

My arguments about the value of gorillas for scientific and psychological research carried some weight in official circles, and I began to get more support than I had hoped. Luckily I had a good manager who could look after the chimpanzee farm for me in my absence. My friend David Bruce, the American ambassador in London as I write, managed to arrange my passage across the Atlantic and when I sailed from New York in February 1944 I actually carried a letter of recommendation from President Roosevelt himself.

I had to travel light. I had arranged to pick up my money from a bank in Brazzaville, and decided to wait until then before I equipped my expedition. All I took with me was a small suitcase with a minimum of possessions, an old battered lightweight suit and a single volume of the collected works of Jane Austen.

This, of course, was apart from my camera. For although this was not a film-making expedition in the way my others had been, I could not bear to think of a journey such as I planned, without taking some means of recording it. So I carried a portable 16 mm. cine-camera and twenty thousand feet of colour film. Altogether the film, the camera and the light meter fitted into a canvas hold-all and weighed just over 45 lbs.

I mention the weight because I remember it only too well on the journey across the Atlantic. I was aboard an old Norwegian freighter zig-zagging its way across to Sierra Leone and every night when the siren went for a U-boat alarm, I would grab my precious hold-all, clamber with it in pitch darkness to the lifeboat and wait on the deck with it between my knees until the alarm was over.

Rather to my surprise we succeeded in dodging the U-boats and once I had reached Freetown and Monrovia, I found I was able to hitch-hike aboard American service planes flying from airfield to improvised airfield all the way down to Brazzaville. It was slow, but it was fairly sure, and I reached Brazzaville by the end of February with my camera and my precious stock of film intact.

At Brazzaville my troubles were only just beginning, for the city itself was in chaos. The French officials there had rallied to de Gaulle and the Free French Government in London, but farther north in the Gabon, the Vichy French were in control. As a result, Brazzaville was alive with rumour and I felt that everyone I met was spying for someone. Several people felt the same about me, and if it had not been for the precious letter from Roosevelt, my stay might have terminated abruptly.

Worse still, as far as I was concerned, was the struggle I had getting official permission to journey north and capture any gorillas if I could find them. It took weeks of lobbying, nagging and waiting before I finally assembled all the stores and equipment I needed, and had my authorisation, with the Governor's heavy blue stamp, safely inside my passport.

It was during these frustrating days of buying and stocking up that I realised how much I missed the blessed self-sufficiency of my earlier expeditions. Perhaps I had planned things too precisely in the past and carried more stores and equipment than we had ever needed, but that was infinitely preferable to this nightmarish trailing round from shop to shop in this sweltering city where the most mundane articles were often non-existent and I had to be grateful for what I could get at black market prices.

Tinned meat was unobtainable, although I did finally discover one shop with a good stock of tinned butter and I was careful to lay in a good supply of dried milk to feed any baby gorillas I might catch. I also had great difficulty getting hold of tools to build the cages I was going to need. Even after a week of scavenging for six-inch nails, I never succeeded in getting as many as I needed.

It was during these weeks I spent plodding around Brazzaville that I picked up the first of many troubles that were to dog me for the rest of the trip. The city must be one of the hottest places in all Africa and I was so anxious about the arrangements for my journey that I forgot to take even the most elementary precautions against the sun. For the one and only time in my life I got sunstroke. Stupidly I tried to ignore it after half a day in bed, but apart from the headaches it gave me and the strange effect it had on my vision I found that for many weeks afterwards I became dizzy if I had to stay on my feet for longer than a few minutes at a time.

But finally I was ready to go. I had bought a second-hand Dodge truck and placed all my stores aboard. I had hired an African cook called Joseph, who had just left the service of the local Corsican chief of police, as well as a boy called Zinga who had picked up some experience of looking after animals in the local zoo. My sunstroke was still troublesome but I was not delaying our departure on account of that, and four weeks to the day after I landed at Brazzaville, I started the truck and headed north up the broken-down track that some French cynic once christened "la Grande Route du Nord," the Great North Road.

It was a moment of high excitement. At last I was on my way in search of an animal that had puzzled me all my life. During the next few weeks I would settle this mystery of the gorillas once and for all; for the strange thing was how little information anyone seemed to have about them even in Brazzaville. Some of the officials had heard about gorillas to the north, but they had no idea of their numbers or where they occurred and it was impossible to find out anything of the strange tribe Rainez had talked about.

Several people had warned me of the road, but it proved worse than all the warnings. The surface was atrocious, loose and treacherous with potholes big enough to bury a sheep in. The going was so tough that in the first thirty miles or so out of Brazzaville the radiator nearly boiled dry, the clutch developed the most alarming rattle and I thought we would have to return to a garage in Brazzaville. But after waiting for the engine to cool down, filling the radiator again and topping up the oil, everything seemed to be all right and we set off again in the cooler atmosphere of the late afternoon.

This time the truck, in that strange way trucks have, made short work of the hills and sandy stretches, and by the time darkness was falling we were able to make camp with more than sixty miles between us and Brazzaville.

Next morning we were off early; suddenly the exhilaration was intense. Not that this was anything like the sort of country I had expected. I had been prepared for the deep virgin forest of equatorial Africa. Instead here we were driving through rolling savannah country with neat rounded hills reminiscent of the Sussex Downs. Most of the time it was too sandy for trees and too open for game, although every so often we would find ourselves driving through a narrow belt of forest.

But it was Africa. It smelt and felt like Africa and for the first time since I arrived I had the sense of being back at last in this continent I loved above all others. I remember the skies that day

better than I remember the landscape, skies that were always changing as they do in this part of Africa, with great tumbled banks of
white and grey broken by patches of the deepest blue beyond, and
all the time lightning was playing across the layer of mauve storm
cloud along the horizon.

Although I was so anxious to find the gorillas I knew that
my sunstroke made the hot hours of the middle of the day a real
danger to me and we took the journey in easy stages, stopping each
day for a couple of hours for a leisurely lunch off the small folding
table I had bought in Brazzaville. At night we pitched tents and
slept rolled in blankets, for the nights were surprisingly chilly.

Each day the road seemed to get a little worse and each day I
would be waiting for the countryside to change to the deep primeval
forest where I expected to find my gorillas. It never did. The rolling
savannah country continued. The only sign that we were getting well
away from Brazzaville came when I noticed that fewer and fewer
of the local tribesmen we passed were now wearing the filthy cast-
off European clothes they insist on wearing when they are close to
civilisation.

By the fouth day we reached the area where I thought the gorillas
should be, and I was beginning to get anxious. For not only did the
terrain seem wrong for these animals but whenever I stopped to
inquire about gorillas from any of the local tribesmen, I was always
met with the same blank expression. I was just beginning to think
my entire journey had been a complete mistake when my luck
changed.

We reached the town of Okio. Perhaps it is being over-polite to
call it a town as it was little more than a cluster of huts and bungalows
where the local French administrator had set up his headquarters.
The administrator himself was away when we called and we were
met by his deputy, a young man from Alsace called Scheler. He was
a quiet, undemonstrative fellow, rather a change from the run of
French administrators in these remote areas who are usually only too
grateful for some company and gossip from the world outside. But
I liked him. He had integrity and an obvious feeling for this forgotten bit of Africa.

His bungalow was a large one and he invited me to stay the night.

It was not until that evening after we had eaten that I raised the subject of the gorillas.

At first he looked surprised that I should have mentioned it at all.

"Well," he said, "there are gorillas in the district." He could not say how many, but it was not advisable to get near them. They were very dangerous, they were a long way from Okio and Europeans were always best advised to keep well out of their way.

But was it true, I asked him, that there was actually a tribe that hunted them?

Again he looked surprised, and paused a while before answering.

"Just what do you want, Monsieur? If you tell me I'll do my best to help you."

So I told him the whole story, about Rainez, about my anthropoid ape farm and my chimpanzees, and about my expedition; when I had finished he puffed thoughtfully at his pipe, still saying nothing.

I was beginning to get annoyed at his silences.

"But is it true about this tribe hunting gorillas?" I asked again.

He shrugged his shoulders.

"Sure, it's true enough. There's one tribe that does regularly, but I must warn you, it's not a particularly pretty sight. And it's also extremely dangerous. I would advise you to leave this business alone. While you are in my district I am responsible for you and it could cause me a lot of trouble if anything happened to you."

I argued with him: I told him that I already had permission for the expedition from his superiors in Brazzaville, I said that if I was silly enough to risk it, that was my affair, and I finally showed him the letter of recommendation from President Roosevelt.

"Mr. Denis," he said, "I see you carry heavier guns than I can cope with. Be ready to set off by eight o'clock to-morrow morning and I will show you your tribe. Whether they will show you any gorillas is up to them."

Scheler was as good as his word. At eight next morning we were on the road pounding along the dried-up track that led westwards from Okio across the bush. We drove most of the morning, not stopping for lunch, and in the early afternoon reached the outskirts of an African village with half a dozen women working away at the threadbare fields that had been cleared from the bush.

The village was half a mile beyond, a sad, tumble-down affair with an abandoned medical dispensary and two or three dozen huts. It was called Oka. When we drew up a few old men came out to stare at us and Scheler called one of them over and introduced him. He was very short with bandy legs and one of the wickedest old faces I have ever seen. Where his left hand should have been there was just a claw with the remains of two fingers.

"This," said Scheler, "is Chief Bamboo. He is a great hunter of gorillas and will give you all the help you need. If you would like to stay in his village he will be highly honoured. I would suggest you camp in the old dispensary, as the roof is fairly sound and you will be no more uncomfortable there than anywhere else. And one last word," he said. "For heaven's sake be careful. These brutes you are after are not just large monkeys. They're devils. Look after yourself."

With that he shook hands and drove off and for a moment I found myself wondering just what I had let myself in for.

But there was work to do. The sooner my camp was set up the sooner I could start looking for gorillas, so we drove over to the old dispensary and started unloading our stores on to its ramshackle veranda. Zinga seemed quite pleased with his quarters and began setting up the pressure lamps and the folding table ready for the evening, but Joseph, my cook, began to wail almost at once and I realised just how incompetent a housekeeper I was. For, as Joseph pointed out with tears in his eyes, I had brought no salt, no baking powder, no laundry soap and no cooking fat.

"Never mind," I said. "To save on the laundry I will do without a shirt and instead of cooking fat we will use Australian butter."

Luckily I seemed to have bought far more tinned butter than we would normally have needed. Instead of baking powder I told him to use the traditional method I remembered from my last trip to the Congo; the cook keeps a bottle full of chewed-up banana which is allowed to ferment and is then added to the bread in the place of yeast. As for the salt we would just have to do without. If all else failed we could fall back on tinned milk and the apricot jam of

which, for some reason, I seemed to have laid in truly majestic
supplies.

No sooner was this settled than I had other business to attend to.
Chief Bamboo arrived on an official visit. He wore only a rag in
lieu of trousers, but in honour of the occasion he had put on a very
torn, very greasy, European dress shirt, complete with clip-on bow
tie. As soon as we had exchanged courtesies he handed me his present
of welcome, a small, sadly undernourished goat with the short legs
and bloated stomach common to all goats in this part of Africa.

I knew that this present called for payment within the hour at a
slightly higher rate than if I had been buying it on the open market,
and accepting it with the mixture of gratitude and casualness that
seemed called for, handed it to the disdainful Joseph for decapitation.

But this was not what Chief Bamboo expected and no sooner
had I passed the goat to Joseph than the old man launched into a
frantic harangue, angrily waving his claw in my face, and telling me
in pidgin French that he wanted immediate payment.

This, I thought, was hardly the way to manage an exchange of
diplomatic courtesies but to keep the old man quiet I took fifteen
francs from my wallet and offered them to him with as much
dignity as I could muster. Furiously he threw them to the ground
and, shouting louder than ever, called the entire village to witness
that the goat was worth twenty francs if it was worth a centime.

Normally I would not have argued, but I felt that here more than
just five francs was at stake. Our whole future relationship depended
on whether I let him get away with this or not. So I grabbed him
by the collar of his greasy dress shirt, propelled him into the road,
and sent his fifteen francs flying after him. The last thing I saw
before I closed the door after him was Chief Bamboo, carefully
picking up his fifteen francs from the road and then, still in his dress
shirt and bow-tie, standing to attention and giving me a cracking
military salute. From then on our relations were cordial in the
extreme.

So cordial in fact that less than two hours later he sent a messenger
round to tell me that some of his tribe from a nearby village had just
returned from a hunt with a young gorilla actually in captivity.
Was I interested?

Without so much as waiting to tell Joseph where I was going I bundled the messenger into our truck and tore off to the village.

It took just over an hour's back-breaking driving to get there and when we arrived the whole of the tiny village was in uproar.

"Come quickly," they shouted to me. "He's over here, in this hut. We've been keeping him for you."

And there inside the hut he was. Not the defenceless baby gorilla I had been expecting, but a huge animal, far larger than I had ever thought it possible to catch, waiting for me in a great cage of branches and vines inside the gloom and stench of the hut.

At first all I could make out was a dark mass of matted black hair, for the animal was sitting huddled in one corner, its hands covering its face. Then suddenly as I peered in at it it saw me and with the shriek and fury of a maniac hurled itself at my side of the cage.

By a miracle the bars held and for the first time I saw its face as it glared at me with a savagery I had never seen in an animal before. This was not the face of a gorilla as I expected to see it. This was something more frightening and more pitiful.

It was like a mask eaten into by some flesh-consuming disease. The lips were gone. The nostrils were eaten almost away and the fangs of teeth were blackened and askew in what remained of the creature's lower jaw. Only the eyes were untouched and they glared at me with indescribable fury.

By this time most of the men who had captured the gorilla had crowded into the hut and reluctantly I had to tell them it was no use. Whatever the disease was the wretched animal had caught I had no idea, but I knew there was only one thing to be done.

So I paid the men for their work and then with a heavy heart ordered them to kill it before it suffered any further torment. They speared it and it died swiftly and without a murmur.

16   *The First Capture*

As I drove back to Oka I had my first sense of foreboding about
the expedition. Obviously Rainez had been right. There
were gorillas here in numbers that no one else had suspected.
With the help of this strange tribe that hunted them with such
evident expertise it would not prove too difficult to capture some;
provided I paid the hunters enough I could make it worth their
while to preserve the animals, instead of slaughtering them indiscriminately. Before leaving, Scheler had explained to Chief
Bamboo the price I would be willing to pay for all the live animals
they could get hold of.

But what about this terrifying disease? I had never heard of it
before. Just supposing all the gorillas in this part of Africa suffered
from it? What then?

I remembered the hunters had mentioned killing another
gorilla when they captured the one I had just seen, so when I
arrived in Oka I sent them a message asking to see its remains as
soon as possible. They arrived that evening. Its body had been much
too heavy to carry and had been cut up for meat on the spot. But
its head remained untouched and four of the hunters brought it to
me in a basket slung from a long piece of wood.

I paid them for their trouble and there on my veranda, by the
harsh glare of my petrol lamp I opened the basket for my first sight
at close quarters of the head of a fully grown male gorilla. My first
fears were groundless. This gorilla had been untouched by disease.

The head was well over a foot long and weighed 28 lbs. It was
covered with coarse black hair forming a mane at the back; the
teeth, a dull, matt brown, were as big as a lion's. Drained of blood,

the lips, gums and tongue had a curious ivory whiteness about them.

Unlike the other gorilla I had just seen, this one's expression was not particularly ferocious. A spear had broken the left cheek bone and the eye on this side was revulsed. Despite this the face remained surprisingly human in expression, reminding me vividly of a lady I knew well in New England, who lived in a village and wrote books. This poor gorilla had the same look of painful concentration that she always presented to the world.

The important thing was that I now knew that the frightful disease I had seen only that morning had not spread to all the gorillas in the district. My expedition was not doomed from the start as I had thought it might be.

By now it was getting on for midnight and I suddenly realised how unwell and exhausted I felt myself. All the excitement and exertion of the day had brought on a recurrence of the sunstroke I had in Brazzaville and I was on the point of collapsing into my bed when I heard shouts and singing from the far side of the village. More shouts followed. People began scurrying out of the huts. Torches were lit. Then across the path in front of the veranda marched an exultant group of hunters. When they saw me they stopped and, calling me in their dialect, began pointing triumphantly to the centre of the crowd. For there, carried on the shoulders of eight men was a great crush litter of heavy branches. Strapped to it with vines, in a semi-sitting position, its huge fists on its knees, was the immense body of an old male gorilla.

At once, my fatigue forgotten, I hobbled down the steps to inspect their prize. This was the first fully grown gorilla I had ever had a chance of examining. At last we got him free from the litter and with the combined efforts of a dozen men stretched the stiff body out flat on the ground, so that I could start to measure it.

He was not as tall as I expected. From the soles of his feet to the bony crest of his skull measured only 5 ft. 2½ ins., but it was the spread of his arms that was so immense. From finger-tip to finger-tip of his extended arms measured 7 ft. 9 ins., and his chest 52½ ins. The figure that impressed me most, however, was the measurement round the neck, 29½ ins., and the rest of the limbs had a circumference in proportion. The upper arm was 18½ ins., the forearm 15½ ins., the wrist 11½ ins., the thigh 25 ins., the calf 16 ins., and the ankle 14½ ins.

Put like this the measurements seem simple enough but when I was faced by the massive body I found them difficult to appreciate and had the carcase turned and placed in position after position just to understand its proportions. The most impressive view was from the back, with the huge buttocks, the massive waist, the terrifying power of the high square shoulders, and the neck so short and monolithic that the head seemed to emerge almost straight from the shoulders.

The chest and most of the back were bare to the black leathery skin, but the rest of the body was thickly covered with coarse hair, some black, but most of it white, giving this old male a distinctly hoary impression of age. The hair was especially thick on the upper arms as if to emphasise the massive strength whilst the reddish colour of the hair on the top of the head, so noticeable in young gorillas, had totally disappeared.

As I gazed on him I felt my first real qualms about catching gorillas. From now on it would be creatures like this I would be facing; this big male made the idea of capturing gorillas a very different proposition from the way it had appeared to me in New York. I also hated the idea of having anything to do with the killing of animals like this. The hunting went on of course whether I was there or not, since gorillas were an important source of meat for the tribe, and I knew that the rewards I was offering for live gorillas should soon bring down the death-rate on the hunts. Nevertheless death like this was not pretty, and had to be set against the excitement of everything I was discovering.

As if to set my mind at rest, Chief Bamboo suddenly appeared through the crowd, grinning all over his wicked old face and waving his claw of a hand at me in greeting. He had good news. The last of the hunters had just returned bringing with them a young 30 lb. gorilla and he was alive. It was the most exciting thing that had happened since I left Brazzaville but even as I tried to follow him over to his hut where the young gorilla had been put I realised I was all in. I could hardly make one leg follow another.

"To-morrow," I shouted, "Let me come and see him to-morrow. Look after him well for me and I'll see you get a good price."

Even then I could not force myself into bed, for the villagers had started skinning the old male by the light of the petrol lamp as he lay in front of my hut, and I found the sight too unusual to miss. So I dragged myself up on to the veranda, and propping myself against the railings watched them long into the night. Opened and exposed the body looked larger than ever with its huge thoracic cage and the mass of muscle on the chest and arms. Most frightening of all were the hands, for once they were skinned and the matted black hair removed they looked grotesquely human as they lay there on the veranda floor.

When I finally went to bed I slept only fitfully and woke long before dawn. My head still throbbed but the dizziness had left me and I found I could walk. I was suddenly anxious to see the young gorilla old Bamboo had told me about the night before, so I took my torch and walked across to his hut. I found the cage at the back and shone the light in at the first successful capture of the expedition.

The young gorilla was obviously needing sleep more than I did, for he was lying on his side, his limbs hunched in a curiously foetal position and his eyes tightly shut. The light on his face did not wake him, and I could see the steady rise and fall of his breathing although his sleep was absolutely silent. For the first time in my life I smelt the strange subtle odour of a young gorilla, a faint, sweetish, slightly choking smell quite unlike the strong wild stench of the adult gorilla that still clung to my clothes from the previous night.

Here, after the weeks of uncertainty and frustration was our first real success. But then I remembered that old male I had watched being dismembered on my own veranda so recently, and made up my mind that I was going to do what I could to stop this killing.

By now I had learned quite a lot about this strange tribe. To look at they were nothing special. The men were slightly under-sized by African standards and the women were mannish-looking and shaved their heads, which did little to improve their looks. But what was remarkable about the tribe was the way its entire existence centred round the gorillas. They had hunted them from time immemorial and the animals had become not only the source of meat for the villages, but also provided the tribe with its one industry, its main excitement in life and the inspiration for its dances.

As a result the villagers no longer spoke about the gorillas as if they were animals. For them they were really a rival tribe and when they went out to kill them it was not a hunt but a war that was pursued ferociously with the sort of wild courage that Africans traditionally put into their tribal battles. For them the big old male gorilla I had seen the night before had been a famous chief. That was why they were so pleased with themselves when they brought me his body, and they would speak of him having wives and children exactly as if he had been one of their own chieftains.

It was because they regarded the gorillas as a hostile tribe that the slaughter was so great. If they had been sensible about it you would have thought that once they had killed enough gorillas to feed the village for the next few weeks they would have called the hunt off and come home satisfied, but it was not like that at all. Once they caught sight of the gorillas the tribe would go mad. Sometimes men would rush straight into the most terrible danger, and the fact that I was offering them a good price to preserve the lives of the gorillas they caught meant next to nothing to them. All they wanted was to kill. I have seen men in the middle of a hunt come up to a gorilla that had already been slain and start to beat it and spear it savagely. It was as if they were still moved by an insatiable hatred for the animal.

If I was to stop that I knew there was only one thing for me to do. From now on I had to go with the hunters and be there at the capture myself. There was no other way of restraining the blood lust that seemed to rise up in these people whenever they got near a gorilla.

The way they hunted was ingenious, and had been passed on from generation to generation.

First the trackers would go out, usually after rain, and once they had picked up the spoor they would follow it for miles across the open savannah. The gorillas lived in families—numbering as many as twenty or even thirty—inside the *galeries forestières*—the patches of forest I had noticed on my journey from Brazzaville. During the day the group would leave the forest and go off in search of food in the open country, sometimes even reaching the village fields and scaring the women away before scavenging for manioc, maize, pineapples or anything they could lay hands on.

Once the tracker had picked up the trail left by one of the gorilla groups in the open country, he could be sure it would ultimately lead him back to the part of the forest where the family would spend the night. These trackers knew what they were up to. They would never risk actually entering the forest themselves. This would have been foolhardy since the gorillas would certainly have heard them and would either have attacked or else panicked and fled for miles.

Instead, if the tracks entered a patch of forest, the trackers circled it completely to make sure that no tell-tale tracks led out again. When they had satisfied themselves that the gorillas were inside they would circle the patch of forest once more, listening. The hearing of these men must have been extraordinarily acute, for in the end, just as dusk was falling, they would pick up the sound of the gorillas settling down for the night—the cracking of branches, the tearing off of twigs, and the puffing and grunting of the big gorillas building their nests for the night. From these sounds the trackers would be able to pin-point the position inside the forest, knowing perfectly well, since gorillas are heavy sleepers, that there they would remain until an hour or so after sunrise the following morning.

As soon as the noises in the forest ceased, the trackers would run back to the village with the news. I would hear them in the middle of the night, while they were still a mile away, singing, and shouting the news of their discovery. They would know from the tracks, how many gorillas were in the patch of forest, and how many "mwanas"—young animals and babies. The whole excited village would hear and understand and prepare for the hunt even before the trackers reached home. Then, soon after midnight, the trackers would start out again with twenty or thirty more men armed with spears and long sharp knives. The trackers would lead them to the edge of the forest and point unerringly to the spot where the gorillas were asleep, and the men would set to work.

Silently, delicately, in darkness so profound that even their night-seeing eyes were useless, they would begin to cut a narrow tunnel through the thick of the forest so as to encircle the sleeping gorillas. It was dangerous and back-breaking work. They would have to feel with their hands for the roots of the bushes and circle round trees too large for their knives to cut. Gradually they would advance. Sometimes they would drive their tunnel so close to the gorillas that they would actually hear their heavy breathing or the crackle of twigs as they shifted in their sleep. And sometimes one of the gorillas would awake and give the alarm. When this happened there would be nothing the men could do, for spears would be useless in the dark and at such close quarters. If they were lucky the gorillas would just escape with the males barking angrily and the females rushing headlong behind them through the forest, carrying their young in their arms. But sometimes the old leader of the gorillas would turn and attack the men and it was in these night encounters that the most terrible wounds of all were suffered by the hunters.

But if all went well the tunnel would be completed just before sunrise and the gorillas would have heard nothing. This was the time when the main body of hunters arrived from the village carrying their spears, their guns and their nets. They would wait on the edge of the forest until the first glimmer of light filtered through the trees and made possible the work they had to do in the tunnel. Long before the sun was above the horizon they would have finished and throughout the length of the tunnel their nets would stretch, tightly fastened every two or three feet to the trees, facing the spot where the gorillas were still asleep.

These nets were far bigger than anything I had seen in Africa before. Thirty to forty feet long and five feet high, they were made out of tightly twisted native rope and were knotted into an eight inch mesh; the tribe would make them and keep them in repair, no small undertaking, since thirty or forty of these nets were needed for a gorilla hunt.

Once these nets were stretched and firmly secured in the tunnel, on the side towards the sleeping gorillas, the hunters could feel reasonably safe and the need for silence and caution would be over. They would all go to work then inside the tunnel with their axes and big knives, widening it to about fifteen feet. This time as they

worked they would sing and shout at the tops of their voices, knowing that the net was between them and their enemy.

By the time the gorillas had woken and seen what was happening
the biggest of the males would pluck up courage and hurl himself
against the net. A circle of spears and guns would be waiting
to meet him, and the battle would start.

17   *The Fight in the Forest*

IT was not until I had been in Oka's village nearly a week that I got my first chance of carrying out my plans to accompany the hunters. For the villagers hunted only when they felt like it or when the witch-doctor decided the auspices were right, and there was nothing I could do to hurry them.

I spent these first few days, working with Joseph and Zinga, building ten large cages to house the gorillas we hoped we would catch. Chief Bamboo assigned several of his men to bring us timber from the forest, but even so it was hard work for the rest of us as I knew that we might have to pay with our lives if there was any weakness in the cages.

Then, late one afternoon, the village was suddenly swept with excitement. Some women who had been harvesting maize just outside the village came shrieking that they had spotted a pair of gorillas near their field. The men started shouting as well. The witch-doctor was summoned to make sure that a hunt would be in order for the following day and as soon as he had pronounced in favour of it, the trackers went off to trail the two gorillas through the bush.

From then on, it was exactly as if the village was mobilised for war. The men were everywhere, sharpening spears and rolling up their nets, whilst the women were preparing the food the village would take with it on the hunt. I took the precaution of presenting Chief Bamboo with a couple of handfuls of the gunpowder I had brought with me from Brazzaville, before asking whether I could go with the hunters. He nodded quite cheerfully, so I loaded my camera in readiness for the morning and went off to an early bed, leaving Joseph with strict instructions to call me at first cock crow.

As it happened I need hardly have bothered him. In the first place, in this part of Africa, the cocks seemed to crow all night long. In the second, the noise of the village of Oka working up its courage for a gorilla hunt would have wakened the dead. For several hours I tried to ignore the din and lay, tossing on my camp bed, cursing the dancers, the drums and every gorilla in French Equatorial Africa.

Finally I gave in, slipped on my sandals, and made my way through the pitch-dark of a moonless night to the spot just outside the village where the dance was being held.

It was a clearing about 30 yards across and everyone was already so intent on the dance that I arrived unobserved. Normally the village dogs would have barked and given me away but in this part there were nothing but a few mission-bred puppies and they were too amiable even to bark at a white man.

A dance like this, when the performers do not know they are being observed, is a totally different affair from the sort of polite performance put on for white visitors, and this one was quite new to me. It turned out to be a well-acted version in mime of an entire gorilla hunt.

I have always been fascinated by the way an African dancer can turn himself so vividly into any animal of his choice, mimicking its behaviour down to the most minute detail. These dancers were superb and what made their performance particularly interesting to me was not the way it demonstrated the methods of the hunters, so much as what it told me of the reaction of the gorilla to attack.

For suddenly I saw the man impersonating the gorilla stand right up, start striking his chest and then drop on to all fours to charge the rest of the dancers. Then in the most fearsome way he began seizing their legs and trying to tear the muscles away from the bone with the sheer force of the fingers—a source of injury from gorillas I had often been told of but had never really believed.

As a dance this gorilla hunt was inferior to the elephant dances I had seen among the Mambuti pygmies of the Congo or the hunting dances of the keddahs of Ceylon—I think the minds of the dancers were too much on the actual hunt which was about to take place— and very soon it was over. The rhythm of the tom-toms slowed down, the shadows from the dying wood fire grew longer and the dance became what dances usually are whether they take place in the jungle or in a night club—a preliminary and an invitation to love-making.

Here I felt the movements were less sophisticated, and the suggestiveness more direct than they might have been in New York. It amused me to see the Holy Virgin medals hanging around the necks of the dancers side by side with their pagan scapularies as they writhed in a frenzy of amorous contortion. They all had them, even the witch-doctor; for in theory they were all good Christians.

I decided the time had come to leave them, and stole away to my lonely air mattress to get a few hours sleep before the hunt began in earnest, long before dawn.

I was awakened at three a.m. by Chief Bamboo in person. He had come to remind me of the gunpowder I had promised for the hunters and as I pulled myself from beneath my blankets I was struck by the chill of the night air. It still seemed pitch black, but the old chief must have had eyes like a cat as he led me across from the dispensary and through the village to where the hunters were waiting.

"We must leave at once," whispered old Bamboo. "The men have found many gorillas and the tunnel is cut ready for the nets. There will be a good battle and we must be ready for the animals when they wake."

After the din and noise of the dancing the silence was now un-canny and it was not until we had reached the far end of the village that I saw that half the villagers were there already waiting to move off.

Bamboo gave the signal and off we went, still in silence, the leaders setting a gruelling pace despite the darkness. We kept to-gether, marching in a long column like a battalion of infantry. For something like a mile we followed a track, then that petered out and we were in open country. The going became rougher. Time after time I found myself stumbling. My head began to throb, but there was nothing to do except follow the faint bobbing figure of Bamboo in front of me and I longed for daylight as I had never longed for it before.

We must have walked like this for nearly two hours before I

"*It was partly the closeness of gorillas to man in the pattern of evolution that caught my imagination*"

The author measures one of the first gorillas to be brought into
his camp at Oka, French Equatorial Africa

The village at Oka

Ritual dance before a gorilla hunt

The net is put up and a spearman stands ready

Waiting for dawn in the tunnel that has been cut round the part of the forest in which the gorillas are nesting

Victim of the hunt

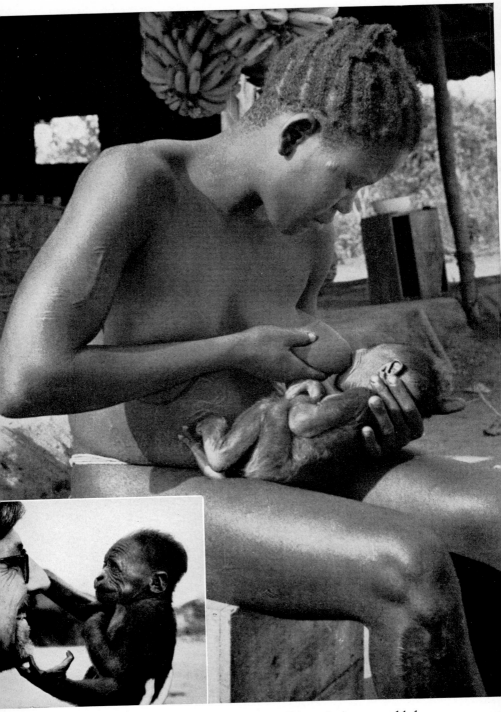

*The author with the orphan gorilla baby which was suckled
by one of the chief's wives*

noticed the first flush of dawn in the sky, and I had begun to dread what Bamboo had meant when he had told me that the gorillas were "not far from the village." To my cost I had learned already that Africans have a highly elastic sense of distance. As long as their legs are in motion they have no idea of time and I knew that if I had to stumble on much farther my sunstroke would soon become troublesome and I would be walking with a constant sense of vertigo and my vision practically obliterated.

Daybreak came with the sudden drama usual in this part of Africa. For the first time I could see the other members of the hunt. There must have been at least two hundred of them, the men stripped down to the most meagre of loin-cloths, and the women, who had come along for the excitement and to help with the food, completely naked except for a girdle of coloured beads and two diminutive aprons.

All the women carried fresh sections of net, rolled into greasy bundles and carried on the head, whilst the men bore a fearsome selection of weapons. A few had ordinary spears. Others had a peculiar harpoon-like weapon I had never seen before in Africa. It had a thick, heavy hardwood shaft, whittled thin in the centre to make a handhold but left thick at each end to increase the weight. On the front was fixed a murderous-looking barbed spearhead, but this was not attached tightly to the shaft. Instead it was tied to the middle of the shaft with a skein of heavy twine, so that when the weapon was thrown at a gorilla, the barb would be driven deep into the animal's body, and the shaft be shaken loose to drag behind as it tried to escape. This shaft would soon catch in the bushes leaving the gorilla trapped and helpless for the hunters.

But most bizarre of all were the guns. As far as I could see there were nearly twenty of them, all proudly carried by the wealthier village notables, immensely long, ponderous muzzle-loaders, the sort of weapons I had never thought to exist these days outside museums.

With the sun, conversation began. Reinforcements joined us from other villages and soon the whole column was singing and shouting with excitement. Before long there must have been nearly four hundred of us. Twice we had passed through narrow patches of forest and I had gratefully accepted the shade of the trees as I trudged beneath them. But most of the time we kept on, straight across open country, and I found myself wondering where the gorillas could be, and whether I would be able to last out until we reached them.

Suddenly, as if an unspoken order had flashed along the ranks, the singing and the chattering ceased, and in the hush I saw we were approaching another of those long belts of forest like those we had already been through. We covered the last three hundred yards practically on tiptoe and it was not until we had reached the edge of the thick, leafy, almost impenetrable forest that I spotted the place where a few bushes had been cut and a narrow tunnel driven through the packed underbrush. Inside the tunnel I could see a man squatting every few feet with his spear poised and almost immediately our men went in with the nets spreading them silently, efficiently, along the length of the tunnel.

It all seemed too peaceful and orderly to be true, and I remember signalling to old Bamboo inquiring in sign language whether the gorillas really could be inside this patch of forest. The old man grinned ferociously and nodded. Just at that moment, as if to confirm what he was saying, a sudden outburst of screaming and sharp, staccato barking, like the noise of a gigantic dog-fight, echoed through the forest apparently only a few feet from where I was standing.

There was a pause, then a deep roll followed, thudding like muted drums. I recognised what it was. I had heard it once before in the Kivu mountains in the Congo and it was the sort of sound that once heard is never forgotten, the noise of the big male gorilla pounding his body with his hands.

I was so excited that I expected the gorilla to come crashing out at us from the forest at once, but none of the hunters seemed particularly concerned and I realised from the way they were going about their preparations that the hunt was going to be a long and complicated affair.

Old Bamboo amused me. He had appointed himself quartermaster as well as commander-in-chief of the expedition and was making the rounds of the men who had guns, measuring each of them out a fistful of the black gunpowder I had given him earlier that morning. Now that I had a better chance to see these guns they caused me more anxiety than the gorillas. They were all muzzle-loaders and two of them were actually old flint-locks, roughly converted to work with a hammer and cap mechanism. Several cracked barrels were held together with copper wire, and another barrel was unmistakably a piece of old gas-pipe, with the screw threads still there at the end of the muzzle. But the marvel of marvels was a home-made two-barrelled contraption which fired both barrels simultaneously, an arrangement which scarcely seemed to increase the victims' chances of death whilst making the firer's practically certain.

I asked Bamboo what these sharp-shooters used for bullets and he produced a precious little bag full of nails, screws, nuts and odd scraps of iron. These missiles, he explained, were rather special, and then showed me the standard bullets used on these hunts. They consisted of tightly compressed wads of metal from old tin cans and I recognised several of my own among them including discarded sardine tins, and cans of Campbell's soup and Heinz spaghetti.

The hunters had something still more disturbing than this in their armoury. I saw several Africans loading their guns not with bullets but with short spears each tipped with a sickle-shaped chisel, the cutting edge of which was about $2\frac{1}{2}$ inches wide. The shaft of the spear was rammed down the barrel on top of a 4-inch charge of gunpowder and an inch of wadding.

The owners of the guns sat quietly by as the last of the nets were being fastened, the blades of their spears poking threateningly towards the wall of trees from behind which the gorillas could be heard, their grunting and cries of alarm becoming louder every minute. After my long march I felt dizzy and was more grateful than I can tell for this interlude. It gave me a chance to find myself a spot in the shade on the edge of the forest where I could rest. I got a good twenty minutes respite and even managed to shoot several scenes of the hunters waiting by their nets. The buzzing in my ears was still as strong as ever but at least my vision was back to normal, and when Bamboo suddenly shouted for the hunt to move forward, I was ready to follow.

ON SAFARI

Although by now the gorillas on the other side of the net hardly stopped shrieking and barking with alarm, they had not yet plucked up courage to attack the net and it was time for the hunters to make the next move. A compact group of them with knives and axes crossed through the net at right angles and working with enormous energy began cutting a new lane right across the area now enclosed so as to divide it into two. They worked rapidly, backing and chopping and shouting as they went, and all the time they were backed up by a team of warriors armed with spears and guns. Once again these provided splendid scenes for my camera.

Bamboo explained that it was usually this cutting team that made first contact with the gorillas and was often attacked, especially by the old male gorilla. As soon as he told me this, I determined to follow them, for by now I was caught up in the whole spirit of the hunt, and did not want my film to miss any detail of it.

Perhaps this seems strange as all my life I have hated hunting. I despise the white man's cult of the hunt with the special clothes, the trained dogs, the expensive precision guns and the careful luxury of the kill. I have never owned or used a hunting gun and simply cannot understand why anyone should ever want to shoot an animal unless in hunger or extreme danger.

But a native hunt is something different and I have often taken the opportunity of observing one. To the protein-starved forest dwellers hunting is a necessity, not a luxury as it is with the white man. The risks are more equal, and I tell myself that it will go on whether I witness it or not. In this case my presence would even be the means of saving the lives of many young gorillas who would otherwise be surely killed.

I used also to love trudging through forest and stream. I used to pride myself on my ability to share all the hardships of the hunters, and I still know nothing to equal the feeling of being at one with them, with the same keenness of eye and ear, and the same casualness in danger. For these qualities are infectious and if I am honest with myself I have to admit that being on this gorilla hunt satisfied a deep urge in me beside which the motor safari and the organised big game hunt would be little more than a joke.

I followed close behind the cutters as they tunnelled slowly
196

on through the forest, but although I was hoping for a sight of one of the gorillas there was another lull in their noise and I could imagine them regrouping somewhere behind the trees and waiting for the moment when they would charge the net and make their dash for freedom.

The sun by now was rising rapidly and for the first time I really noticed the heat and my thirst. So I left the cutting party and came back through the net to the rough seat of branches I had made myself in the shade. The men with the spears had stopped shouting now and were sitting around talking in casual groups. The sound of the men cutting into the forest gradually died away as the leaves muffled the noise. The hunt was obviously going to take its time.

So I crept back to where the women had left the provisions. Most of the food consisted of rolls of manioc, retted in water and roasted in banana leaves. I could not face these. They were as tough and resilient as india-rubber. Nor did I particularly fancy any of the meat the women had brought. It was probably goat and was very old and very high. But I did find some bananas and a pineapple. They were more to my taste and when I had eaten I went back again to drowse at the foot of my tree until something happened.

Of all the tropical forests I had ever been in this was probably the most comfortable. True, hundreds of tiny sweat flies had taken a fancy to me and covered my arms and knees. But there were no ants, no mosquitos, no ticks and no leeches. After a while my head nodded and I left the flies to make what they could of me.

I have no idea how long I sat there asleep opposite the net, but suddenly a faint shuffling and cracking of branches jerked me awake, nerves tingling. As I watched I saw that in a tight mass of branches on the other side of the net something was moving. I dared not make any noise to attract the other hunters who by now were mostly dozing quietly along the net. But slowly the branches parted and the huge head of a male gorilla peered through.

For a moment I thought that my sunstroke had caused me to imagine him. Then I heard my heart pounding so loudly that he must surely hear, so close was he and so silent the forest.

I watched the great eyes roll and then peer towards me. But I was in deep shadow. He could not see me, and I saw the head turn as he caught sight of the group of seven or eight men relaxed and unprepared a few yards to my right. Before I could do anything to warn them, the head was withdrawn, and the curtain of branches closed. Then the next instant he was crashing through the bushes towards us like an express train.

I am sure he was not trying to charge me or the men, and I am sure he never so much as saw the net. This was the old leader's one wild dash for freedom. He paused for a fraction of a second when he saw the open space behind the net, and then rushed headlong towards us, tearing the net bodily from the trees on each side.

For a moment the net held and he was thrashing in it in the middle of the lane. I ran forward and tried to focus my camera.

This was extremely stupid of me. I had not realised that the men on my right had come to their senses and that I was now between them and the gorilla. They seemed to be rushing straight for me, a yelling horde with spears and harpoons raised and I had no time to get back to the shelter of the trees.

To this day I have no idea how they missed me. Perhaps they were better shots than I thought. But one of them actually had one of the fearsome muzzle-loaders with its chisel-ended spear pointing straight for me. He stopped, raised it at arm's length in the general direction of the gorilla and holding it as far away from him as he could, he shut his eyes, turned his head away and fired.

What happened then has remained photographed in my mind. I saw the man yank wildly at the trigger. For a moment nothing happened and the gorilla went on roaring and thrashing at the net. Then there was a tremendous WHOOF, more like the noise of a rocket than a gun. The gun flew back, cracking the man on the side of the face and knocking him clean over and the air was suddenly filled with a cloud of acrid smoke.

I crouched where I was, unable to see a thing. Two more WHOOFS followed as other marksmen rushed to join in, and then the gorilla screamed. It was a cross between a shriek and a roar, infinitely prolonged and dropping down to a growl, gurgling deep in the animal's throat.

I could still hear him thrashing away with his arms, and when the smoke lifted I saw that he was held precariously by the net.

Someone else fired. Three men hurled their harpoons simultaneously and then scattered as the great gorilla with a last effort tore free from the net.

Then I remember the wounded animal coming straight for me, its arms outspread, its mouth open and bleeding.

I tried to run. The animal was perhaps eight feet from me by then and even as I dodged for the bushes my foot caught in a creeper and I fell, violently, right in the path of the charging animal.

I remember thinking, almost dispassionately, that this was the end of my expedition and lying there, winded, waiting for those terrible teeth. But nothing happened.

I heard shouting all round me and more shots and then realised that the old gorilla, although terribly wounded, had got away. In his escape he had jumped clean over me, and as I stumbled to my feet I could see that I was covered with the excrement he had dropped as he ran. Had I not fallen I would have stood straight in his path and would certainly have been attacked.

Although the gorilla had gone I could see the hunters were still worried and when I had a chance to ask him, old Bamboo told me why. Apparently it was quite common for the "tata," the powerful old male gorilla, to escape like this and whenever it happened it spelt trouble. He would usually stay quite close and later in the hunt, when he heard the screams for help of the females, he would return to attack the hunters ferociously from the wrong side of the net.

It was this that spurred the men on for the climax of the hunt was approaching. The female gorillas had picked up the shrieks of the old male and the forest was filled with the din as they joined in. Three times, isolated females charged the net and three times they were repulsed.

All the time the work went on, with fresh tunnels being cleared and the nets being moved steadily forward until the enclosure with the gorillas inside had shrunk to less than a few hundred feet across.

By now all the men were swarming around the nets waiting for a mass break-out from the gorillas, and it was not until I saw old Bamboo squinting anxiously up at the sky that I realised we were in for a storm. Half the sky was already pitch black and I knew as well as Bamboo did that a tropical downpour at this crucial point in the hunt would be disastrous. The rain would be so heavy that none of us would be able to move and we would be floundering in a sea of mud.

Bamboo started calling urgently in the local dialect and a few minutes later the ancient witch-doctor came waddling into the clearing with the tribe's rain ju-ju borne ceremoniously before him on the end of a long pole.

As far as I could see it seemed to be the extremely greasy skin of a civet cat, but everyone treated it with great respect as it was shaken eloquently to the heavens.

And it worked. Whatever it was it worked, for although the clouds massed and the forest darkened, the rain kept off.

A few minutes later there was a commotion from farther down the net. A shot was followed by a great cry from the hunters; by the time I had hurried to the spot they had already started their triumphal song over the body of a large female that had been plugged neatly through the head with the compressed remains of one of my tins of Dominion Apricot Jam.

I know it was apricot jam because I had seen it being loaded that very morning into the gun belonging to the boy who now stood beside the gorilla, a grin all over his face and an ugly gash in his chest caused by the recoil when he had fired.

There was another shout followed by a fusillade of shots, and I looked up into the trees to where some of the men were pointing. Two huge bodies were swinging from branch to branch with the smooth assurance I had admired so often in orang-utans but had never thought possible for the far bulkier gorillas.

These were both young adult male gorillas weighing 300 lbs. or more apiece. If I had seen them walking I would have thought them incapable of lifting themselves up off the ground; yet here they were, high overhead, swinging expertly from tree to tree.

All my sympathies were with them, and I held my breath, hoping that they would get away. Certainly the larger one looked as if he was going to make it. He was high and moving fast and had got right to the edge of the enclosure unscathed. But by now so many trees had been felled that he faced a wide gap, with the rest of the forest stretching away beyond. Somehow he had to get across if he was to escape and we all watched as he moved out on to the last slender branch. Slowly it buckled beneath its weight and with a despairing cry the animal threw himself off and tried to reach the forest beyond.

It was too far, even for a gorilla, and he had hardly touched the ground before a dozen spears pierced him.

Then the other one came to the gap. He saw how far he had to jump, and at the last minute his nerve failed him, leaving him hesitating high overhead until the guns could be reloaded and a lucky shot finally reached him. He fell in one long wheeling motion, turned over twice, and crashed at our feet just outside the net.

The score stood at four dead. The hunters were overjoyed. The village would have meat now for several weeks to come and that was as important to them as the rewards I had promised for the gorillas they could capture alive.

By now the morning had gone and the storm was threatening again. The sky overhead had become completely black and the civet cat was being walked round and round the slowly shrinking enclosure. I realised that the area enclosed by the nets could only be as big as a suburban garden and the men were working furiously to confine it still farther, constantly chopping at young trees and moving the nets.

Rain would begin any moment and any delay would be fatal. I suggested to Bamboo that while we waited on one side of the net, the rest of the men should go round the other side of the enclosure and at his signal put up a great shout to try to stampede the gorillas towards us.

It was a fearsome noise the men made and it succeeded beyond our expectations. First to appear was a young adult male; before he could so much as charge the net four spears were hurled at him from deadly range and he was down inside the enclosure.

This was the last of the big gorillas. Now it was time for the small ones I was so anxious to capture. To catch them every tree and bush standing in the enclosure had somehow to be levelled. There were scarcely twenty square yards left uncut when the first shout was raised and a biggish youngster came charging out, raced across the clearing and became entangled in the net. A dozen men jumped on him trying to pin him to the ground with forked branches, but he was too strong for them, caught one by the ankle and broke free. In a second he was racing across the clearing again, scattering men right and left and they were so scared of his strength and ferocity that I had the greatest difficulty in stopping them using their spears on him.

Then he was in the net again and this time it caught him cleanly so that he could neither move nor get hurt. I had several basket-work cages made for me and although they were really too small for an animal of this size there was nothing else to put him into; so net and all, trussed up like a sausage, my gorilla was bundled in. He had skinned his hands but was otherwise completely unhurt.

Then suddenly the hunt was over. With only a few feet of bush left uncut we saw two very young gorillas hesitating whether to make a dash for it across the clearing and almost before they could move we had the nets over them. That seemed to be that. But then, just as we were about to go there was another great shout of excitement from the hunters and they came grinning all over their faces holding the smallest gorilla baby I had yet seen. He looked very frightened and pathetic and had been nearly overlooked as he clung to a small tree. But he was perfect, healthy and completely unharmed and I realised excitedly that my plan had worked and out of the hunt I had won nine young captive gorillas.

The hunters seemed as excited as I was and gathered round them to sing their traditional song of triumph for the end of a successful hunt. Even as they sang, the first spots of rain began to fall and soon it was sheeting down in a blinding hissing deluge. The last thing I noticed was the witch-doctor wrapping his rain ju-ju carefully in a banana leaf to keep it from getting wet.

IF I had known what was to be involved in the day's hunting I had just seen, I think I would never have left America in the first place, but that evening, back in my camp, I tried telling myself that it was no use being too squeamish about the deaths that had occurred. Even if I packed and left that night the gorillas would still go on being hunted and I had the knowledge that although seven gorillas had been killed that day, my presence on the hunt had saved nine young ones from the slaughter.

Together with Zinga and several men from the village, I transferred these nine animals from their light carrying-cages to the big cages we had built and gave them fruit to eat and water to drink. When I examined them I was relieved to see that they were all fine specimens and that none had been injured in the capture.

Then, when I was satisfied that my gorillas were as comfortable as I could make them, I went off to eat my first proper meal of the day—a corned beef hash that seemed to be one of the few dishes Joseph could remember from his days with the Chief of Police. Afterwards I sat outside on my veranda and read a few chapters of *Pride and Prejudice* by the light of my big petrol lamp. The glare soon attracted a cloud of insects but I took no notice of them and as I sat there I heard my gorillas for the first time calling to each other. It was the strangest of sounds, a low clucking noise, exactly like the noise a mother hen makes calling her chicks. I never heard them make it except at night and I can only suppose that it was some form of message of reassurance, for it would often break out in the middle of the night, a strange concert of barnyard noises that would last a minute or two and then die away as the gorillas, satisfied that they were not alone, turned over and went to sleep again.

I used to wish that I could sleep as easily as they could. The old dispensary was riddled with white ants. There were rats in the roof and I could find no way at all of getting rid of the bugs that infested my room. They were a particularly powerful local breed and no known brand of insect powder seemed to have the slightest effect on them.

But during the day I was so fascinated by these gorillas of mine that I hardly noticed the discomfort and the lack of sleep. I would be up early to supervise their first meal of the day. This would usually be of pineapples or manioc of which they all consumed fantastic quantities, and by now I had half the men in the village working on fresh cages for me. I had an official permit from Brazzaville to export up to thirty gorillas, and if my expedition was to justify itself I really needed to catch my full quota.

During these days Chief Bamboo became the most valuable of friends. Through him word got round to the neighbouring villages that I would pay five hundred francs for a live gorilla and as other hunts returned so my stock of gorillas grew.

Soon I knew my gorillas as well as if they had been members of my own family and I was struck by the remarkable resemblance of personality shown by gorillas captured from the same family group, resemblances that made the gorillas from one family quite distinct from those of another. The group from my first hunt were an easy-going lot who were soon inclined to make the best of things, rolling over on their backs when I came near, experimenting with their cages, and showing a decided interest in their new surroundings.

But the next group brought in, consisting of two young males and a nearly adult female, appeared far less intelligent, never seeming to identify me with the source of their food and spending their days lying listlessly in their cages.

As I gathered more gorillas still, I even began to notice marked physical similarities between animals from the same family. They might have shorter legs or longer legs than the average. Their colouring would tend to be the same, and I would even imagine I could detect the sort of facial similarities you find among members of the same human family.

The rarest of all my captives was a day-old baby. In those days

gorillas had never been bred in captivity and I was particularly
thrilled to have the chance of raising this tiny gorilla virtually from
birth. For one of the hunters had found him abandoned by his
mother less than an hour old and had brought him to me when the
hunt was over.

He was very small and very appealing but it was something of
a problem to know how to feed him as he was really too young to
be bottle-fed on dried milk. It was Chief Bamboo who suggested
an answer, offering one of his young wives as a wet-nurse for him.
To my surprise this was a great success. The girl had no objection
to feeding this unlikely infant, and for the rest of my stay in Oka
the young gorilla lived among the other children of Bamboo's
household.

In total contrast to him there was my largest captive of all
who was also a male. Incidentally it took an acrobatic *grand écart* on
his part before I could be sure of this fact, so small, set back and well
concealed are the sex organs of the gorilla. Despite his size he was
still very young—perhaps eight to ten on the human scale—but his
face retained none of the appearance of childhood. Most of the time
his expression was one of complete despair.

I would watch him silently for a few minutes. To start with he
would avert his eyes. Then reluctantly he would turn to meet my
gaze. As soon as our eyes met his face would contort with hatred
and with a great shriek he would hurl himself towards me against the
wire of the cage. Then he would pick himself up and go back to his
hunched, sullen position, nursing his knuckles from the battering
they had received against the wire.

He would take food occasionally from Zinga, but whenever he
saw my fingers holding some tit-bit or other for him it would set up
such a conflict of simultaneous hatred and desire that after snatching
it from my fingers he would invariably drop it or else completely
miss his mouth with it. If he did accept a pineapple, his black teeth
would tear at it with such fury that I could actually hear them
gnashing together.

I had been in the village over a fortnight before I had a chance of
seeing what teeth like these could do to a human limb.

It was a female that had done the damage. An old man had

fired his converted flint-lock at her and missed. The gorilla in her turn had grabbed him by the leg and managed to bite him just once before a dozen spears had pierced her body. That one bite had been sufficient for the upper teeth to gash clean through to the bone and practically sever the calf muscle.

Despite this shocking wound, the old man lay quite expressionless, not flickering an eyelid even when I drenched the gashes with cresol and camphor, the only antiseptics I had. The cuts were far too big for me to sew with my cotton thread, and as there seemed just enough of the muscle left to hold and allow the leg to heal, I dressed it, bound it up with Kodak film can tape for an adhesive, and took him in the truck to Okio, where there was an African medical assistant who, by general assent, could work wonders with his *pique-pique*, his hypodermic syringe.

I am not normally a creature of habit, but at Oka I soon found myself slipping into a routine of catching and tending to my gorillas and became strangely attached to the village and the people in it. I have memories of the times we hunted together, of being up with the *premier coq* in a chilly night with the sky brilliantly clear and studded with stars and of travelling miles across the open bush before dawn. Often we would be waist deep in the wet grass. My shoes would squelch water and the dripping stalks of elephant grass strike my face. But we would keep up a good pace, and when the sun rose and the dew steamed and every blade of grass sparkled we might rest for a moment to regain our breath. At times like this it was enough just to be in Africa again and I found myself hoping that we might miss the gorillas this time and be spared the sight of bloodshed on a day as perfect as this.

But the hunting played too important a part in the economy of the villages to allow sentiment to come into it and I never knew the hunters to fail to find their quarry once they had set out. Gradually my stock of animals grew and after two months I had the satisfaction of owning thirty young gorillas that would certainly have perished if the hunters had had their way. I also had succeeded in shooting some of the most exciting sequences of animal photography of my life. I had not only filmed a hunt in its entirety but had also managed to film individual gorillas in the wild in a way that had never been done before.

By waiting on the other side of one of the patches of forest from where the hunters were advancing, I was able to film a mother gorilla clutching her baby just before she rushed out to escape across the savannah beyond. I also filmed one of the old males pounding his chest as the hunters approached. This chest-pounding was quite different from the way it is described in most books on gorillas.

The actual noise is not particularly loud or fearsome and the gorilla does not use his fists. He slaps his body just below the chest with his open palms, moving his hands in an upward circular movement, exactly as a man on a bicycle moves his feet. Although the gorilla I filmed was clearly doing it as a gesture of defiance, it is not always done in anger or to inspire fear. The animal seems to do it when anything has agitated him and I even saw one gorilla pounding himself while sitting down.

There was another sound I heard the gorillas making which carried much farther and seemed to be a means of summoning the rest of the group in time of crisis. This was a curious clapping noise the animal made by beating the slightly cupped palms of the hands together, in much the same way as old colonial settlers used to clap to summon a servant. I never heard them make it in captivity but during a hunt this strange sound of clapping would echo through the forest, and I would know that the old male was calling the family for its last stand against the hunters.

When my film was complete and I had as many gorillas as I could hope to carry back with me, I told Chief Bamboo that I could buy no more from his hunters and prepared for the long journey back to Brazzaville. It was now that I had my first hint of real trouble.

I had gone down early that morning to make the rounds of the gorillas at the back of the hut. They were being well looked after and I was pleased to see that even the sullen young male I had been so worried about seemed to have settled down. But there was just one gorilla that I did not like the look of. This was a young female, one of the first we had captured, and she had always been one of the brightest animals I had.

But now she was looking as miserable as only a young female gorilla can. Her food lay uneaten before her in her cage. Her eyes were running slightly and she was huddled in one corner whimpering to herself. I tried coaxing her with a pineapple which normally she would have jumped at. Now she just sat where she was and still whimpered.

At first I thought she had caught some sort of a chill, for gorillas, despite their size, are surprisingly delicate creatures. But by that evening I was thoroughly alarmed. She still would not take any food and had now developed violent diarrhoea as well. Her state was so pathetic that I stayed up most of the night nursing her, but her whimpering never stopped and I could not persuade her to take anything.

I had never seen anything like this before. The rest of the gorillas were eating their morning meal with their usual noisy relish and there she was, still huddled in the same corner where I had left her, too ill even to crawl forward for a bowl of condensed milk.

As it happened it was on this very morning, just as I was trying to coax her to try the milk, that a group of tribesmen arrived from a neighbouring village. They asked to see me and seemed very excited, shouting that they had travelled all night with a fine male gorilla for me. I walked over to them and saw that whatever they had was bundled into one of the roughly woven basket-work cages that are usually made to keep small antelope in. It had been slung from a pole by ropes and if the men really had been travelling all night the animal must have had a rough time of it.

When I peered in what I saw was not the sort of half-grown young gorilla I was trying to collect, but a real monster. He must have weighed about 280 lbs., all shoulders and chest, and of course was far bigger than anything that I would normally handle. Also I had all the animals I needed by now. But I felt I could not refuse him. The men had come so far and taken such pains to bring him that it would be churlish in the extreme to tell them to take him back again and I knew that if I did do this I would simply be signing the animal's death warrant. He would certainly be butchered and eaten by the following morning.

So I paid them their five hundred francs and had a closer look at my latest gorilla. He was in bad shape. He had not been wounded, but the long journey he had had to endure in his cramped little cage had chafed his back badly. Gorillas are highly strung at the best of times and I could see that he was terribly restless and agitated.

What worried me almost as much as the state of the gorilla was the state of his cage. These jungle cages are made by the villagers out of any materials to hand and they are not meant to last. Once you tear one part of it the whole thing falls apart and as far as I could see this was in danger of happening now. I had no bigger cage to put my new captive into as I was stocked to capacity.

So, uncomfortable though it was for the gorilla, I had no alternative but to try temporarily roping the damaged end of his cage, leaving him food, and putting a couple of men to warn me if anything happened.

I had more than enough to do that day. I had arranged to return to Brazzaville in two days' time and the preparations for transporting thirty assorted gorillas single-handed across 300 miles of Equatorial Africa are on a par with moving a large hotel or stocking a medieval army. The invaluable Scheler had promised me the use of his truck and had found me another that I could hire, so that transport was the least of my problems. There were all the emergency stocks of this and that to think about, the hiring of extra animal men, the distribution of final gifts to the villagers, and the collection of our own food supplies. What with fussing over a thousand and one details like these, there was little time that day to spend worrying over my sick female gorilla or my agitated and highly uncomfortable male, apart from instructing Zinga to make a new cage for him as fast as he could.

As far as I remember I was with Joseph, checking over the remains of our kitchen stores early that evening, when one of the men I had left guarding the big gorilla came rushing across the veranda screaming that the animal had gone mad and was escaping.

There was not a great deal I could do. I had no gun and could not have used it if I had. But I had no illusions about the gorilla. In the mood he was in he was a killer and I did not like to think what would happen with him loose in the village.

So I hurried over to the cages and was just in time to see the gorilla pulling himself through the broken end of his cage. I could see that his back was raw from the rubbing it had received the night before, and as soon as my men saw him standing beside the cage they rushed off into the village to spread the alarm.

The sight of half a dozen scampering Africans was just the thing the gorilla needed to make up his mind for him and he set off in pursuit. By now the village was in uproar. The women were screaming and I could see that several of them had already climbed up into trees, although quite what use this was supposed to be with a gorilla around I am not sure. All the noise obviously irritated the gorilla more than ever and he screamed back with rage before setting off along the deserted village street.

I realised that if any villager was hurt by one of my gorillas I would inevitably be held responsible; trouble of this sort could have the most serious consequences for an expedition like mine. If I was to stop this happening it was up to me to do something and to do it quickly.

The first thing was to get the gorilla out of the village. So I ran up as close as I could get to him and began tempting him to come after me. To start with he did not seem too keen on the look of me and stood there in the dim light sniffing and grunting.

Then I shouted at him and that annoyed him. Finally he did move, shambling after me back down the street; I led him on purposely until I was level with the door of the dispensary. Then I dodged inside, hoping that he would follow.

I should explain that in the middle of this room was a large wooden table piled high with the cages in which I kept the baby gorillas. These made a pretty effective barrier. Certainly nothing could have jumped over it. Also the windows had fortunately been crudely barred as protection against leopards which were a constant danger to my gorillas and to myself.

By this time the enraged gorilla needed no encouragement to come after me. I waited for him at the far end of the table. He lunged round it after me, shrieking with rage, but I just had time to skip round the other side of the table and out through the door. As soon as I was outside I slammed the door on him, and he was caught.

But we had not got him back yet by any means. The lock on the

door was not strong enough to hold an animal like him for long. I
yelled for some of the men to come and help me, and while they
were putting their shoulders against the door to stop the frenzied
gorilla from bursting out, I tried to think of a way to get him back
inside a cage.

The only hope was to catch him with the nets, but this was more
easily said than done. We could not risk letting him escape again,
and no one would have stood a chance trying to net him alone in
the room.

Then I remembered the windows with the bars that had been
put up against leopards and had an idea. If we could induce him to
reach out for something we had a good chance of grabbing his hand
and holding him tight. The bars, provided they held, would stop
him reaching us with his teeth.

This plan worked far better than I had ever expected. I had no
sooner started rattling my stick against the bars than a great hand
reached out to grab at it and three of us managed to grasp his wrist
and hold it tight. We tried the same trick with the other hand and
again it worked.

Now came the crucial point of the capture. I shouted to the men
to hold on for all they were worth and, grabbing a net, unlocked the
door. Everything depended on the strength of those six men outside, but by the dim light that filtered into the room from outside I
could see that the gorilla was pinioned tight against the window. I
managed to loop the net under his legs and up over his head. More
men came in with nets and when he was safely trussed I shouted to
those outside to let go.

By now Zinga's cage was ready for him, and although it took
another couple of hours to get him safely inside and disentangled
from the nets, it was not until then that the first of the women came
cautiously down from the trees.

It was now just after eleven. I had not eaten all day and I felt
weak with relief at getting the gorilla back. But the worst shock of
all was still to come.

I suddenly remembered the young female gorilla who had been
so unwell earlier in the day, and thought I would have a look at her
before going to bed. Her cage was at some distance from the

dispensary and the light from the petrol lamp on the veranda hardly reached it so that at first I could not see what had happened to her. I could make out her bulk at the back of the cage and saw she had shifted her position from the corner where she had lain all that morning. It seemed a good sign to see her sleeping so peacefully.

But then my eyes became accustomed to the darkness and I saw her back was towards me with her head doubled beneath. When I opened the cage I saw that she was dead.

I was suddenly afraid. I had seen countless animal epidemics and diseases in my time, but never anything that killed with the speed of this. I remembered the scare I had over the first gorilla I had seen captured and the loathsome disease that had attacked his face. But I had since learned that this was comparatively rare among the gorillas in this area and was closely connected to the disease of yaws that occurs among the African tribes along the coast. Yaws kills very slowly.

Instead, this was something that could kill a healthy young gorilla stone dead in under forty-eight hours; everything depended now on whether the other gorillas caught it.

There was no chance to start looking for symptoms that night. But the rest of the gorillas were sound asleep and although I fetched my torch and shone it anxiously round the cages none of them awoke.

So I went off to bed dreading what I would find next morning.

Although I was so worried I slept well, a deep, dreamless sleep, so that I woke later than usual feeling refreshed and inclined to look on all my anxieties of the previous night as much exaggerated. Beyond the veranda I could see two of the boys giving the gorillas their morning rations of yam and pineapple and they all seemed to be eating well. Even the big male there had been all the fuss over the night before was behaving himself.

So I gave myself time to shave before going to the cages and examining every gorilla for symptoms of disease. There was nothing wrong with any of them. They were beautiful creatures, and as I examined them, one by one, I could hardly wait to get them safely back to Florida before there was any more trouble.

The villagers were indignant when I insisted on burying the re-

mains of the dead female gorilla. This seemed to them mere super-
stition, coming between their families and a good meal. But as soon
as it was done I felt free to get on with the last arrangements for our
convoy back to Brazzaville next morning. These took much longer
than I had expected. The news of our departure had got round the
village and all day long a stream of villagers was making its way to
the dispensary to say its farewells and satisfy its insatiable African
curiosity.

On top of this round of sociability, I found that almost all the
cages needed some repairs if they were to survive the journey down
to Brazzaville. That was really hard work. It kept us up most of the
following night sawing and hammering and roping until I was satisfied we were going to be ready on time.

We managed it and when Scheler and his two trucks rolled up,
punctually at 9.30 the next morning, we were ready to load and be
off. But first the formalities had to be observed and the village of
Oka was all set on an official farewell. Old Bamboo turned out in his
dress shirt and bow tie, the women piled the trucks with fruit, the
witch-doctor carefully fixed a grass figure to the front of my radiator
and only after I had distributed the last of my cigarettes and gunpowder were we allowed to leave for Brazzaville.

The journey back was uneventful. Scheler came all the way with
us as he had business in Brazzaville and I was glad of his company.
He would lead in his truck. I would follow in mine, with the third
trailing behind. With him in the lead we made such good progress
that we were back in Brazzaville by the evening of the third day.

The gorillas had behaved impeccably. There was no further sign
of disease, and miraculously, even the most jerry-built of the cages
survived.

It was with Brazzaville and civilisation that things became difficult
for the first time. No one had ever driven into town with thirty
gorillas before and the idea of them seemed to throw the authorities
into more excitement than if they had been thirty fully-armed
Vichy Frenchmen arriving to take over the garrison. The first night
I managed to camp with them just outside the city, but the next
morning it seemed highly doubtful whether I was going to be al-

lowed to stay at all. When I drove into the city the police, the military, the health authorities and the immigration people all shook their heads when I asked them for help.

"Gorillas, Monsieur," they would mutter as if I was trying out a practical joke on them, "don't you realise this is wartime?"

The difficulty was to get my gorillas on to the next leg of the journey back. This involved crossing the broad Congo River over to Leopoldville, capital of what was then the Belgian Congo, and getting them on to the railway that runs the two hundred miles from Leopoldville to the port of Matadi. At Matadi I would have to trust to luck for a ship back to the United States.

An operation as complicated as this needed active official assistance. Without the help of Scheler I would never have got it. During that first day back in Brazzaville he was indefatigable. With his old-fashioned pith helmet pulled down round his ears and his pipe clamped firmly between his teeth he strode from government office to government office, explaining, insisting, cajoling, and at the end of the day I had the permission I needed.

The only trouble was that the line down to Matadi was overloaded and no one on this side of the river could say when I would be able to get the animals on to a train. I would just have to wait.

Scheler was a resourceful fellow. He remembered he had a friend working as a technician in the Brazzaville Pasteur Institute, and through him some of my gorillas were offered the hospitality of the Pasteur Institute's farm outside Brazzaville.

Meanwhile I had taken the ferry across to Leopoldville and made a similar arrangement, through the kindness of some Belgian officials I knew at the Leopoldville Zoo.

These were useful places to leave the biggest and most dangerous of the gorillas but they accounted for only fifteen of them. The rest had to remain in my camp, and for several days I spent all my time moving them across to Leopoldville on the ferry. Once more I was engulfed in the intricate problems of housekeeping for a family of gorillas.

Finally I got all my gorillas across to Leopoldville except for the six in the Pasteur Institute's farm at Brazzaville and the Belgians promised me that there would be only a day to wait for an empty wagon on the train down to Matadi. In fact there was nearly a week —a week of anxiety and sheer misery.

It all began the morning after I had brought the last of the cages across the river to Leopoldville. I was staying at a small hotel not far from the railway station and just after eight there was a telephone call for me from across the river. It was Scheler's friend from the Brazzaville Pasteur Institute and very worried he sounded.

"Sorry to trouble you," he said, "but it's that big male gorilla you left with us. Don't like the look of him at all. For nearly a day now he's not eaten a thing and he just sits huddled up and whimpering in the corner of his cage."

The Brazzaville line was bad but I could hear quite enough. Resignedly I told the man I would catch the next ferry over and thanked him for the trouble he was taking.

So we had brought the disease with us after all, and I knew for sure now that it was contagious. It sounded as though it had almost won its second victim already.

By a particular stroke of irony this turned out to be the big male that had caused all the fuss when he had escaped from his cage just before we left Oka; he was very different now from when I had seen him last. The experts in the Institute said they had never seen anything like this illness before; although they were treating him as a suspected case of food poisoning and had somehow forced some medicine into him. This treatment was obviously producing no improvement. The poor thing was just sitting at the back of the cage and whimpering even more pitifully than the female I had seen dying of the same disease.

I did not tell the man at the Institute more than I had to. I knew nothing with any certainty, and there was no point in alarming him further; but as I caught the afternoon ferry back to Leopoldville I knew I was going to need extraordinary luck if I was to avoid a full-scale epidemic among my gorillas now. I had no idea how it spread or what caused it, but I was not going to give in to it without a fight.

One fact gave me hope. This was that the new outbreak was among the six gorillas I had left in Brazzaville. There was no trace of it among the far greater number of them I had with me in Leopold-ville, and there was just a chance that I might have isolated the disease safely inside the Brazzaville farm with the broad waters of the Congo River to stop it reaching the rest of my gorillas in camp.

As soon as I got back to camp I organised as many men as I could find to work in relays fumigating every cage we possessed and scrubbing them out with disinfectant. This work went on all night. So did my work of inspecting each gorilla individually for ticks or insects or anything that could be the cause of this illness, and every animal, as it was put back into its newly cleaned cage, was thoroughly dusted with insecticide.

When it was finished I was satisfied that I had done as much as I could to prevent the disease. More important, I could see no signs of it among any of the gorillas that had been through my hands.

At 11.30 next morning the telephone rang for me again. It was the Pasteur Institute technician from Brazzaville. My gorilla had died that morning at 7.15. An autopsy had been carried out but nothing had been found to account for the animal's death. My technician friend seemed embarrassed. I thanked him as well as I could for all his trouble and asked him how the other five were. Rather hesitantly he said that they were all right, and when did I plan to take them away from the farm? I replied that in a day or two at the latest I would be coming to collect them to ship them down to Matadi. That same afternoon one of the boys who fed the gorillas at the camp mentioned casually to me that a couple of them seemed to be off their food at the mid-day meal. The nightmare had begun in earnest.

The worst thing about it all was that I felt so responsible for these animals. I had organised a 10,000 mile expedition to deprive them of their freedom and all it seemed that I could offer them in return was this silent death. I had been so near to getting them all safely back to the United States. The dangers, the hardships were behind me but now with success so close it looked as though I was to be beaten by the one thing I had never taken into account.

The one awful thing about the disease was the unhurried way it began picking off the animals. It was almost as if someone had found a way of destroying my gorillas and was patiently doing so in ones and twos to prolong the agony.

The symptoms and the course of the illness never varied. The pair that had sickened that lunch-time grew steadily worse and were dead within forty-eight hours. Not a single gorilla that caught it survived, but until the moment the disease struck it would be as healthy and unconcerned as any animals I had ever seen.

I did what I could to find out about the disease. I carried out minute autopsies myself on each animal, but there was never much to show. I called in the help of the Pasteur Institute in Brazzaville, and of the Prince Leopold Institute in Leopoldville; they carried out endless tests on the dead animals but even they were defeated.

At the institute I begged the director to allow more research to go on in the hope of finding some cure before it was too late. He was a kindly man although he was badly understaffed at the time and had many things to think about besides gorillas. He shrugged his shoulders.

"I'm sorry for you and your gorillas," he said. " Believe me I'm sorry, but we've gone as far as we possibly can. We've found out something. It's a virus disease they're dying of. We've eliminated all the other possibilities."

"But what virus?" I asked.

Again he shrugged his shoulders. "If we had the latest equipment they have in London, or New York—if we had a fully trained research team to spare for a couple of years—and if we had a lot of luck—we might be able to tell you after two or three years of hard work."

Within six days the death roll stood at sixteen, and I had given up hope. I had come to Africa as a collector. It looked as if I would be leaving it as an undertaker. I was getting no sleep, as the animals needed nursing and most of the time there was no one else to do it; on top of everything else the people in Leopoldville had started to turn against me. The rumour spread that I had brought disease into the town. Insults were shouted at Zinga and Joseph and I found it more difficult than ever to get supplies for the animals.

I hardly know what I would have done if the railway had not chosen this moment to discover that it had some empty wagons on its next train down to Matadi. We still had fourteen gorillas alive; I got them all aboard that night.

In Matadi there was the same trouble I had had at Brazzaville.

Everyone was suspicious of us and it seemed impossible to find anywhere to camp. Finally some Swedish missionaries took pity on us and allowed us to camp in the back of their garden while we waited for a ship back to the United States.

But the U-boats were busier than ever in the Atlantic by now and a ship never came. The one thing in the whole of Matadi that never waited was the disease. On it went, steadily, neither increasing nor decreasing, and still there was no animal that caught it that ever recovered.

The people turned completely against us too, just as they had in Brazzaville. Without the missionaries I cannot think what I would have done. Our pathetic camp at the bottom of the garden was soon like something in a siege. Each week the survivors were a few less.

Each day I would visit the docks. Occasionally there would be a boat and my hopes would rise, but it was never going to America.

Finally, the last of the gorillas died. By a strange chance this was the youngest of them all, the baby I had first seen on the day of its birth and that had been nursed for me in Chief Bamboo's family. Ever since the outbreak of the disease in Brazzaville, I had kept it in my own room, trying to isolate it from the rest. To the last I thought I might have succeeded.

A three-month-old gorilla can be very appealing, especially when you have lived with it as closely as I had with this. His death upset me more than I would have thought possible.

By now everything about Matadi and about the expedition was odious to me. The very place seemed implicated in the death of my animals and all I could think of was how to get away and back to the States as quickly as I could. The attempt to form a collection of gorillas had ended in disaster. My only consolation lay in the unique film I had shot.

With supreme irony, exactly two days after my last gorilla died a freighter docked at Matadi. Her name was the *Tamesis*, she was registered in New York, and she was bound for Boston.

The *Tamesis* was a slow ship and in the mood I was in I was confident that I could hitch-hike back to America by air very much quicker than if I relied on her. My own problem in trying to go back all the way by air was that I now had nearly a hundred pounds of baggage. Apart from the camera and the completed film, there was a pile of diaries and notebooks I had kept during the expedition along with a mass of photographs and scientific data on the disease that had killed the gorillas.

I felt I could hardly leave these behind, and so, when I discovered that an American priest from Leopoldville was travelling back to the States aboard the *Tamesis* I asked him whether he would mind taking charge of my belongings. He was kind enough to agree and the following day I said good-bye to Joseph and Zinga and the Swedish missionaries, and caught a train up to Leopoldville.

As I had no baggage at all, I found little difficulty in hitch-hiking back the way I had originally come. There was an army Dakota flying up to Liberia, and from there I took a clipper to Brazil and army planes again to Miami and on to New York. I was in New York again in the autumn, just as I had been the year before, and without realising the coincidence, booked in at the same hotel overlooking Central Park where I had been staying when I met Rainez, the Brazilian gold prospector, and heard the first story of the gorillas of French Equatorial Africa.

I waited anxiously for news of the *Tamesis*, for now that I was back in New York I felt that the film I had made of the gorillas might still provide something of a justification for my disastrous expedition. It could not bring my gorillas back to life, but it was a unique film and could have covered the expenses of my expedition many times over.

But the *Tamesis* never did arrive in Boston. She was involved in a collision just off Bermuda, and sank without loss of life. I met the American missionary a few weeks later. He apologised about losing the film.

19 *Okapi*

IT was to be four long years before I saw a gorilla in the wild again. I had to spend my time in Miami, struggling to keep my colony of chimpanzees together. I soon realised that the only research anyone was now interested in for chimpanzees was the one sort I would never agree to.

From the start I had made it plain that my chimpanzees were to be used solely for painless research into immunology and psychology but as the war progressed the authorities began to appreciate that a chimpanzee was a useful double for a human being when it came to testing out any particularly hazardous piece of equipment. In increasing numbers chimpanzees were now being used in ways that were to culminate in their pioneer rocket flights for the American government's space programme. I knew that sooner or later I would be asked to allow my animals to be used in this way, and that my refusal would place me in a very difficult position. Rather than run this risk I finally decided to discontinue the entire project.

It was a hard decision to take as I had known the animals so long. Many of them, like Mugwump and Katie were almost personal friends but I could see no way out and finally they were all sent to the safety of a new anthropoid ape farm at Lake Wales in Florida. I could be sure that there they would be in good hands.

After this there was nothing else to keep me in America and I spent every spare moment I possessed planning my return to Africa. But even with the end of the war it was still virtually impossible to get together another expedition. Passages to Africa were restricted. Cameras and film were in short supply and although I found no difficulty getting the backing of RKO for another full-length film on Africa it was not until the spring of 1946 that I had assembled the equipment and personnel I needed and was ready to start.

My plans were ambitious. They included what were to be my third and fourth overland crossings of Africa. I have always liked these long drives across continents and I now intended to make up for the four years I had been away. I had been starved of travel so long that all I could think of was how to cram as much as I could into the precious time at my disposal. I wanted to see what had happened to the Africa I knew and I planned my route accordingly. I wanted to see the elephants again in the savannah country north of Stanleyville. Then there were the pygmies of the Ituri Forest and Pat Putnam if he was still alive, whilst from Putnam's Camp it would be possible to strike farther east to the East African plains that I had seen in their splendour with Al Klein six years earlier.

Our plane landed at Leopoldville, and we went by train to Matadi to pick up our trucks and cars. It was uncanny how little Matadi had changed. The docks were just as I remembered them. The garden behind the Swedish mission was exactly as it had been when I had made my camp there and watched my gorillas die. Even Brazzaville seemed virtually untouched by the war and as we jolted our way up the *Grande Route du Nord* I kept asking myself how long this miraculous immunity to change would last.

I found my answer when I reached the village of Oka and Chief Bamboo came out to greet us in person. He was even more outrageously dressed than when I had seen him last, with boots and gaiters and the tattered remains of a Norfolk jacket.

"You're still hunting your gorillas?" I asked him, as I shook hands with his claw-like hand with its two remaining fingers.

"Of course," he said, grinning and patting the barrel of a large shotgun he had somehow acquired since I saw him last. "We have killed many since you were here last."

"But are there as many gorillas as ever in the forests?" I asked, thinking of the unknown disease that had carried off my gorillas so swiftly.

He nodded and grinned again. "You can see for yourself. Come with us when we hunt to-morrow. There are always gorillas to be caught. We will capture as many for you as you want."

I explained that this time I did not want to capture gorillas, only to film them, and during the days that followed I discovered that what old Bamboo said was literally true. Whatever the disease was it was obviously one that occurred only when the gorillas came in contact with human beings. Luckily the animals were too widely scattered and the whole area too inaccessible for this contact to be very frequent. Apart from Bamboo's tribe, the Africans themselves preferred to leave gorillas strictly alone and I realised on this trip that the animals occurred across an even wider area than I had previously suspected. As we drove we found their tracks in many places across this little known savannah country and after the experience I had had of the gorilla disease, I was relieved to find that the forest gorilla was as plentiful as ever.

Although a so-called guest-house had been built in Bamboo's village since my last visit, the whole place was still as poor and broken-down as ever. The thatch of the guest-house roof had already acquired several large holes and we all slept rolled up in our blankets on the hard mud floor. Because of this, none of us was sorry when we finished our filming and were able to get on the move again, driving south-east through the Congo that had provided such a rich and happy part of my life.

Again the changes I had feared among the animals did not seem to have occurred and despite my anxiety we were able to film the leopards and elephants and monkeys of the Congo as freely as the last time I had been there. Where I did find the signs of change was among ihe people I met. We visited my old friends the Watusi, the giant race of Ruanda and found them in a sad state of decline. There was their king for instance. The first time I had met him had been before the war and he had been easily the most impressive monarch I had ever set eyes on. Nearly seven feet tall in his brightly coloured robes of state, he had received me surrounded by his ministers in the remarkable palace of plaited straw where he lived on the outskirts of his capital.

Now he drove out to meet me in his latest model Chevrolet. In his grey pinstripe suit he was not quite the man I remembered and he drove me back for drinks at the Ostend-style villa the Belgian administration had helped him build. His old palace with its

symmetry and decoration and great beauty had gone. When I
mentioned it the king looked embarrassed. It was almost as if I
had mentioned an unsavoury episode from the past, and he shrugged
his shoulders quickly—"*Le progrès, Monsieur Denis . . . le progrès.
Il faut accepter le progrès.*"

As I found out as soon as I tried filming the Watusi, it was not
only their appearance that *le progrès* had altered since I had been
there last. When I persuaded them to put on their tribal dress and
practise their war dances again I found that all their most impressive
warriors were comparatively old men. There were young men there,
but they had nothing like the height or physique of their fathers.
The old men would all seem to be nearly seven feet tall, but the
young ones would be six or eight inches shorter. And just as the
Watusi were declining in stature, so it seemed to me that they were
declining in their consciousness of themselves as a race. They no
longer cared for their tribe as they used to. The king was losing his
power, the elders their authority. The old arts were no longer
practised and the young men were marrying outside their own
people. Within a few years one more unique part of old Africa
would have been merged and forgotten. That same progress I had
seen and hated a quarter of a century before in Bali was here in
Africa. Like Bali, Africa was yielding to it, and as in Bali it was
destroying everything that gave the country its character, its
colour, its culture and its charm.

There was one race where I thought this could never happen—
among the pygmies of the forest—but even when we drove through
the Ituri Forest to visit Putnam's Camp again we still found our
evidence of *le progrès*. As we drove along the road from Irumu towards the camp a tiny figure in a tattered European suit and a brown
fedora appeared from nowhere and raced alongside our truck.

"Me pygmy, me pygmy," he shouted in English as we slowed
down to see what he wanted. "You take picture. Me pygmy. Ten
francs."

Putnam himself was still there, as defiantly resistant to change as
ever, and I was relieved to see that his camp was almost exactly as I
remembered it. The museum was there, still heavily padlocked in
case any unwelcome visitor attempted an unauthorised peep at its

bizarre exhibits. The swimming pool was still waiting to be finished and the hotel looked more than ever like something that had grown spontaneously out of the very depths of the forest.

He greeted me absent-mindedly.

"Hallo," he said. "Where have you been?"

I tried explaining that I had been in America because of the war, but he hardly seemed to hear what I was saying.

"There's so much to do, in a place like this," he grumbled. "That's what people like you won't realise. You just drop in and think everything's ready for you at a moment's notice."

I tried saying something about not needing a room, but he was not listening and a few moments later he pointed to one of the huts.

"There," he said. "That should do you. No one's slept in it for three or four years, but if you care to use it you can stay as long as you like."

In the end we stayed nearly a fortnight at Putnam's Camp, and I soon realised that the years he had spent in the Congo Forest, virtually isolated during the war, had left their mark on him after all. The restless interest in everything and everyone that I remembered so well seemed to have gone. His disappearances into the forest were more frequent and there were long periods when the only people he would have anything to do with at all were the pygmies.

One thing that had not changed about him was his passion for animals. It was almost as if they were taking the places of the human visitors who no longer came and he allowed his chimpanzees and antelope to roam the camp on terms of complete equality with himself. Naturally all this appealed to me greatly, but there was one animal above all that Pat Putnam possessed that I found particularly exciting. This was an okapi.

Putnam was very proud of it and with some cause. For the okapi is one of the strangest and most elusive animals Africa possesses. It is a great curiosity, a sort of living fossil related partly to the giraffe and also to an animal called a samotherium that roamed Europe during the lower pliocene period. For me it held the added interest of being the last important animal to be discovered in Africa. Before nineteen hundred there had been highly coloured reports about this strange animal lurking in the depths of the Semliki

"*There was one animal above all which Putnam possessed that I found particularly exciting. This was an Okapi*"

"Hippo in a river are among the most difficult of all animals
to film satisfactorily"

A jacana pirouettes on the back of a hippo

The first stage of capturing a giraffe

After it is successfully lassoed the giraffe is hooded for the placing of the harness

The giraffe arrives in its temporary enclosure

The author with a baby jumping hare

Forest between Lake Albert and Lake Edward. Native belts would be brought back to Europe made of the skin of this legendary animal that was still unknown to science and it was not until 1902 that the famous consul general Sir Harry Johnston finally solved the mystery and obtained the first correct description of the okapi.

At first everyone assumed that the okapi was extremely rare, and they were placed under the most rigid protection by the Belgian government. Then it gradually appeared that they were not so much rare as virtually uncatchable. Far from being in any danger of extermination they occur over a huge area of the Congo Forest but being shy, nocturnal and superbly camouflaged with their chestnut skin and black and white stripes they are hardly ever seen in the wild. Normally the pygmies are the only people who catch sight of them and it was of course the pygmies who had brought Putnam the okapi I saw him feeding now.

They are delicate creatures although they have a kick to them that could easily kill a man, but Putnam had a way with animals and as I watched him offering the animal the tender leaves it normally lived on in the forest I could admire its great brown eyes, and the long, remarkably sensitive tongue it used for gathering the foliage.

I asked Putnam whether he often had these animals brought to him like this.

"Sometimes," he said. "I've had one or two in my time. I've managed to persuade the pygmies that if they catch an okapi in their nets they should bring it to me. I have to hand it over to the Belgian authorities in the end for they've a monopoly of all the okapis caught in the Congo, but at least it saves the animal's life and the Belgians usually let me keep it until it's used to being fed by hand."

"It looks as if you're taking over where Brother Joseph left off," I said.

He looked at me and laughed. His beard was white now but when he did laugh he looked splendid, like some Old Testament prophet enjoying a good joke. "Oh, you knew Brother Joseph, did you? It's a bit hard on the old boy's memory comparing him with someone like me. Besides, I could never handle an okapi as well as Brother Joseph."

This was certainly true, for Brother Joseph Hutsebaut, by a strange quirk of fate, had been the greatest practical expert on the okapi that Africa had ever known. I had met him before the war at the large Catholic mission at Buta where he lived most of his life as a simple lay brother. By then Brother Joseph was a man of some age and his fame had been considerable. Naturalists from all over the world would make a point of visiting Buta especially to see him, but Brother Joseph had remained entirely unimpressed by his fame and never pretended to be anything but the simple Flemish peasant God had made him.

He had come to Buta originally to look after the vegetable garden. His lack of education had made him unable to become ordained as a priest, but one day some Africans had brought him a baby elephant that had been orphaned and he had looked after it with all the skill he had picked up with the animals on his father's farm in Belgium. The elephant was only a start. From then on when anyone for miles around found an animal in need of care they brought it to Brother Joseph. One day he was brought a young okapi. He had never seen one before, but since it was one of God's creatures he looked after it and the animal flourished. News of it finally reached the Belgian authorities at Stanleyville. By chance this co-incided with a period of extreme official interest in okapis. They were still virtually unknown outside Africa and the King of the Belgians was anxious to acquire one that he could present as a gift to some foreign monarch visiting Brussels on a State visit. Brother Joseph's okapi was duly commandeered and shipped off to Belgium. From then on whenever the king wanted an okapi the governor at Stanleyville would be instructed to contact Brother Joseph, and Brother Joseph, anxious to oblige his king, began to encourage the local Africans to capture them for him.

At once this brought them into conflict with the strict game laws that had been enacted to protect the okapis and Brother Joseph found himself in the middle of an absurd situation. One week he would hear that two Africans had been arrested for trying to catch an okapi for him. The next he would have the authorities at Stanleyville saying desperately, "The king has asked us for another okapi. Get us one for him at all costs." It was hardly surprising that the poor lay brother became a little tired of these duties that were being thrust upon him, and when I saw him I remember him complaining to me in his thick Flemish accent, "I never wanted any of this. I didn't come to the Congo to catch okapi. I came to worship God."

But however much he complained, he had a great gift for tending animals and it was through this legendary old lay brother from the mission at Buta that most of the early specimens of okapi were brought out of the great Congo Forest alive.

Putnam and I chatted about him for some while. "You know who's catching okapi for the Belgian government now?" he said.

"Who?"

"De Medina," he said. "You remember him. He used to be an elephant hunter. Well he's given that up now, and the Belgians have appointed him official custodian of okapi for the whole of the Congo. He's living at a village called Banalia, about three hundred miles west from here on the other side of the forest."

"How does he catch them?" I asked.

"Well, he's trapping them in pits. I don't know how he does it but he's supposed to be quite successful at it. Last I heard of him he had caught seven or eight and was looking after them on behalf of the government."

As soon as I heard this I determined to find de Medina. I was not entirely surprised to hear the news about him. He was half Portuguese, half African and I had got to know him on my previous trip to the Congo when he had been a freelance guide and hunter, only too eager to be of any assistance to the foreign visitors coming to the Congo in search of wild animals. If he really was catching okapi now on the scale Putnam said, he would certainly be well worth filming.

The journey to his village took longer than I expected; we spent two days driving across the great forest area east of Stanleyville. This forest, of course, was the home of the okapi. We were always hopefully on the lookout for one, but there was really no chance of seeing so shy a creature in this dense tropical forest and I could understand how the okapi had avoided discovery so long.

When we found it, de Medina's village turned out to be exactly like all the other small African villages on the edge of the forest and there was nothing to distinguish it as the home of the official *Conservateur des Okapis* for the whole of the Congo. But de Medina was obviously taking his job seriously. He was wearing an official-looking peaked cap when he came out to greet us and I soon saw that Putnam had been right. Neatly corralled at the back of the house were no less than eight adult okapis—probably the largest group of these animals that had ever been brought together in one place.

De Medina had put on weight since I had seen him last; he had an African wife and an immense family swarming all over his house. But he was as energetic and enthusiastic as ever. He invited us in, produced an enormous bottle of gin for us, and proceeded to talk non-stop about okapi.

"Never try catching okapi for a living," he said. "I don't mind leopards or lions or even elephants, but these okapi are quite impossible."

"You seem to be doing all right with them," I replied, pointing across the yard to the animals he had caught.

"Those," he said. "Do you know how long it took me to capture those eight okapi? More than six months. At the moment I've nearly two hundred pits dug in different parts of the forest. We catch everything in them except okapi.

"I'll tell you what happens," he went on. "We dig our pit and cover it with leaves and earth so that not even you would know there was anything there. But the okapi is suspicious. He won't go near and while he is keeping clear of it a little water gets in the bottom and a bull-frog or two get inside. Then the next night the okapi comes near he hears the wretched frogs and they tell him all he wants to know. That's another okapi we don't catch."

Despite de Medina's pessimism, we were luckier than I had expected and while we were there two okapi were actually caught. This was a great event. It was also the signal for the entire village to turn out and assist in the hazardous business of bringing two fully grown okapi unharmed from the pits to the safety of de Medina's corral. We went with the crowd of villagers who swarmed out into the forest to see what had been caught but the actual pits were harder to reach than I had thought. We followed a track of sorts for three or four miles into the forest and then struck off to the left, forcing our way through the undergrowth guided solely by the shouts of de Medina's men who were already guarding the pit.

It was only then that I understood the difficulties de Medina was up against in trapping his okapis. For these pits of his were sited in the densest parts of the forest and the work of visiting them and keeping them in repair must have been formidable. De Medina was there already when we arrived, still wearing his peaked cap the government had given him and desperately trying to organise the crowd of helpers that seemed to grow every minute.

Several of his men were already digging away at one end of the pit so as to make a ramp up which the okapi could be driven. Cautiously holding on to a nearby branch I tried to peer down through the hole the animal had made as it fell into the trap. It was dark inside, but I could just make out the long neck of the okapi with its black and white markings. I could hear it shuffling as it tried to find a way out.

"Careful," shouted de Medina, when he saw what I was doing. "If you fall in with the okapi there won't be much of you left by the time we pull you out."

"How are you going to get the animal out anyhow?" I asked.

"Oh, you have to be patient," he said. "First we must dig our ramp, but even when we've finished that we must still get the animal down to the pathway for the truck to come and pick it up."

"How do you do that?" I asked.

"That's always what takes the time," he said. "We have to clear a path and fence it in both sides so that we can drive the animal, otherwise it would be sure to escape."

By this time de Medina's villagers were working away at this too, laboriously hacking at the undergrowth, and weaving the vines and branches into a tough double line of fencing that would have to stretch nearly half a mile down to the path.

It seemed a lot of effort, even to catch an okapi so I asked de Medina why he did not try backing his truck up to the pit.

"We'd never do it," he said. "The forest is far too thick to allow any truck through."

"Why not try mine?" I replied. "It's got a four-wheel drive.

I'm sure it would save you hours of work." But for some reason de Medina would not hear of it, and when I went off with him to find his second okapi we left half the village behind us digging and hacking away.

The second pit was even more inaccessible than the first had been and by now I was seriously worried for the animal that was in it. It must have been inside nearly twelve hours already. At the rate de Medina's men were moving, I could see it would be the following day before they tunnelled their way through to it. So again I suggested using our four-wheel drive to try reaching it.

De Medina was obviously getting tired of my advice by now. "All right," he said, "try it if you like, but I'm going back to supervise the first pit. See you this evening."

It took more than an hour to get back to the village and I managed to pick up several of de Medina's men on the way, so that I had all the guides and assistance I needed when I drove back towards the trapped okapi. At first I thought de Medina was going to be right about the forest and for a while we could make no headway at all once we left the path. But gradually, by pushing and reversing and then pushing forward again in bottom gear we managed to inch our way forward. Occasionally we had to chop the vines and undergrowth away from the front of the truck but we made it far quicker than I had thought possible and after much slithering and grinding of gears I managed to back the truck a few yards from the end of the pit.

There was no sound by now from the imprisoned animal. This pit was deeper than the other had been, so that it was difficult to make out what had happened to the okapi. I knew it was there because I could just make out its shape in one corner of the pit, but all the time we were digging the ramp it never moved and I was half afraid that by the time we were ready to bring it out we might find it had injured itself or even died.

By now it was midday. It was hot. We had worked hard, and the flies and midges were swarming around us. But there was no question of stopping. The only way we would find out about the okapi now was to have all our preparations complete so that we could try coaxing it up the ramp and into the truck. To do this meant

230

fencing in the sides of the ramp, and building the earth right up to the tail-board. It was this that took the time.

Finally we were ready and pulled the branches away that had shut off the end of the pit from the ramp. Still the okapi did not move. So we shouted, trying to frighten the animal up into the truck. There was still no reaction. At this I was convinced that the animal really was injured and that one of us would have to go into the pit and see what had happened. But fortunately, one of de Medina's men had had more experience of okapi than I had.

"He's all right," he said. "He is just a little frightened. He's not used to people yet. Leave him and see what happens."

So we all moved away from the pit and sat waiting silently in the strange gloom of the Congo Forest. For ten minutes or more nothing happened. There was only the buzzing of the insects and the occasional shriek of a monkey from the tangle of branches high above. Then I saw a faint movement from the edge of the pit. Two delicately shaped ears appeared. The head followed, eyes wide open, nostrils sniffing suspiciously. Then slowly, delicately, this most beautiful of animals emerged and stood, undecided, on the ramp we had built.

The rest was easy. As soon as we got behind it, the okapi ran up the ramp of its own accord and I was glad that we were able to get it safely back to de Medina's house without causing it any further distress. I felt doubly pleased with myself when a very tired de Medina returned that evening with his okapi, only to find mine already settled quite happily in the corral.

Although the okapi is so timid in the wild, he becomes surprisingly tame in captivity and I found these animals of de Medina's a source of constant delight. I was particularly interested in the okapi we had brought in ourselves and stayed on for several days to film him and watch how he adapted to civilisation.

I found him a temperamental animal. He was very highly strung and would go off his food if the slightest thing upset him. I would also be careful never to get behind him as I distrusted the power that he certainly had in his hooves. But he soon grew to recognise me. I would bring him his favourite leaves from the forest and when I fed him he would never attempt to bite. He would

231

recognise people more by their smell than by their appearance and I found that like many short-furred animals, he was particularly fond of having his neck and shoulders stroked with a stiff brush. After I had been at the camp a few days, my okapi would wait for me every morning by the side of the corral and refuse to budge until I had given him his morning brush down.

Apart from actually catching the okapis, de Medina's biggest problem was to adapt them sufficiently to civilisation to allow them to survive the journey down to the coast and on to the zoos where most of them would finally live. To do this he had to slowly change their diet from the leaves and vegetation of the forest, to the sort of food that could be obtained in Europe and America. But again I was surprised at how quickly the okapis could be persuaded to eat hay. Brother Joseph had found that it was unsafe to allow okapi in captivity to pick up food from the floor as they quickly infected themselves with their own droppings, and de Medina used to follow his practice of placing the bales of hay in a rack three or four feet above the ground.

Because of this the okapi could eat quite easily but I was never able to get an adequate film of the animal's magnificent tongue in action. For their tongues are very long and in the wild they use them for gathering leaves from the trees. I tried countless ways of filming them, even going as far as to place a dab of honey on the shoulder of my okapi when I had finished grooming him in the morning. I knew that he loved anything sweet, and hoped that he would turn his head and lick the honey off. But not even this would work, and to this day I have never managed to film, as dramatically as I would like, the tongue of an okapi.

20 *Savage Splendour*

I HAD always thought of the huge plains of East Africa as the most exciting game area in the world. I had seen them last in 1940, teeming with their herds of buffalo and zebra, wildebeeste, gazelle and giraffe, and now, six years later, I could hardly wait to return. I had been saving this part of Africa as the climax of my film, and finally decided we would have to say good-bye to de Medina and his okapi and begin our thousand mile drive from the Congo across to Kenya.

It was an impressive journey, with the landscape constantly changing as we wound our way up from the Congo Forest, descended the escarpment to cross the plains of Rwindi, and then climbed again through the hilly country beyond Rutshuru to Uganda and the shores of Lake Victoria. But there were few animals to see and as we drove I kept preparing in my mind's eye the sort of scenes I was hoping to shoot once we reached the big herds.

"You wait," I told my assistant, who was growing tired of filming nothing but scenery. "Soon you won't have enough film in your cameras for all the animals you'll be seeing."

We skirted the southern shores of Lake Victoria and headed east. This was the edge of the country I remembered, but the game never seemed to turn up. We reached the great depression of the Rift Valley, which had always boasted the richest wild life of all, yet even there there was hardly anything to see apart from a few lonely zebra and Thomson's gazelle plucking nervously at the grass.

I had no idea what could have happened and we drove slowly down the valley searching for the herds that had been here only six years before. We searched in vain. Occasionally we would find three or four giraffe or half a dozen ostriches, but this would be in

233

places where I remembered watching scattered herds stretching as far as the eye could see.

Now there was nothing but emptiness and silence. The very life had gone from the country, and the animals we saw were nothing but the survivors of some massive disaster.

There was nothing to film so we headed for Nairobi and on the final lap of the journey towards the city, I halted the trucks halfway up the Rift escarpment to take one last look back at the lifeless floor of the valley. An elderly settler had chosen the same place to stop to allow the steaming radiator of his overloaded van to cool off. I saw him looking once or twice in my direction, and just as I was about to start off again he called out my name. I did not recognise him until he came over to the cab and introduced himself.

"I met you in 1940," he said. "You were with Al Klein. The two of you stayed a couple of nights at my farm on Kinankop."

I remembered him then. He had been most hospitable to us although his farm had been very small and very cold, nine or ten thousand feet up in the Aberdares. He was a short, rather quiet man and was still puffing at the same briar pipe that I remembered when I had seen him last.

"Pity about Klein," he said. "Pity he died so suddenly."

"Perhaps it was as well," I said. "It would have broken his heart if he'd seen Kenya in the state it is to-day."

"You mean the game," said the old man. "Not so good, is it? Still, what do you expect? There's been a war."

"What's that had to do with it? There's been no fighting in Kenya."

"No," he replied, "no fighting, but plenty of shooting."

"What sort of shooting?"

He took his pipe from his mouth. "Well, you know how it is when you get a lot of troops in a place like this. They soon get bored. They've got plenty of guns and ammunition and the valley's full of game. The boys are only human."

"But a bit of shooting wouldn't account for the state the valley's in to-day. Just look at it."

"Well, it wasn't just a bit of shooting. It was rather a lot of shooting. You see, many of the lads had never seen a wild animal

234

before outside a zoo. Most of the game wardens were away at the war themselves and there was no one to stop them doing as they liked."

I asked just what they did do.

"There was quite a bit of machine-gunning of buck and zebra. You can do a lot of damage to a herd of zebra with one bren gun. Then there were the giraffe, of course. Anyone can get a giraffe with a service rifle and an ostrich too for that matter. The troops were here nearly four years and the game doesn't last for ever."

From the people I met later in Nairobi, I learned that the shooting the troops did was only part of the story. The damage they had done had been followed by something more organised and equally unforgivable. After the campaigns to the north of Kenya's borders in Ethiopia and Somaliland, the country had been used as a detention centre for many thousands of Italian prisoners of war. The Italians had to be fed, and purely in the interests of economy some inspired bureaucrat had decided that the best way of supplying them with meat was to feed them game.

For anyone with the instinct for really large-scale butchery, this offered the chance of a lifetime. The techniques of mass production could be applied to the simple business of killing. European contractors hired gangs of Africans and issued them with rifles to shoot down buffalo, a hundred head at a time. The slaughter went on for many months until nothing but the remnants of East Africa's game were left, and those only in the most inaccessible country.

Even in the still relatively unfrequented area of the Serengeti which we visited a few weeks later there was evidence of the most savage destruction of wild life. You may not be able to feed Italian prisoners on lion meat, but the sportsmen had come here with their rifles and blazed away at the lions for the fun of it. Until then the Serengeti lions had rarely been hunted and they must have made sitting targets.

More serious still, from a long-term view, was the rapid erosion of natural resources right across East Africa. Wood had been needed during the war, so great chunks of forest had simply disappeared. Because of the overriding urgency of war, nothing had been done to repair the damage, and in those five years the habitat of the animals had suffered more seriously than in twenty-five years of normal evolution.

With the ending of the war, the whole idea of normal evolution in this part of Africa had vanished anyhow. Peace had brought an explosion of development to East Africa. Huge areas of bush were being cleared. More and still more areas of forest were being felled. Migrants were flooding in and clearing the land and everywhere roads were being cut and farms established. Suddenly it seemed as if everything was converging to bring about the doom of East Africa's wild life.

At first I was so depressed at what we found that I thought there was no point in going on with my film. What I had thought of as the climax of my journey looked like becoming its epitaph. But I stayed on in Kenya for some months and began to realise that this threat to wild life made work by people like myself more important than ever. If there was to be any real hope of preserving what was left of East Africa's game, public opinion outside Africa had to be told what was happening and I knew that there should be some way of using films like ours for this purpose.

Of course, there was no chance of using the commercial cinema for the sort of propaganda for animal conservation that I was to put on television a few years later. If a film was to sell, it had to be first and foremost entertainment and it took me some time to find a theme that would combine all the excitement that the film companies would expect with something of relevance to the plight of the animals. Finally I found the subject I was looking for in the way that wild animals were being captured alive. The result was my film, "Savage Splendour."

Ever since I had directed Frank Buck's "Wild Cargo," I had been unhappy about the way the vast majority of animals were being captured for zoos. To me this presented a virtually insoluble dilemma. I believed, and still strongly believe, in the value of zoos. They are essential to the study of animals and they give young people the chance they must have of seeing what animals are really like. For me it would be as inconceivable to allow a child to grow up without seeing a lion or a rhinoceros as to prevent him seeing a green field or a seashore.

On the other hand, I know something of the cruelty that all too often goes on in the bringing of animals out of the wild into captivity. I had seen young orang-utans captured in Sumatra by chopping down the trees where they lived, shooting the mothers and then keeping the young drugged on opium for days on end while they were being smuggled out of the country. With some of the big game animals methods of capture seemed even crueller and more wasteful. This was particularly so with the rhinoceros. For a long time, virtually the only way of catching a young rhino for a zoo was to shoot the mother and hope that the young animal would be hardy enough to survive the journey to civilisation.

I had always thought this barbarous and wasteful. On the average, as many as four rhinos would be sacrificed to get one safely to its destination and while I was in Kenya I began to wonder if I could devise a way of capturing rhinos without this steady toll.

The chief problem was the mother rhino. Her highly aggressive maternal instincts are more than matched by her sheer strength; after I had seen a three-ton lorry tipped over bodily by one irate female and had had one of my own tyres wrenched off by another, I realised that they were not to be trifled with. For even if you managed to separate a mother from her young she would always come back in the end and determinedly charge anyone or anything she saw trying to interfere with her offspring.

I discussed all this with several professional big game trappers and all of them seemed to agree that however much of a pity it might be, the only really practical way of capturing a young rhino was still to shoot its mother.

"But have you never tried lassoing the mother?" I asked one of them. "It should be perfectly easy to get a noose over her head and provided you used a good strong rope you could surely stop her breaking away."

"You could stop her breaking away all right," replied the trapper, "but you couldn't stop her breaking into your truck. If you tried lassoing a mother rhino from a truck, she would just smash it to pieces."

He was obviously quite right. Straightforward lassoing from a moving vehicle was impractical. But the more I thought about it, the more convinced I became that there must be some way of getting a lasso over a rhino's head—and of rendering your rhino harmless—without having your truck smashed in the process. Finally I had an idea.

The theory was simple. We would try lassoing our rhino, but we would leave the back of our truck open. Inside there would be a length of heavy log and the end of our lasso would be securely tied to it, so that once the noose was over the rhino's head, the log would be pulled out and immediately slow the rhino down. Then, if my plan worked, the truck could drive away, and wait until the rhino had grown tired of struggling with the log.

If necessary, this would be the time to repeat the lassoing with yet another log. It should be easier this time as the rhino would have slowed down considerably and once we actually had two nooses on her, her capture should be almost complete. For I knew that then five or six men on foot could grab at the ropes, hold her secure and tie her legs until we wanted to free her again.

That was the theory and I knew that if I could make it work it would ultimately save the lives of many rhino that were still being unnecessarily killed. But to do this we first had to learn how to lasso a fully grown mother rhino. It was not quite so simple as it seemed.

I naturally discussed my plans with the game department and got their interested co-operation in the experiments I began to carry out on the plains at the foot of Mount Kenya. Even so, it took several weeks before we had developed an effective technique.

The first problem was how to get a rhino on the run, for if we were ever to lasso a fully grown female, she would have to be running from us, and not we from her. This alone seemed difficult enough, but luckily I knew from past experience that if you can catch rhino off-guard, they are fairly easy animals to panic into flight; during these early experiments we found that if we charged a rhino head-on with our truck the very moment we saw her, and without leaving her any time to evaluate the situation, she would invariably turn tail and run.

This initial charge at an animal weighing over a ton never ceased to be a nerve-racking affair, but once the rhino was actually in flight, our capture was relatively straightforward. For luckily a rhino runs fairly straight. Its top speed is just over twenty miles an hour and once it has reached this, it had none of the powers of manœuvrability or acceleration of a sixteen-horse-power truck. These were the two advantages we relied on for my plan to work.

As I drove, I would gradually draw the truck level with the rhino. She would be lumbering along, as fast as she could go, and I would see her eyeing us suspiciously just a few feet away from where I was sitting. Once we were as close as this, I would have to watch her intently for this would be the crucial moment of the whole operation.

There would always come a moment when she decided she had put up with enough nonsense from us. Her head would suddenly lower and in an instant she would change from pursued into pursuer, swerving and trying to charge us as she ran.

This would be the point when my foot would have to go down hard on the accelerator and, provided I judged things properly, the charging rhino would pass safely, three or four feet behind our tail-board. At this moment, someone in the back would have no difficulty dropping the noose neatly over the animal's head.

During our weeks of experiment we used bags of flour instead of the lasso until our sense of aim was perfect and we could get the bag to burst every time on the very point of the rhino's horn. I found that, with practice, I could calculate the moment of acceleration with some accuracy, and after one or two slightly hair-raising near misses by the rhino we could always get her to pass the prescribed distance behind the truck.

By now I was confident that our technique was as near perfect as we could make it. It was just a question of using it to lasso a fully-grown mother rhino. Before doing this I had a last minute discussion with the Game Department who came up with an objection I had not thought of.

The area chosen for captures obviously had to be one with smooth level country, suitable for a truck to drive over at speed. But what would happen, asked the Game Department, if a rhino, with a lasso and a log trailing behind it, broke away from this level country, and escaped into rough terrain where we could no longer pursue it? Unless someone could get the noose off its head fairly quickly, the animal might easily become trapped or starve to death.

This was clearly a possibility we had to reckon with and unless I could find an answer, there could be no question of going ahead. At first, I tried working out a complicated timing device that would automatically release the log from the noose after a certain period and so give the rhino back its freedom. But I knew there must be a simpler way than this if we could only think of it.

Finally I found that if I soaked a piece of rope in a heavily diluted solution of battery acid, it would at first lose none of its strength—but after a few hours, as the acid became concentrated through evaporation, the rope would slowly disintegrate. The speed at which it did this would naturally depend on the strength of the acid, and after several experiments I found exactly the right strength we needed.

One morning, we set off on our first serious attempt to capture a mother rhino and her calf. Our lassos had been carefully soaked in weak acid beforehand so that we knew that if anything went wrong the nooses would fall apart exactly four hours later and give the animals back their freedom.

I was in the first truck. With the vibration there was no chance of using a camera on a fixed mounting, and I was relying on shooting the whole scene with a hand-held camera from the cab of my own truck. The two nooses of three-quarter-inch rope were lying, carefully coiled in the back, securely tied to a pair of sturdy two-hundredweight logs. Close behind us followed a second much larger truck, with another camera, two of my assistants and a dozen African helpers aboard. Once we had the nooses over the mother rhino, they would be there to help hold her and I hoped to use this same truck to bring back the young rhino to camp.

We soon sighted a female rhino with a one-year-old calf, and when we had charged her, we set off in pursuit according to plan. The first time we tried lassoing her, the noose missed; it took two more attempts before we could get the rope where we wanted it, squarely over her head.

Then we veered off, the rope paid out, jerked taut, and the log was pulled after the charging animal. It was like putting a brake on an express train. For a while the rhino continued her charge, but the log was too heavy, even for her, and she soon stopped, puzzled and more annoyed than ever. For a moment we were forgotten, for she now had a new opponent—the log. For nearly fifteen minutes, at intervals, she vented her rage on it, charging it and trampling it and trying her best to break free.

Finally she began to tire of it all, and we found that the second noose was far easier to put on her. Again she tried to set off in pursuit of us, but by now she had almost had enough and I was anxious not to tire her too seriously. So as soon as she stopped, we halted the trucks, and although she protested, there was not a great deal she could do as we passed the ropes around her legs and tied her securely.

As soon as this was done, we all rushed up to her and with eight or so of us pushing against her, we managed to roll her on to her side so that there was less chance of her breaking loose or doing herself any damage. She was snorting and puffing with rage and trying to thrash around with her head, but as her legs were tied she was too heavy to get on her feet again, and we were free to turn our attention to catching her calf.

Even now we had to be careful, for a year-old rhino can be surprisingly powerful and this one had kept fairly close to his mother all through the pursuit. At the moment he was about a hundred yards away, bleating in the strange way young rhinos do, but already looking as if he was making up his mind to come charging in to the rescue. So rather than take any risks with the men, I decided we would lasso him from the truck as well.

In his case, we would not need to use the logs, but would rely on a simple noose with one end tied to the truck.

This time we managed to place the noose over his head at the first attempt. I was glad of this for he had already run quite far enough for an animal of his weight and age, and I knew that if he had been pursued too far there would have been a danger of over-straining his heart.

But once we had lassoed him, there was no great difficulty in pulling him to a halt and then tying him up safely in the same way we had tied his mother.

The whole capture had taken less than an hour. It had made a unique sequence for my film; as far as I know, it was the first time that a fully grown rhino and its calf had been captured together without injury.

At first we had intended letting the mother go free and bringing the young rhino back to the camp of the professional game trappers, who were helping us at the time. But they had the official permits to capture rhino; we had a fine specimen of an adult female already captured and in good shape, and we had adequate transport for her. Why not keep her as well as her calf? There were plenty of foreign zoos that would be delighted at the chance of adding a fully grown female black rhinoceros to their collection. That afternoon, we sweated away at the back-breaking task of lifting a large female rhino into a three-ton lorry.

A shallow pit had to be dug so that the lorry could be backed down it until the tailboard was roughly at ground level. A large sledge had to be built out of branches; when all was ready, the female rhino was lifted on to it, roped securely in place, and the sledge was winched slowly aboard the lorry.

I was extremely pleased at the decision to have both the young rhino and its mother brought back to camp: I had never had the chance before of observing these animals immediately after capture. I wanted to film them, and I also wanted to see how soon they would become tame enough to be used to human beings. To my surprise this was much sooner than I had ever imagined.

The animals were put in a substantial pen, and although they spent the first day refusing to eat and trying to batter their way out, they suddenly accepted their situation far sooner than I had expected. They stopped charging the sides of their pens, and forty-eight hours after lassoing the old female, I was actually feeding her through the bars with chunks of euphorbia tree that are one of the favourite delicacies of a rhino in the wild.

I was greatly interested also in seeing their reaction to the different diet they would have to live on in civilisation. Again this proved much less of a problem than I had imagined. Within a few days, the mother rhino had been shifted quite successfully on to a practical zoo diet and the young one seemed to do particularly well on a great bowlful of porridge and tinned milk three times a day.

Despite our success with these two rhinos, I was not really keen to take part in further rhino captures now that I had my film and had proved that rhinos, of all ages, could be caught without loss of life and without cruelty. What interested me was to see how we could adapt these methods to improving capture techniques for other animals. For by now I knew that this whole question of capturing animals had an importance far beyond the mere stocking of zoos. If a man was to make a serious attempt to preserve Africa's remaining wild life, it was clear that he would have to devise an adequate means of capturing and transporting animals from areas where they were threatened to National Parks and places where they would have a proper chance of survival. In the past if man wanted to take over a new area for cultivation from the wild, the animals would simply be shot or driven off.

This had to stop. But it was useless getting too indignant about it, if you offered no alternative. So for several weeks more we continued our experiments near Mount Kenya and near Mount Kilimanjaro areas, and filmed as we went. For a while, we concentrated on catching giraffe by lassoing from a moving truck, using a long noose on the end of a bamboo pole. Here, the chief difficulty was not so much the actual capture—anyone can catch a giraffe in the end provided he is prepared to chase it in a car until it is exhausted. Instead, we wanted to find out how to catch it quickly, for the best method of capture and the one that does the least harm to the animal is usually the swiftest. So we used to work very fast, and once we had lassoed the giraffe we would quieten it by throwing a large black cloth over its head.

When it could no longer see, it would stop struggling. Then we would be able to tie ropes to its legs and body. Eight or ten men would be needed to hold the ends of the ropes, but provided we took our time and were careful, we could slowly remove the cloth and then, pace by pace, walk the giraffe to a waiting lorry. With an animal of this size, transport was something of a problem; we used to place our giraffes inside a type of large packing case, which would support them during the journey, and prevent them kicking or hurting themselves. A space would be left at the top for their heads to poke through, and the giraffes would peer mournfully over the top of the cab as they were driven away.

Apart from the giraffes, we also lassoed eland, zebra and ostriches; I became convinced that lassoing was the most effective and humane method of capture in existence. It has only been quite recently that I have changed my mind about this, with the remarkable advances that have been achieved in techniques of anæsthetising wild animals with hypodermic darts. Attempts of this sort had been made for many years, but at the time I made "Savage Splendour," they were still far from perfect, tending either to leave the animal totally un-affected or else to prove fatal.

The real problem was to discover exactly how much anæsthetic the animal needed and several scientists now seem to have solved this in different ways. We have worked closely on this recently with Dr. Harthoorn of Nairobi, and the methods he uses have proved particularly successful. As an anaesthetic, he uses a mixture of four drugs—a hypnotic, a narcotic, a tranquilliser and a muscle relaxant—and fires his hypodermic darts by means of an air-gun or a specially constructed gun using a small charge of black powder. We have shown his work on our television programmes; the most impressive demonstration of the success of his methods occurred a few months ago when they were used to capture sixty scarce white rhino in an area needed for cultivation in Natal and to send them to National Parks where they had a chance of continuing to breed. Eight were even sent quite safely as far as Southern Rhodesia.

Although animal captures played a large part in "Savage Splendour," they did not form the whole of the film by any means, and the scenes I was probably proudest of in the end came almost entirely by chance and featured some animals I had not even considered when I first planned the film. These were the hippos of M'zima Springs.

I had heard about these legendary springs several times in the past, but it was not until I had finished filming my captures and was actually back in Nairobi that I had a chance of visiting them. For in those days, M'zima Springs were difficult to get to. They lay one hundred and sixty miles east of Nairobi in particularly rough country and for the last two or three miles you had to make your way there on foot once the trail petered out and you would risk a broken axle if you tried taking a truck any further.

I decided to break our journey at the Springs on the way down to Mombasa. I had been taken in by too many stories about African beauty spots in the past to be expecting anything particularly unusual, but from my first sight of M'zima Springs, I knew that this place really was unique.

It was a natural spring surrounded by palm trees, with the water forming a large pool. Part of it was very deep, but because of a rocky bed and the quality of the water it was absolutely clear. The nearest thing to it I had ever seen was Silver Springs in Florida, but M'zima Springs had something that even Silver Springs lacked. Swimming quite undisturbed in this sparklingly clear water were fifteen large hippo.

Even as I watched them, I saw the possibilities offered by this strange freak of nature. Normally hippo in a river are among the most difficult of all animals to film satisfactorily. You see little more than their mouths or their nostrils breaking occasionally above the surface of the water. But here I could actually watch the movements of their bodies as they swam. I had never seen this before and never realised quite how graceful a hippo can be when he is in the water.

Even so, there was no really effective way of filming all this from the edge of the Springs. The picture would be distorted and we would not be able to get close enough to them. I knew that the only way we would ever do justice to this remarkable scene would be to film from under the water myself.

As I thought of it, this seemed quite impossible. We had no underwater cameras, and no diving apparatus, nor did I know anyone in Africa who had. But the more I watched these hippo, the more determined I became that this was not going to stand in my way. If we could not get any special diving apparatus, we would have to make our underwater film without it.

That very afternoon I turned our trucks back the way we had come and we reached Nairobi again by nightfall. Next morning I was out early. My first point of call was the largest hardware shop

in Nairobi. I was relieved to find that they stocked large, gal-
vanised iron water tanks, and I bought one—a sturdy, rectangular,
coffin-shaped object, eight feet long and three feet wide and just
over three feet deep.

I think this tank cost five pounds ten. I had it loaded on to one of
my trucks and then drove off with it to a blacksmith on the other side
of town who had done several repairs for us in the past. He had an
oxy-acetylene blowlamp, and I told him that I wanted the top cut off
the tank, and a small window cut in one end. While this was going
on, I had a sheet of toughened windscreen glass specially cut to fit it.
When the glass had been bolted into position and the joint water-
proofed with a thin strip of rubber, the equipment for our first
underwater filming expedition was complete.

The following morning we were on our way back to M'zima
Springs with some African helpers. It was quite a struggle, carrying
our iron tank on our backs for the last three miles, but as soon as we
reached the water I had it launched. The window was perfectly
watertight, but the tank itself was top-heavy and at first had a
tendency to capsize when I tried getting inside. We cured this by
lashing a large tree trunk along each side.

Apart from this, the tank was perfect. I could lie almost full-
length inside it with a sixteen millimetre camera placed against the
window and see everything we wanted beneath the surface of
M'zima Springs. When I was inside, I found that it was necessary to
cover over the top of the tank with a tarpaulin to cut out the glare
from the sun; visibility then became perfect; three of my Africans
pushed me slowly out to where the fifteen hippos were swimming.

When I think of it all now, I suppose we should have taken more
care to find out the reactions of the hippos, for if one had become
even a little playful this submarine of ours would soon have dived a
little deeper than was intended. But we were too excited at our
success to worry very much at the time, and the hippos were too
contented in the clear waters of M'zima Springs to bother themselves with us.

When they were swimming, they were like a monumental underwater ballet. At other times, they simply basked near the surface of
the water, their great legs scarcely moving for hours on end.

We spent several days filming them and returned to M'zima Springs on two occasions. As the hippo ignored us so completely, we soon became bolder, approaching to within a few feet of them to take close-ups, and even getting to recognise them by their particular characteristics. There was one old male we never tired of filming who was something of a clown. His tusks were curiously distorted, giving him an expression of rather startling good-nature, and he would leer at us from under the water as if he knew what we were doing all the time.

I was particularly pleased with these scenes we shot of the hippos as they seemed to prove something I had always believed about film-making—that the simplest methods are invariably the most effective. A few months after I made my film, a team of Italian cameramen arrived at M'zima Springs to film the hippos under-water as we had done. They were superbly equipped. They had collapsible boats and aqualungs and diving suits and underwater cameras. No sooner had they begun than the hippos left M'zima Springs. It was three weeks before they came back.

21 *Michaela*

THE town of Potosi in Bolivia is one of the oldest Spanish cities in South America. A strange relic from another age, it is the place where the Spanish conquistadores came to dig their silver from the Andes. It is 14,000 feet above sea level and is generally said to be the highest city in the world. But for me Potosi has another claim to fame.

When I returned to the United States from Africa after making "Savage Splendour," I had one outstanding ambition—to get back to Africa to make films showing the threat hanging over its wild life. But this was not even remotely possible at that time. Film backers are not particularly concerned with starting crusades and those I knew seemed anxious to go on getting the sort of films I had made in the past. I was known chiefly for my long-distance car expeditions overland and it was finally suggested that I ought to make a film on a journey through South America from Guayaquil in Ecuador through Peru and Bolivia down to Argentine and Buenos Aires.

So I set off, travelling light. I had a single large Dodge truck and touring car to carry my camping and photographic equipment. I imagined, somewhat hopefully as it turned out, that in South America it would be easier to live off the country than in Africa.

After Africa, this journey seemed too easy. There was none of that air of constant uncertainty that made Africa so exciting and often so nerve-racking.

But what the start of my journey lacked in excitement it more than made up for in spectacle. The road led across the Altiplano, the high plateau of the Andes and the Cordilleras that runs for several hundred miles parallel with the coast of the Pacific. Most of the time we were at least ten thousand feet above sea level. The climate was superb, and we drove on across those long plains with a brilliant sky above and the snow-covered peaks of the Andes glistening on the horizon away to our left.

Only occasionally would something remind me of the work I knew I should be doing in Africa. Most of the time the grasslands of the Altiplano were devoid of wild life, but suddenly I might notice a pitifully small herd of llama or vicuña and remember the early descriptions I had read of the way these animals had abounded before the Spanish invaders arrived and massacred them nearly out of existence. It is because of the rarity of vicuña to-day that their fine, superbly soft wool is the most expensive in the world.

As I drove on across these beautiful, almost empty plains, I understood as never before the way the life seems to go from a country when it loses its wild animals.

Apart from this, the journey was most enjoyable, and the sense I had of this being something of a holiday grew when I met Michaela. I had already known her in New York, where she worked as a fashion designer. Now I suddenly found her here in the middle of South America, travelling through obscure villages of Bolivia and Peru in search of traditional Indian patterns and designs as an exotic inspiration for her work. Our paths crossed on several occasions while I was filming, but it was not until we became snowbound together, on the road to Potosi, that I proposed to her and was accepted.

From the start, Michaela made it clear that she was as prone to sudden decisions as I was, and we decided to get married at once. This was easier said than done. First we had to reach Potosi, and after driving up the spectacular road that zig-zags across the Andes towards the city, we arrived just in time to catch the registrar before he closed his office for the night. After some argument he agreed to marry us and the ceremony took place in his office. One of the witnesses was the president of the local Bolivian-American club. The other was the town drunk.

Despite the haste and light-heartedness of our marriage, I have always felt myself particularly fortunate in having Michaela as a wife. Right from the start I found that she shared my passion for travel and for animals and throughout our marriage our enthusiasms have always seemed to coincide on the things that matter to us.

Michaela's toughness as a traveller was soon put to the test on a journey we made into the thick forests of Ecuador. There cannot be many women who would care for a honeymoon under the conditions in which we spent ours. There was no chance of taking a vehicle along the jungle tracks we had to follow and we jogged our way for many miles into the forest on horseback. Sometimes the going became so rough on mountain trails that not even the horses could continue and we travelled on foot, alone with our Indian guides.

We were searching for the survivors of the once powerful tribe of the Colorado Indians. There is a small, semi-civilised group of them living near San Domingo in Ecuador; but there were said to be still a number of families living in complete isolation, in the forest. As far as I could discover, there were barely two hundred of them left, although they had once been among the most numerous of the Indian peoples of Ecuador. Now they were a doomed tribe, living their furtive life deep in the forest, their numbers shrinking year by year.

Apart from this, the chief reason why I was prepared to make such efforts to find them and film them was that the Colorado Indians had somehow managed to preserve their distinctiveness as a race, still decorating themselves in the unique and colourful way that they always had. They derived their name from the way they dyed their bodies brick red with the juice of the anyoto seeds. An elegant young Colorado would not consider that his appearance was as it should be until he had also blackened his teeth, drawn broad zebra-like stripes on his face and body with a black vegetable dye, and daubed down his hair with the sticky anyoto juice into the semblance of a solid, tight-fitting helmet.

To travel through their country we had to cross several rivers on a jungle ropeway. You sit in a rope harness and pull yourself from bank to bank, a few feet above the river, by tugging on the pulley. This looks far more hair-raising than it actually is; Michaela and I soon found that by far the greatest danger was of catching our fingers between the pulley and the rope.

Finally we saw our first Colorado Indian. He was a young boy on his own in the forest, and despite the greetings of our Indian guides, he ran as soon as he saw us. This was bad, for I feared that unless we managed to catch up with him before he got back to his village and reassured him that we meant him no harm, he would report that we had tried to attack him. The last thing I wanted was to be the centre of the warlike attentions of a tribe like the Colorados.

Se we had to set off in pursuit, blundering our way along the overgrown forest paths the boy had taken. Luckily our Indians were as at home in the forest as the boy and could run considerably faster. At last they caught him and at the price of a packet of American cigarettes, we managed to convince him that we wished him and his tribe well.

As a result of our new friendship with the boy, we were soon made welcome by the whole tribe and were able to stay several days with them filming their weaving and the daily life in their primitive village in the forest. It was here that I had my first chance of observing one of Michaela's particular talents from which I have benefited many times since—her remarkable ability to win the friendship of primitive peoples. For without speaking their language, she was soon on the warmest terms with these Colorado Indians and before we left, they insisted on making us both honorary members of the tribe by painting our faces with the traditional red and black stripes of their race.

During the next few days of our journey back through the forest, we found that the red dye soon washed off but the black remained. For several weeks after we had left the forests of Ecuador, we were striped like a pair of zebras with the tribal marks of the Colorado Indians.

Although Michaela had done so well during our first trip, there was one thing that seriously worried me about her during these first months of our marriage; she seemed so engrossed in South America that I used to wonder how I was ever going to get her to come with me to Africa.

"Don't fall in love too much with South America," I used to say to her. "One of these days I'll take you to Africa. Save your affections for that. Africa really is a place worth falling in love with."

She would laugh and tell me I talked about Africa too much and even when we returned to New York, she was still busily at work, planning a return trip for us both to South America. But then, once again, chance intervened and before Michaela's South American plans had come to anything, we had both been offered a totally unexpected chance of working together in Africa.

This began a few weeks after our return to New York with a cable from Hollywood asking me to fly out to meet the producer Sam Zimbalist at the Metro-Goldwyn-Mayer studio as soon as possible. I was not anxious to become involved with Hollywood at this point of my career, but when I made inquiries I found that M.G.M. was just starting production of a new version of Rider Haggard's highly romantic novel, "King Solomon's Mines." It was to be made on location in Africa with no expense spared, and I was being considered for the position of technical adviser to the film.

At first I was slightly puzzled why M.G.M. should be considering me for this particular job. It was not until I had reached Hollywood and been ushered into the middle of a story conference to meet Sam Zimbalist himself that I discovered why.

"Gentlemen," said Zimbalist, introducing me to the rest of the conference, "this is Armand Denis who made that wonderful sequence you saw of the hippos swimming under water in his film 'Savage Splendour'."

I was suitably flattered and tried to thank him but he went on talking about my film. "You know," he said, "the hippos were great, just great, but it wasn't just the hippos that made me decide you should be our technical adviser on this film.

"No," he went on, "it was the splendid way you pretended to shoot it. Do you know," he said, turning to the conference, "Armand here actually made it appear in the film as if he shot those scenes of the hippos from an old iron tank with a piece of windscreen glass stuck in one end. That's what I call real showmanship."

"But, Mr. Zimbalist," I said, "I really did shoot those scenes like that, just as I showed them in the film."

"Oh, now, now, Armand," said Sam Zimbalist, "don't try

taking us in. We've been in the business longer than you have and we know that you couldn't have shot a scene like that without at least 25,000 dollars' worth of equipment."

I would have gone on arguing, but I suddenly realised that everyone around the conference table was in deadly earnest and that if I persisted in this absurd story of mine, I would soon be annoying people and lose my chance of the job.

So instead of carrying on the argument, I just said, "Well, Mr. Zimbalist, I must say that film took in most people, but I suppose I should never have expected it to fool you."

At this, everyone smiled knowingly and the following day my appointment as technical adviser to "King Solomon's Mines" was confirmed.

Under normal circumstances I would not have been quite so anxious to work for Hollywood. I have always valued my freedom and independence too much. But this film had an unexpected amount in its favour as far as I was concerned. Production was due to start in Kenya so it offered me a unique chance of getting back to the one country I wanted to and be handsomely paid for my trouble. It also turned out that M.G.M. needed a double for Deborah Kerr, the star of the picture. Michaela had such an unusual resemblance to her that she was offered the job: the two of us could therefore travel and, we hoped, be together during the entire production of the film.

The only thing I had to worry about now was how Michaela was going to react to Africa. We flew together out to Nairobi in the autumn of 1949, and all the way there I remember thinking how disastrous it was going to be if she did not like it.

Within an hour of landing I knew I need worry no further. Whatever it is about Africa that claims its followers for life, began to win her at once. She fell in love with Kenya, just as I had, and before long she was busy driving round the outskirts of Nairobi in a hired car, looking for a likely spot to buy land and one day build a house of our own.

Our assignment with M.G.M. lasted six months and we spent the time flying in chartered planes to different locations in Tanganyika, Uganda, Ruanda and the Congo, sleeping in luxury camps specially built for the film staff, working with vast crews of camera-men and technicians and never ceasing to marvel at Hollywood's way with the jungle and with Rider Haggard.

I was never particularly happy about the film as it finally appeared. As it progressed I felt it was presenting altogether the wrong view of wild life and that scenes glorifying the hunter and the killing of animals contributed to exactly that view of Africa that I disliked when I met it back in America. For this reason I finally asked that my name be kept off the film's credits and decided that wherever my own future lay, it was certainly not with this sort of large-budget film-making in Africa.

Apart from the film, our stay in Africa was a great success, particularly for Michaela, who made an excellent double for Deborah Kerr. In the end she also found her plot of land. It was on the side of a long wooded ridge, in a district called Langata, eleven miles south-west of Nairobi. It was isolated and untouched. There was a wild ravine with a stream at the bottom and an immense view across the plains beyond. When the weather was right, the distant outline of Mount Kilimanjaro appeared on the horizon, 132 miles away.

Most important of all, this place had the feel of Africa about it. It had space and freedom and as soon as we saw it we knew that if ever the day came when we could settle and build a house, this was where it would be.

For everyone else who had come from America to work on "King Solomon's Mines," the conclusion of the film marked the end of their work in Africa. For us it was only the beginning. We had the time and the money now to make a film of our own, and when the last of the chartered airliners had roared off from Nairobi airport, carrying M.G.M.'s technicians back to Hollywood, Michaela and I stayed on, relieved that at last we could work in our own way.

We planned what was to be my fifth overland crossing of Africa, driving from Mombasa across Kenya, Uganda, the Congo and Angola to Luanda and the Atlantic. As I completed the preparations for this journey in Nairobi, things seemed to go smoother than ever before at the start of an expedition.

To start with, there was no difficulty buying all the equipment we needed at bargain prices. Much of it had been left behind by M.G.M. The stores in Nairobi that specialise in fitting out safaris and expeditions had more equipment than they knew what to do with, and our pots and pans, our tents and sleeping bags and pressure lamps had all seen service earlier on location with "King Solomon's Mines."

I also found that Michaela made a great difference to the efficiency of preparations for a safari. After the early days when I had taken such pride in arranging the food supplies of my expeditions, I had been getting increasingly haphazard in the stores I had been laying in. For some reason I would always seem to buy great quantities of herrings in tomato sauce, most of which would remain uneaten throughout the journey; and when I was driving I would find myself living on sandwiches and tinned sardines for days on end.

Michaela did her best to put a stop to this, and spent several days putting the housekeeping of our expedition firmly in order, so that by the time we were ready to leave our two trucks had a good supply of potatoes, a large bag of onions, boxes of dried apples and apricots, packets of dried soups, tins of condensed milk and several cases of the only tinned meat I consider worthy of a man's eating—corned beef.

This expedition of ours produced a film that was a successor to "Savage Splendour." We called it "Below the Sahara," and for all the early scenes, I had the particular satisfaction—unthinkable under the M.G.M. regime—of working as my own cameraman. This was something I particularly liked doing as the result was always a film that I felt to be particularly my own. By this time I had finally sold my old travel-scarred Akeley cameras and was shooting the whole film in colour with a 16 mm. Bell and Howell, a camera I always enjoyed using because of its convenience and high mobility.

I appreciated the new freedom and flexibility this gave to the camera work when we were filming among the tribes I knew in the Congo. We visited the pygmies again and the giant Watusi, and all the time I was pleased to see how well Michaela was taking to this life on safari and how here, as in South America, she seemed to show an almost uncanny knack for getting on with even the most outlandish tribes.

The scenes of animal capture in "Savage Splendour" had proved so popular that I planned to continue the same theme in this film. After we had been joined half-way through the trip by a new assistant, called Tom Stobart, who was later to acquire fame as photographer to the successful Everest expedition, we set off down to South Africa where I was hoping to film the capture of some animals that had long interested me—particularly the sea-lions that still breed at a few rare places along the Atlantic coastline of south and south-west Africa.

The first place we made for was a small island off the coast, not far from Cape Town. In the past the sea-lions had been hunted almost to the point of extermination along this coast, but on this particular island the animals had managed to survive. It was practically inaccessible from the mainland, with rocks and treacherous currents that made it impossible to land except on the calmest of days. In time, this island had become the last refuge for the sea-lions, the place they came to every season to breed and raise their families before disappearing into the Atlantic again. I was glad to see that by now the South African government had understood the uniqueness of the island, and placed it and its sea-lions under the most strict protection.

Luckily we had no difficulty getting permission to land and do our filming. We also received permission to capture one of the sea-lions provided we let it go almost immediately afterwards, which suited us as I had been specially asked by one of the local universities to obtain for them a sample of the blood of a fully-grown male sea-lion for research.

A fully grown sea-lion can weigh anything up to 800 pounds and I knew it was going to be no easy task to catch one unharmed. Unlike a giraffe or a rhino, there was no chance of catching one with a lasso, and I finally decided that the only feasible way of doing it was with a large net. But I knew how powerful a sea-lion was and nowhere in Cape Town could I find a net that really seemed to me strong enough.

Finally I decided that the only thing to do was to design a net

*The author at Macchu Pichu, the mystery city of Peru, with its discoverer
Senator Hiram Bingham. The Incas "anchored" the sun to this stone
at the solstice*

Ecuador. A Colorado Indian painted with the traditional red and dark blue stripes. Below, crossing a river a few feet above the water by tugging on the pulley

*The author and Michaela shortly after their marriage in
Bolivia, 1948*

"*Most of the grasslands of the Altiplano were devoid of life but suddenly I might notice a pitifully small herd of Vicuna*"

Filming Birds of Paradise from a platform in a dead tree, New Guinea

The everyday costume of the Wahgi Valley people, New Guinea

"*Luckily Des Bartlett was with us again: that first year in Africa our very lives seemed to be divided between the Land Rovers and the editing room*"

of our own and have it made by the fishermen in one of the villages along the coast. So we bought several hundred yards of government surplus nylon parachute cord and had a net made from it with a two-inch mesh, twenty-five feet long and about eight feet wide.

By now we had our net and our permit, but we still had to reach the island. This was the most difficult thing of all. For nearly three weeks we waited along the coast, but the seas were as heavy as ever and the fishermen told us that the surf breaking over the island would make it highly dangerous to attempt to land.

We were getting highly impatient, but finally the seas did drop a little. Several students from Cape Town University, who were all strong swimmers, were keen to come with us and help with the landing, so we decided to risk it.

We had one sailing boat and a couple of dinghies with outboard motors. Our cameras were in waterproof plastic bags, and we had placed our film and smaller pieces of equipment inside biscuit tins and sealed them with tape so that if necessary they could be floated ashore.

For as we came closer to the island, I saw that there was nowhere we could land the boats. The waves were still crashing on to the rocks. The only way to land was for everyone to swim the last thirty yards and scramble ashore as best he could. This was good enough for all of us except for Michaela, who hates the water and can hardly swim a stroke.

If I had known how dangerous it was going to be, I would never have allowed her to come. As it was, if it had not been for the students from the university, she would have had to spend the day waiting for us in one of the dinghies, for we could never have got her ashore. But one of the best swimmers we had dived through the surf with a line and we were able to use this to pull her to the island with nothing worse than a ducking.

Once we had landed and could turn our attention to the sea-lions, we were fascinated by what we saw. The animals were everywhere. The island was minute, scarcely 400 yards across, and every square yard of it seemed to be carefully allocated to a particular family of sea-lions. Several times we saw the old grey bull sea-lions fighting. They would charge and gash each other with their razor-sharp teeth and on each occasion the dispute seemed to be over the territory their families were occupying.

But it was these families that we found most interesting and that we spent most of our time filming. The females seemed to enforce the strictest family discipline on their young and some of the best shots we got were of the young sea-lions being fed and learning to climb on the rocks, while the very young babies lay and sunned themselves beside their mothers.

Unfortunately the weather began to worsen and the fishermen who had brought us were soon looking anxiously at the waves. I still wanted the chance to try capturing one of the bulls, but finally I was told that if we waited another hour, we might be stuck on the island for a fortnight. Reluctantly, we packed our cameras, sealed the film into the biscuit tins again, and battled our way back through the surf to the waiting boats.

We spent another week or so waiting for the weather to change, but it never did. We were getting seriously behind schedule with our film, but we still had not captured our male sea-lion nor obtained the blood samples I had promised the university. I was just getting ready to abandon the whole idea when one of the old fishermen who had been helping us made a suggestion.

"If you really want sea-lions," he said, "this isn't the place for you. You should go to Cape Cross. There are more sea-lions there than in the whole of this coast, and it's not an island. It's part of the mainland so you won't have any trouble getting there when the seas are rough."

"But where is Cape Cross?" I asked him.

"Oh, it's quite a way," he replied. "Right up the coast of South West Africa. Not far from a town called Swakopmund. But it would be worth your while going there if you're really interested in sea-lions."

I knew Swakopmund. The only trouble about it was that it was nearly 1,500 miles from Cape Town and there was no regular air service.

I waited on another two days at Cape Town to see if the weather changed. But the seas remained as rough as ever, and I realised that if we were to complete our film in time, it was Cape Cross or nothing. I had found that it was possible to fly as far as Windhoek by scheduled plane, so Michaela, Stobart and myself set off, trusting that we could find some way of completing the journey when we got there. Our luck was in. At Windhoek we found a stunt pilot who was willing to cram us into his plane that he normally used for aerobatics, and fly us the rest of the way to Swakopmund.

It was a terrifying journey for the pilot seemed determined to show us that there still was some wild life in the parched, semi-desert we had to cross. We never saw an animal in this entire wilderness, but the pilot seemed to think that if he could only fly low enough he would find something in the end, and finally we were nearly hedge-hopping across the desert.

The town of Swakopmund itself was something of a curiosity. It had been built by the Germans during their period of colonisation, and still remained a completely authentic German provincial town in the middle of Africa. The African waiters in the hotel said "Mahlzeit" and clicked their heels when they took your order. There were men in the streets in *lederhosen* and Tyrolean hats, and although the year was 1949, there was still a war memorial in the town square showing a fallen German soldier being taken off to Heaven by a solid Teutonic angel.

Cape Cross was about twenty miles away, and we drove there that afternoon. Everything the old fisherman had said about it was true. The sea-lions were there in great numbers. They were not protected in the same way as those on the island near Cape Town, but a local company had a concession to kill a limited number each year for their skins, and they seemed to have been able to protect the animals against poaching, and see that their numbers remained fairly constant.

We got in touch with this company and obtained permission to film and capture what we wanted. For the capture, we hired about a dozen local men and drove off with them, the net and the cameras to the beach. We soon picked a magnificent group of three males and decided that we would try for one of them.

The way I intended using the net was to hold it out with eight or nine men behind it, and try to persuade the sea-lion to charge it while he was still on land. We soon found that these males were only too anxious to oblige. They were all extremely aggressive, and surprisingly fast on land: the sight of an 800 pound male sea-lion charging straight for you is one that you do not forget in a hurry.

Luckily we were able to isolate one heavily scarred old male, and after a great struggle we had him firmly enough in our nets to use the hypodermic and get the blood samples we needed. Several of us were badly bruised and when we let him go, he stood roaring aggressively after us across the beach. We decided then that the capture of one male sea-lion was enough for us.

22 The Last of the Head-Hunters

I HAVE always been slightly horrified at the time it takes to make a film. "Below the Sahara" occupied us for eighteen months and we must have driven over ten thousand miles from location to location across Africa while we were making it. We never had a day off, we worked long hours, and we shot nearly 50,000 feet of film. Yet when we arrived back in New York to deliver our work to the R.K.O. film company, who had bought the rights and were undertaking the distribution, I had to watch as their editors relentlessly cut my material into a film that would run for a bare eighty minutes.

The editors did their work well; the film was a success, and I seemed to be the only person who was at all concerned that it had taken eighteen months to shoot eighty minutes of feature film. But the more I thought about it, the more dissatisfied I became. I was sure it must be possible to cut down the wastage on this sort of film making and just to see whether we could do it, I planned an expedition that was to last exactly six months. In that time we would make not one, but three full-length films.

To-day when we regularly make one television film every three weeks, this seems almost leisurely, but in those days it was practically unheard of. As we know now, the secret of this sort of high-pressure film making is to plan your itinerary as thoroughly as you can beforehand so as to cut down delays to a minimum. At the same time, you have to accept the fact that things will go wrong, so that within your plans you must leave yourself as many alternatives and as much flexibility as possible.

It was with this in mind that I planned the three films we were to make. The first was to be in Northern Australia, the second along the Great Barrier Reef off Eastern Australia, and the third, if everything went as it should, was to be among the stone-age people of New Guinea. Each of these areas fascinated me, and I knew that each possessed a sufficient variety of people and wild life to give us a wealth of material. Where our skill would come in would be in making the most of it in the limited time we had set ourselves.

On each successive expedition I have undertaken, it has always seemed that I have travelled lighter than on the one before. I dislike equipment for its own sake, and when Michaela and I flew to Sydney in the spring of 1952 for the start of our journey, almost the only pieces of film-making equipment we had with us were our tape recorders and the 16 mm. Bell and Howell camera that had served us so well on my last two expeditions. Even so we had something of a battle while we were finishing our packing. If Michaela had her way she would always go on safari with several suitcases full of the most glamorous dresses she has, and with an extraordinary array of lotions and cosmetics she claims to be indispensable. I have found that the crucial point in any of our expeditions always comes when I have to start reminding her about excess baggage and persuading her that there is simply no room for everything she wants. The problem tends to be aggravated if we spend a few days in Paris, as we did on our way to Australia. Every woman—and every husband—will understand what I mean.

These arguments of ours always finish in an uneasy compromise; and when we took off from Orly to Sydney our luggage was still considerably overweight.

From Sydney on our journey was by road, driving several hundred miles north up to Cape York, the peninsula that forms the northernmost tip of the continent.

The country we had to cross was difficult and singularly devoid of charm. It swarmed with flies. It was scorched and airless and apart from an occasional gum tree or two, there was little vegetation of any interest. As we were working to such a tight schedule, the worst thing of all was the roughness of the country which caused us endless delays. Time after time we had to stop and laboriously winch the trucks across the treacherous sandy beds of the dried up rivers with which this part of Australia abounds.

One thing alone alleviated the discomforts of the journey—the birds. This bleak countryside was alive with them and as we drove on we would be preceded by great flocks of parrots and cockatoos and budgerigars. We would glance casually at a flock several thousand strong and then one of us would notice that it was entirely made up of some unusual species of parrot or cockatoo, a single one of which would have had a sizeable price-tag in a New York pet shop.

Exciting though they were, we had not come all this way to this uncomfortable country just to watch birds. Our real destination lay farther north, and our film-making would not begin in earnest until we had reached a town called Normanton, and contacted a man there called Norman Smith.

I had heard a lot about Normanton, but nothing had quite prepared us for what we found when we arrived. A pair of bony cows were asleep in the main street as we drove in. The shops were empty, and no one answered when we sounded our horn. For Normanton is one of the ghost towns of Northern Australia. At the beginning of the century it had been the centre of a famous gold rush and had mushroomed like one of the boom towns of the Yukon. For a few years it prospered. Its population grew to several thousand. Then the gold suddenly petered out. The people began to leave, and within a few years all that remained of Normanton were its empty houses, its deserted casino, and its theatres with the sun-bleached playbills still outside dating from the beginning of the century.

But the state of the town hardly worried the man we were seeking. Norman Smith's real interest in life lay beyond in the mangrove swamps and along the estuaries of the muddy rivers which run from the Cape York peninsula to the sea. For he was one of Australia's leading experts on crocodiles and we were counting on him to help us film and capture a good specimen of the biggest crocodile in the world—the famous marine crocodile that inhabits the seas between Northern Australia and the islands of New Guinea and Indonesia.

I have already described how I encountered with one of these monsters in Bali in 1929. On that occasion I had had no chance of filming it and now, nearly a quarter of a century later, I wanted to make up for the chance I had missed then. According to some reports, a fully grown marine crocodile could measure anything up to thirty feet in length and although a lot of them had been shot in recent years, I hoped it would still prove possible to find an impressive one.

The crocodile hunting is done for the most part by so-called "sportsmen" from other parts of Australia. Almost every large city in Southern Australia appears to have its crocodile-shooting club, the members of which charter planes to the north for week-end parties and then pop away enthusiastically at anything that remotely resembles a crocodile.

Although this part of the coast had always been a favourite spot for these outings, Norman Smith was hopeful that he could show us something. During the last few days he had sighted several good-sized crocodiles in the estuary and he thought that with patience we should be able to capture one.

To do this we had to follow a strange procedure. First we had to catch some bait for the crocodile. This in itself was exciting enough as the most effective bait for a marine crocodile proved to be a 200 pound grouper fish caught with a rod and line. Our first attempt to find some suitable bait resulted in pulling ashore a nine-foot sawfish with a three-foot saw on its nose, but Norman Smith rejected it, insisting that the crocodiles in this part of Australia had a particular taste for grouper.

The trap itself was a strong stockade of logs driven deeply into the mud just above the high tide mark along the shore. The bait—a ten-pound chunk of grouper—was placed at the far end of the stockade and across the entrance Norman Smith had stretched a long steel cable tied in a noose and attached to a delicately balanced baulk of timber that would jerk the noose tight if anything disturbed it. To reach the bait the crocodile had to enter the stockade and the piece of fish was placed in such a position that when the crocodile reached it, the noose would be almost exactly around the centre of his body.

To me it seemed a strange and complicated way of catching a crocodile, but Norman Smith was highly experienced and confident that it would work. So at dawn we all made our way down to the estuary, set the trap with great care, smothered ourselves in mosquito repellent and waited for our crocodile to appear. We were so anxious to film the crocodile actually coming out of the water that we waited all day, although Norman Smith had told us that this would almost certainly be a waste of time, as marine crocodiles usually come ashore only at night.

It was nearly sunset before we left, but there had been no sign of life from the river. Nor was there for the next day, nor the next, and it was not until the fourth morning after we set the trap that we came down to the estuary to find that we had actually caught something. A few yards from the shore there was a great commotion. We had caught our crocodile at last. He had been able to pull himself out of the stockade and into the water, but the cable around his middle had held him tight, and now he was twisting and fighting and thrashing the water for all he was worth.

We had a struggle pulling him in. Finally he tired a little and we were able to film him and measure him and examine him closely before releasing him later that afternoon. He was a fine crocodile, a most handsome olive green and certainly larger than anything I had seen in Africa. But compared with the great crocodile I remembered seeing swimming beneath my canoe in Bali, he was a disappointment. From his snout to the tip of his tail he was exactly nineteen feet long.

These sea monsters are not the only crocodiles Cape York produces. The "billabongs"—the fresh water ponds and waterholes near Normanton—provide a perfect breeding place for the Australian fresh water crocodiles as well, and a few days later Norman Smith took us to a place where they were still plentiful. For unlike the marine crocodile, the Australian fresh water crocodile is not hunted for his leather and is in no danger of extermination.

As well as filming these crocodiles, Michaela and I were anxious to capture a few of them. We had half promised some to a friend in Southern Australia who was planning a crocodile farm on the lines of the alligator farms of Florida. So we took a couple of nets with us to the billabong, and squelched our way across the mud to where we could see a couple of crocodiles basking in the sun.

The estuary where we had spent the day waiting for our marine crocodile had been bad enough, but this was unspeakable. In addition to the flies, the mosquitoes and the stench of decaying vegetation, three cows had got caught in the mud several weeks before, and now their carcases were quietly putrefying, half buried in the congealed mud.

But the sight of the crocodiles soon took our minds off the smell, for there were far more of them than we had ever expected. They were five to seven feet long and, in the first few throws of the net, we found that they were surprisingly easy to catch.

It was this that was our undoing, for we soon became absurdly carried away by success. Instead of being content with the few crocodiles we had originally wanted, we went on a sort of crocodile catcher's orgy. Soon we were taking off most of our clothes and wading into the mud after them, despite the smell and the sharp fresh water mussel shells that cut our feet and legs.

We really were extremely foolish. These crocodiles may have been fairly small, but with one snap of their jaws they could easily deprive you of an arm. Despite this, we were soon following Norman Smith's example, and pulling them ashore by the snout. By the end of the day we had over sixty. We had not expected to catch anything like this number, and by then were so carried away by our success that we scarcely gave a thought to how we were going to look after them, much less to how we were going to get them all the way back to Southern Australia.

Instead we loaded them aboard Norman Smith's truck, and drove them back to our camp, where we tied them up for the night by putting a rope around their middles and attaching them to every available tree around the camp.

It was not until the middle of the night when the first of the crocodiles slipped his rope and came blundering through our tent that we had our first doubts of the wisdom of our day's work. Several more escaped during the night, and by the morning we decided that we had had enough. If our Southern Australian friend really needed fresh water crocodiles, he had better come and fetch them for himself. So we went round our remaining crocodiles, one by one, cutting them loose and then watching gratefully as they waddled back in the direction of the odoriferous billabong.

After our brief visit to the crocodiles, we travelled north up the Cape York peninsula, filming as we went, and making the most of our chances of observing the rich variety of the local fauna. What I found particularly fascinating about this remote part of Australia was that it provided an almost classic object lesson on the dangers of indiscriminately importing foreign species into countries that are not prepared for them.

Originally, Australia possessed no destructive carnivores of its own, and a wonderful fauna must have flourished of small mouse-sized and squirrel-sized marsupial mammals. But here in Cape York I could see the way the descendants of the common domestic cats, imported by the early settlers, had already begun to work havoc with this small marsupial population. These cats appeared to be doing so much damage that it seemed to me that they must ultimately result in the total destruction of the defenceless small fauna.

Whenever I see a hollow tree, I usually make a point of looking to see if there are any animals inside. Whenever I did this in Cape York, nine times out of ten a pair of green eyes would glare out at me belonging to an enormous tabby or ginger cat. These cats looked like any well-fed suburban pet tom, but were actually as savage as the wildest of wild cats, and were said to be virtually impossible to tame again.

For some reason Australia seems to be free of many of the germs and bacteria that, in other countries, usually prevent foreign species establishing themselves. Because of this not only cats, but descendants of many other species, thoughtlessly brought into Australia, have finally escaped and settled themselves, usually to the detriment of the existing Australian fauna.

This does not merely apply to the rabbits and wild dogs that have been such a plague in parts of the country. Australia now has a sizeable wild population of horses, pigs, goats and even camels and wild buffalo.

During our trip to Cape York, our filming was not confined to the animals. We also spent several weeks with the aborigines, filming their customs and unique way of life. We saw the way they hunted wallabies by driving them for miles across open country until they passed an ambush of men waiting for them with spears. This was a scene Michaela refused to watch, but I thought it should be recorded on film. This was not hunting for sport, but for much-needed food. I could not help admiring the marksmanship of the aborigines, and the skill with which the hunt was organised.

But the side of aborigine life that interested us most was the children. The first thing we noticed about them was their cheerfulness and talkativeness since it provided such a contrast to the almost excessive seriousness of most African children who have adult responsibility thrust on them so early in their life. Here the children were remarkably carefree, constantly laughing and chattering among themselves, and we spent some time filming their games which must have been handed on from generation to generation and were surprisingly complex. The most interesting of them were hunting games in which the children imitated turtles or wallabies with the most lifelike skill, whilst in another game one child played the part of a falcon swooping on to the nest of another bird.

Of course there are few aborigines these days that have not been touched by civilisation in one form or another, but I had not understood quite how quickly they adopt the standards and prejudices of the white man until we had left Cape York and reached the town of Cairns.

It was then that I realised that it would be useful if we could shoot some general scenes of groups of aborigines, to act as establishing shots for the film we had already made in Cape York. The shots were not enough to go back to Cape York for, and I was going to forget about them, when an Australian friend told me that at a small nearby town he knew local farmers who employed casual aborigine labour.

These men were real aborigines who had lived most of their lives in their tribes and who came into the farms for short periods when the farmers needed extra hands. When we spoke to them they said that they knew all their tribal dances, and would be quite willing to perform them before our cameras. The only trouble was that we soon found that they insisted on keeping their shirts and trousers on.

This was clearly no use for the film, but no amount of talking would make them take them off for their dance. By this time I was getting exasperated, and finally said, "Don't be ridiculous. Why are you so worried about taking your clothes off? There's nothing wrong in nakedness. It's the proper way for your dances to be performed."

But this had no effect on them at all, and finally I thought that the best argument of all would be that of example.

"Look," I said, "just to show you that there's nothing to be ashamed of in nakedness, I will take my own trousers off first."

This I proceeded to do. They watched me with shocked amazement. Then one of them began laughing, and soon this entire group of aborigines was standing round me chuckling away. I hurriedly pulled my trousers on again and decided that this was one scene the film would have to do without.

It was during the time we were in Australia that a young Queensland cameraman, called Des Bartlett, came to work for us. He shot most of the footage that went into our Australian films, and made an important contribution to our work in New Guinea. But we had no idea that he would be staying with us up to the present day, becoming our close friend as well as our collaborator.

He was with us, of course, when we flew back to the East Coast of Australia to make our second film on the Great Barrier Reef. When I had planned the trip I had arranged to meet, on the Barrier Reef, Noel Monkman and his wife. Noel, who is himself an excellent photographer and movie-cameraman, is perhaps the greatest living authority on the Barrier Reef and its fauna. Our schedule was planned so that we arrived on the Barrier Reef on one of the two occasions of the year when the tides are at their greatest. At this time at low tide huge areas of the great reef are suddenly exposed, and you are able to walk for miles over stretches of coral that are normally hidden beneath the Pacific. This gave us a chance to film the entire submarine world that was suddenly thrust on view.

I was afraid by now that we were falling behind on the six

month time-table I had set, so to catch up lost time we hired an old Catalina flying boat. This also gave us a spectacular view of the Reef, and nothing had quite prepared me for its size and endless variety. There would be the dark outline of the islands, fringed with sand and bearing occasional coconut palms. Beyond would lie the coral, beneath the sea except for the short hours of low tide, and this would be of every imaginable colour—from olive greens and purples through to the darkest blues.

When we had finished filming on the Reef, we prepared for the third and most hazardous part of our journey—the expedition to New Guinea. Michaela and I were both looking forward to this more than to any other part of our journey. We had arranged to stay at a place called Kup, in the Wahgi Valley, in the heart of the still largely unexplored mountain hinterland of New Guinea, which is an Australian mandate. From what we heard, this was one of the few places remaining in the world where civilisation had still not penetrated, and where we would be free to study a primitive people who had allowed the last ten thousand years of history to pass them by.

The Wahgi Valley can only be reached by plane. So we chartered an old Norseman aircraft, loaded our equipment aboard, and then spent the next three and a half hours wondering whether we were ever going to reach Kup in one piece.

Every flying trip in New Guinea is an adventure, and later we almost became used to it, but that first flight was a nightmare. Below us lay the most tormented countryside I had ever seen, a place of abrupt hills and sudden valleys, covered in dense jungle and shrouded in a low blanket of cloud. The plane would roar inland, up one of the valleys, just skimming the tops of the trees, and all the time just managing to keep below cloud level.

The farther we went, the worse it got and I soon had the feeling that we were flying along an endless funnel as the floor of the valleys rose and the ceiling of cloud came continually lower. Before long ice began forming on the carburettor. Every few minutes the engine would sputter and stop. Quite unconcernedly, the pilot would point the plane's nose down towards the jungle beneath to keep the propeller turning until the engine picked up and started firing again.

Finally we did reach Wahgi Valley and the pilot brought us nonchalantly down on to the precarious ironing board of a landing strip that had been cut on a narrow ledge on the top of a steep hillside. Because of the jungle there was no runway to spare at Kup.

As soon as we stepped out of the plane we realised the sort of climate we had come to. It was either damp and foggy or stiflingly hot. It was unhealthy and insect-infested, whilst the thick cloud that almost always seemed to swirl above the valleys stopped the sunlight reaching the dank jungle beneath.

The valley had been discovered from the air less than twenty years before and the ways of living of its inhabitants had not changed.

The most striking thing about our villagers, as with most New Guinea people, was their passionate addiction to self-decoration. The men carried this to fantastic lengths. With the weird objects they thrust through their noses and the elaborate head-dresses they contrived for themselves out of the skins and feathers of the local birds of paradise they appeared, at first sight, as fearsome as any tribes dreamed up in the feverish imagination of a Hollywood producer.

We found the appearance of our tribesmen was slightly misleading. To all of us they were most charming and friendly, and these stone-age primitives, with their stone axes on their shoulders, showed a love of flowers and an instinct for growing them that struck us as remarkably civilised. When we went visiting to neighbouring villages we would find that fresh flowers had been picked and scattered on the last mile or so of the trail leading into the village, as a sign of welcome. I found this love of flowers quite astonishing in a stone-age tribe, and saw it as differentiating them quite sharply from most of the other primitive peoples I had met.

Of course it is difficult to generalise about the people of New Guinea. The country is so broken up with its mountain ranges and ravines that there is nothing like the contact between the people in one area and the next that you find in an open country like Australia. As a result the tribes vary enormously. In one valley there is a race of pygmies. In the next there might easily be people twice their size, and since the people in the valleys beyond were always mysterious and hostile and unknown, it is easy enough to understand why such anti-social conduct as head-hunting and cannibalism occurred.

While we were there this sort of inter-tribal distrust and hostility was still common enough. To tell the truth, there was not overmuch control of the people in the interior and nobody wishes to establish relations with a neighbour whose primary ambition is to add your head to his collection of trophies.

Des Bartlett found out a great deal about head-hunting when he went to stay on his own among the Sepik River people. This was in the very centre of head-hunting country and from what I learned from him and from tribesmen from outside the Wahgi Valley, I discovered that the motives for this unpleasant activity were not exactly what I had expected.

It seems that head-hunting derives from a long-standing tradition in this part of the world that you gain prestige by being able to prove that you have been responsible for the deaths of a number of other people. This is all that the possession of a head signifies. It is in no sense a proof of valour or of manly victory over an enemy. The head of a woman or a baby carries just as much prestige as the head of a fully grown warrior. Any fond father in this area who wishes his son to start out in life with all the advantages he himself has enjoyed goes to a neighbouring village and actually buys a child. He brings the child home, quite unconcernedly ties it up somewhere in the garden, gives his son a knife or an axe and tells him to kill it, so that in his tenderest years he may acquire the prestige of having a head on his belt.

Mercifully this sort of thing is dying out, but although I found it repellent, I could not bring myself to believe that the primitiveness of these people was any argument for trying suddenly to thrust them headlong into the twentieth century. A situation similar to the one I had found in Bali could so easily develop; here was a simple, uncontaminated race, on the verge of the white man's progress and civilisation. Their culture of course was rudimentary, in contrast with the rich culture of the Balinese, but there was even less hope of these people surviving happily if their traditions and way of life were suddenly kicked from under them. I could think of no occasion when a white race had come in contact with a primitive one like this and the primitive people had really benefited. It was all too easy to see the old pattern recurring. The white man's drink, his politics, his diseases would infect the people. Instead of progressing they would degenerate; like the Red Indians of America and so many of the tribes of Africa, they could end up only as third class citizens of a world that had no real place for them.

The Australian Government was making a praiseworthy effort to protect the valley against undue contact with the outside world, but I fear it is an attempt doomed to failure. Not even in New Guinea is it really possible to protect a primitive people on this scale, and the outside world is inexorably closing in on them. The Wahgi Valley already boasted an American missionary and had been visited by a small expedition from the American Museum of Natural History.

But while the New Guinea people will almost certainly make a show of accepting some of the habits and culture of the white man, I believe that beneath their apparent acceptance they will tend to remain much as they always did.

I remember a story the good Catholic Bishop of Papua told us about some of his parishioners. Michaela and I stayed with him on Yule Island and he became a close friend of ours. One evening when we were talking after dinner, he told us how he had found, to his sorrow, that some of the people of his diocese were still practising occasional cannibalism. No bishop likes to find out this sort of thing about his flock, so he descended on Yule Island, preached a stern episcopal warning against the faithful eating the flesh of their brothers and departed with the protestations of the islanders that never, never again would they think of eating human flesh.

Shortly after this the villagers were presented with something of a dilemma. For no sooner had the bishop sailed back to New Guinea in his motor launch—Yule Island is one of the small islands off the Papuan coast—than a neighbouring non-Christian tribe, with whom they happened to be on good terms at the moment, arrived with a peace offering. It was a human arm and for any excannibal a human arm is still a tempting delicacy. Naturally they did not want to offend the other tribe by refusing a princely gift, but neither did they want to offend their bishop. After much thought, they found a solution to satisfy everyone.

They gave the arm to their children to eat. In this way they would not offend their neighbours. The could honestly tell their bishop next time he called that they had not eaten human flesh, and a good arm would not have gone to waste.

In the end the film we made on New Guinea concentrated almost entirely on its people, for there were very few animals on the island. By far the most interesting of these are the island's birds of paradise, but many of the species which survived the cruel fashion for bird of paradise feathers in Europe and America at the beginning of this century are now threatened with extinction through extensive deforestation in the areas where they breed.

We made several attempts to film the wonderful birds by building large platforms in the forest close to trees they were known to visit, but although we spent much time patiently waiting twenty feet above ground, we never did get a really satisfactory shot of one.

Apart from the birds of paradise, the animal on the island that interested me most was the pig. Pigs are not indigenous to the island and I have never discovered when or how they were introduced, but among the Wahgi Valley people the pig has become a vital part of the people and their economy. So much so that the pig is treated quite literally as a member of the family, and a piglet often gets more attention than a child. It always amused me to watch the congregation in the mission hut at Kup on a Sunday morning and to see a New Guinea matron sitting at the back during the sermon with a child at one breast and a baby pig at the other.

It is this devotion to their pigs that makes the New Guinea people's ultimate behaviour towards them so inexplicable. For one day, after a delay of a year or even longer, word would go round among the villages that a feast was to be held. At this feast the villagers would bring out the pigs that they had cared for so religiously for so long and butcher them. This would be done with extreme brutality. Then a great pit would be dug. A layer of nearly red-hot stones would be placed in the bottom. A layer of fresh green leaves would be put on the stones, then a layer of pigs be placed on top. Then more stones would be put in, then more leaves, then more pigs, until the pit was full. This would then be left to sizzle and steam for several hours, and when the pigs were cooked the villagers would indulge in an orgy of pig eating, devouring in one grand fling what it had taken them years to grow.

For me the New Guinea people provided the most fascinating part of this entire journey to the Antipodes, and thanks to them we were able to finish our three films well within the six months we had set ourselves.

But it was a pet that we picked up just before we left Kup that made our flight back to New York one of the most eventful plane journeys we have ever got involved in. It all began when Michaela and I were watching a beautiful sulphur-crested cockatoo flying around the top of a very high tree near one of the platforms we had built to watch the birds of paradise. The cockatoo kept disappearing into a hole high up in the branches and from the sounds which we could plainly hear, it was obvious that she was feeding a fledgling inside.

I pointed out the hole in the tree to one of the young village boys who was with us. He thought we wanted the bird, so before we could stop him he had swung his way up into the tree like a monkey; we suddenly saw him sixty feet above us with a tiny, squawking baby cockatoo in his hands. There was no way of telling him to put it back, so when he brought it down to us, still squawking and desperately flapping its wings, we felt there was nothing to do but adopt it.

I think we have never had a more amusing or lovable creature as a pet. He was far from helpless and very alert. We decided that for safety he should sleep at night in the hen-house in which our chickens were kept; being an excellent mimic, like most cockatoos, he soon picked up their language. He also picked up a few words from us and every morning when we let them out, the chickens would come strutting out first, full of their own self-importance, while the cockatoo would trail behind them, blatantly making fun of them by producing all the sounds a hen makes when it has just laid an egg and interspersing them with an accurate imitation of Michaela saying, "Hullo, hullo. How are you to-day?"

Apart from this, the experiment of keeping our cockatoo with the chickens was not too great a success because he was so difficult to feed. Michaela had fed him by hand when he was very young, and he insisted on this continuing. Michaela used to take far more trouble over feeding him than I would have done: he was fed mainly on boiled rice, and his feeding habits were deplorable. He never swallowed things properly; his boiled rice was always dripping out of his mouth on to the feathers of his chest, which were soon so matted and disgusting that Michaela finally had to make him a bib. Once he had seen it he would never be parted from it, and at every meal his bib would have to go on before he would agree to let Michaela start feeding him.

We had taken it for granted that before we left we would release our cockatoo in the forest where we had found him. We were in New Guinea to take pictures, not to collect cockatoos and besides there are immense complications these days in taking animals with you in a modern aircraft half-way round the world. But although we took him into the forest several times, he would not leave us. He had become too dependent and we knew that without his bib and without Michaela he would probably starve. Clearly we would have to take him with us. So I found a nondescript-looking wooden box for him. It had a small flap in front, and some film labels on the side, and I put the cockatoo inside, making sure that there was enough room in front for him to put his nose through to get some fresh air.

I was not too worried about getting him through the customs in New York as restrictions there were not too severe, but I was worried about Paris. We had to change aircraft there and this meant a wait of two hours at Orly. I was hoping that there would be a simple switch of baggage from one plane to another, and that the French authorities would take no notice of us as we were transit passengers. But when we got to Paris something went wrong. The New York plane was delayed, all our luggage was piled in the customs hall, and along came the most inquisitive customs man I have ever faced in my life.

THE LAST OF THE HEAD-HUNTERS

He went through everything we possessed—cameras, personal effects, clothes—and in the end inevitably caught sight of the wooden box.

He went through everything we possessed—cameras, personal effects, clothes—and in the end inevitably caught sight of the wooden box.

"What's in that box?" he asked.

"Oh, a bird," I said, vaguely.

"What kind of a bird?"

"Oh, a sort of pigeon," said Michaela.

It might have been all right if the cockatoo had been as discreet as we were, but he chose this very minute to stick his head through the flap in his box. He eyed the customs man disapprovingly with his beady black eye. Up went his crest, and he said, "Hullo, hullo, how are you this morning?"

The customs man obviously was no animal lover. He turned purple.

"You take me for a fool," he shouted. " You think I don't know a pigeon. This is no pigeon. This is a parrot and there are laws against bringing parrots into France. I'll have this bird of yours destroyed at once."

I tried to calm him down, but only seemed to make matters worse.

"I'll give you a pigeon," shouted the customs officer; "people like you should be taught a lesson."

It was at this point that Michaela decided things had gone far enough. When she wants to she can make an enormous amount of noise and she obviously felt that if anyone needed a lesson it was the customs officer, so she shouted back at him that we were on an important expedition and that if he so much as laid a finger on her bird he would never hear the last of it.

It takes a stronger man that that customs officer to stand up to Michaela, and I could see him beginning to wilt. Obviously he was scared that he might get into some sort of trouble, but a crowd had collected, he had taken his stand, and it was more than his dignity was worth to budge from it.

By then the whole situation had turned into a complete farce. I could hardly keep a straight face and the cockatoo kept poking his head out of his box to say, "Good morning, good morning. How are you to-day?"

277

Michaela was at her best, loudly proclaiming that she would cut her own throat, right there in the middle of Orly's customs hall if anything was done to her bird, and pointing out how embarrassing this would be to the French authorities. She was collecting a good deal of sympathy from the crowd.

"You tell us that you cannot allow this bird through," I said to the customs officer. "Who can then?"

"Nobody," he replied dramatically, "except the Minister of Agriculture in person."

"Very well," I said, " we must get the Minister of Agriculture on the phone."

"Very well," said the customs officer, "we will."

Of course none of us believed we would ever get through to the Minister, but we dialled his number and incredibly, within a couple of minutes, I was speaking to him in person.

The conversation that followed was pure Marx Brothers.

"Hullo, this is Armand Denis."

"Hullo, this is the Minister of Agriculture."

"I am at Orly Airport. I am having trouble with my cockatoo."

"I am the Minister of Agriculture. Cockatoos are not my responsibility."

I tried to explain what was happening, but the poor man became more puzzled and exasperated every minute.

"If the law says you are not to bring a cockatoo into France, the law must be right and there is nothing I can do about it."

"Monsieur le Ministre," I said, "be human. This cockatoo belongs to my wife. She is devoted to it. In an hour's time we shall be in an aircraft on its way to New York, but if anything happens now to that, my wife will never forgive me or you or France or the French government. Just consider what you're doing."

At this, the Minister of Agriculture decided he had had enough.

"Mr. Denis," he said limply, "get yourself, your wife and your wretched cockatoo on to the next plane to New York. But if you ever come through Paris again with a cockatoo, God help you."

23   *Return to Africa*

OUR return to America was to mark an entirely new episode in our lives, but it hardly felt like that when we arrived in New York. The city was wet and bitterly cold. We found ourselves longing for the sun before we had been there a week, so purely on impulse we took a plane down to Cuba and finally stayed there three months in a rented apartment on Malecon, putting together our material into three full-length films. Although we were spending twelve hours a day editing film, both of us looked on this Cuban interlude as something of a holiday. We found the life of Havana much to our taste. We loved the food, the music and the people, and in those days an occasional shooting affray never seemed much to worry about.

After three months in Cuba our work was finished, and we flew to New York to try and sell our three completed films. Once more I immediately found myself caught up in that endless delay and frustration that always dogs me when I have any dealings with film executives. One company thought the material was wonderful, then added that they would buy it only if I would consent to having my three films cut together into one.

This I firmly refused to do although the price was good, and in an effort to find a market where my work would not be chopped about, I decided to bring the films to England. One of the first people to see them was Sir Michael Balcon, in those days head of Ealing Studios. He liked the films and through him a deal was arranged almost at once. There was no talk of cutting or condensing the films. Ealing Studios and the Rank Organisation agreed to distribute them for me much as I had shot and edited them.

It was now that chance began to work very hard in our favour.

Just after we arrived, "Below the Sahara," the last film we had made for R.K.O., happened to be due for release in England. Quite casually, our good friend, David Jones, head of R.K.O. publicity in London, asked us whether we would mind giving a short talk and showing some film on television to boost the publicity for "Below the Sahara." Equally casually I agreed. David dug out some film extracts from my "Dark Rapture" and "Savage Splendour," and a few days later, on the 5th October, 1953, Michaela and I did our first television show in England—a ten minute live interview with Peter Haigh, followed by twenty minutes of film.

The public response was quite extraordinary. In all my years of film-making I had never known anything like it. A week or two later, at the request of Cecil Madden of the B.B.C., we did another half-hour programme—on our own this time—and on the strength of these two short appearances on television it seemed that we had become famous. The B.B.C. offered us a contract that would mean giving up films entirely and concentrating all our time on television.

This was all highly flattering, but there is something frighteningly unreal about being at the centre of this sort of overnight success and we had to think very hard about what we really wanted to do. If we accepted the B.B.C.'s offer we knew we would be adopting an almost completely new way of life. Although, on the face of it, television work might sound very similar to the sort of thing I had been doing for years, the differences between working for television and for the cinema are immense.

As dispassionately as possible we tried adding up the pros and cons of the two careers.

The arguments against going into television were strong. We would have to work far harder and produce results far quicker than when we were filming for the cinema. In the past we had taken a year to a year and a half to produce a feature film. Now we knew we would have to organise ourselves to turn out half-hour films at the rate of one a month with the possibility of this being narrowed still further to one every three weeks. Also, in the cinema one was working for a medium that could and usually did pay big money. This was not true of television.

The arguments for going into television were quite different. After the delays and disappointments of the previous months, the very idea of working for quick results was in itself a great attraction. We also knew that we would enjoy complete freedom to go where we liked and, within the broadest limits, to say what we wanted. There was much I wanted to say to the widest possible audience about conservation of wild life. The film companies, of course, were not really interested in this, but television offered us direct contact with millions of people and an opportunity, which no other medium could match, to make them interested in the things we loved and considered important.

Of course these were early days in television and a lot of what we might be able to accomplish was still highly problematical, but for me the really deciding factor that made me choose television was that for the first time in my life I would be doing something that depended entirely on the two of us. Making films for Hollywood had always been something of a compromise and had never suited my temperament. Once you have shot the film, a dozen people seem to step in—the editors, the scriptwriters, the musical arrangers, the effects men—and the best I could ever hope for was the dubious satisfaction of having had just one of the dozen fingers that finally went into that particular pie—while I would bear the responsibility for all the assininities of a script which I would not even have had a chance to check.

Now everything was to be under our control—the shooting, the editing, the scripting—and if something did not work there would be only ourselves to blame.

I think Michaela's motives for choosing television were slightly different from mine. She was thinking of that plot of land outside Nairobi, and even before we had signed the contract with the B.B.C., she was trying to convince me that Nairobi would be the ideal spot for us to have our headquarters to operate from and produce our films. At last, as she pointed out, we would be able to do what we had so long dreamed of. We could live in Africa, make our home there and work as we had always wanted to with animals and wild life. Real freedom would be ours at last.

Not that Michaela had to try very hard to convince me. I

was as ready to live in Africa as she was, but the dream took a long time to turn into reality, and signing our contract with the B.B.C. was only a beginning. First we actually had to get to Africa, and I found that there was a considerable difference between going there on an expedition as I had in the past, and going there with a wife bent on making a home. This time our disagreements about packing were even greater than when we had been preparing to go to Australia and although I kept reminding Michaela that we still had no house, and only twenty-five acres of uncleared forest, she insisted on taking almost everything we possessed.

Apart from this we were obviously going to need more equipment than I had ever taken on a normal expedition, if we were to do what I planned and actually turn out finished films in Africa. We needed projectors and Moviola machines to edit our films on. We had to have full-scale sound recording gear to record our commentaries for the programmes, and we would obviously need to add greatly to our movie and still camera equipment.

Altogether there were a thousand and one things to think of, and it was not until after several months of feverish preparation that we arrived in Nairobi. Even then the rush continued. If anything, it grew worse as we started on our programmes. Luckily Des Bartlett was with us again, but none of us had reckoned quite how hard we would have to work to keep up to schedule. For that first year in Africa our very lives seemed to be divided between the Land-Rovers and the editing room.

One week we would be down in the Serengeti, shooting a film on lions. The next we would be on the road for Entebbe and a feature on Lake Victoria. Then we would be back in Nairobi for a frantic fortnight, editing and scripting the films we had made before sending them on by air to London. There was scarcely time to think about building the house, let alone to get out to indulge in the luxury of consulting architects and builders. The house had to wait until we had more time to think about it.

Even then, we always seemed to be picking up animals: from the very first we made it a rule never to turn away an animal that needed help. This in itself gave us our problems since any animal you cure or help seems instinctively to attach himself to you, and before long we found our family growing to include several unexpected newcomers.

Some of them were hardly the kind you expect to make pets of. There was Voodoo the vulture for instance. We found him by chance when we were out filming. Michaela noticed a vulture sitting motionless on the ground about a quarter of a mile from our Land-Rover. The only thing that normally lures a vulture to the ground is a kill of some sort. We slowly drove over to investigate. To our surprise the vulture did not move as we approached. To our still greater surprise there was no sign of a kill or a dead animal.

"Look," said Michaela, "there's something wrong with his wing," and sure enough, we could see that the left wing drooped slightly. He made a pathetic attempt to fly as we got towards him, but despite the flurry of feathers he could not rise. When he realised it was useless to try to get away he seemed to accept us and stood patiently as Michaela stretched out the wing and I felt along it as gently as I could to find what was wrong. It was fractured. Vultures often are surprisingly foolhardy when they feed on the kill of another animal, and many times I have seen a lion charge them to drive them away. I can only suppose that this vulture had not got out of the way quickly enough.

Whatever the cause it was clear that unless we set the wing as soon as possible this vulture's chances of survival were nil. So we lifted him on to the back seat and, trying not to jolt him more than we had to, drove back to camp. Normally a vulture is not a particularly sociable bird as far as people are concerned, but the remarkable thing about this one was that he seemed to realise instinctively that we were trying to help him. We were careful to keep out of the way of his beak but he accepted everything we did for him with considerable patience. Back in camp we placed him on a table, and while Michaela held him, I set the wing and bandaged it to his body with a thin wooden splint.

This was the start of the long and agreeable friendship we had with Voodoo the vulture. It was Michaela who called him Voodoo and soon he would answer to his name and come waddling over with his bandaged wing whenever we called him. Once he had accepted us, he had no fear of anyone in the camp and wandered round, everlastingly on the search for any titbits he could find.

I have always been annoyed by people who speak of the "ugliness" and the "evil faces" of vultures. For me they are among the most beautiful of birds and their action in flight is magnificent. This was particularly so with Voodoo. He stayed with us, living quite happily in camp when we were on safari, and once his wing had healed we had a chance to appreciate him for the exceptional bird he was. He was a hooded vulture with a wing span of nearly five feet and often when we were driving he would leave the Land-Rover and follow us, a tiny speck in the sky above.

"That can't be Voodoo," Michaela would say, but when we had made camp the speck would come swooping down to us and Voodoo would be there ready to squabble with the dogs for his food when we cut up the meat for their evening meal.

With Michaela and myself he was always remarkably gentle. He would never peck or misbehave, although he did have one habit that took some getting used to. This was to follow us whenever we were out walking and then suddenly swoop down on to our heads. With a smaller bird this would have been rather endearing, but with a fully grown vulture it can be extremely painful, especially as he would then try perching on our heads, holding on to our hair with his claws.

Luckily he finally grew out of this provoking habit. Our success with Voodoo showed something I had long been aware of— that there is no better way of taming an animal than to help it after it has been injured. It is surprising how an animal that will normally snarl and bite will accept you while you are treating it, and be grateful afterwards.

This does not mean that you no longer need to exercise elementary caution with an injured animal you are treating. Only recently I was setting the broken leg of a large secretary bird that had been found injured by some Africans, and brought to us as a matter of course, in the expectation of some reward. I had never thought of a secretary bird as being particularly dangerous, but while I was fixing its splint it kicked out with its good leg with surprising violence. Its foot caught the side of my face and I was badly bruised for many days afterwards.

It was while we were on safari that we adopted the most pathetic of all the animals we have ever looked after.

We were camped near Malindi, filming mudskippers and the other strange creatures on the coastal mud-flats near the Indian Ocean.

I had a new short-wave transceiver, with which I could hear police calls and eavesdrop on quite a number of private transmitters. Early one morning I picked up a call, apparently from some telephone men installing a phone line somewhere between Malindi and Lamu, who were talking to their headquarters. A tiny baby elephant, which they said was only thirty inches high, had wandered into their camp. They had chased it away, but it had come back. It had been there three days by now and they had nothing to feed it with. What should they do? This was too much for either of us to resist.

Two hours later we had found the camp, and there, sure enough, was the elephant; and there also were the telephone men, glad enough to have us take him off their hands. He was the most appealing infant. He was actually thirty-two inches high, a little taller than the men had said, about the size of a St. Bernard dog; but he was like a fully grown elephant in miniature except for the furry down still covering his forehead and most of his body. It is rare to find an elephant abandoned as young as this, and its mother had almost certainly been shot. This meant that for the three days it had been in the camp it had had nothing to eat, apart from the condensed milk of which the men had somehow forced a little down his throat, but which certainly does not suit baby elephants. As soon as we saw it, we could tell that it was ravenous.

Had we been nearer Nairobi, this would not have been such a problem. But here in the middle of the bush it was difficult to see just what we could do. Clearly if we did not get it some food within a few hours, it would die, but how were we to find any?

Luckily, Michaela remembered that there was a dairy farm at Malindi, a good hour's drive away along the coast. There, at least, there would be sufficient supplies of cows' milk to satisfy the constant thirst of a growing baby elephant.

The difficulty now was actually getting the elephant to the farm. We had driven up in our old Dodge saloon car—certainly not the sort of transport one normally associates with carrying elephants, even when they are thirty-two inches high. But there was no alternative if the baby was to survive. So I lifted him into the back of the car—I can actually boast that I, single-handed, have carried an elephant—and we climbed aboard ourselves. I drove and Michaela courageously shared the back seat with our passenger.

He was not an ideal travelling companion. He forgot his manners. He squealed: he slobbered: he rolled about. He put his trunk down the back of my neck. Michaela suffered worst, for while she was trying to hold on to him and prevent him climbing on to me, she was being buffeted and trodden on until she was black and blue all over. By the time we reached the dairy farm it felt as if we had driven half-way across Africa.

Even then our troubles were far from over. How do you artificially feed a week-old elephant? No baby's bottle would be big enough and he was too stubborn to open his mouth and allow us to pour the milk in. We tried all sorts of ways to persuade him to drink; finally I thought there was only one way left. I noticed a large tin bath hanging up in a barn, and asked if we could borrow it. We half filled it with milk and getting all the help we could we lifted the elephant into it bodily. He tried to splash and kick it over but we held on tight and finally, by pushing his head right into the milk, we persuaded him to drink. When we drove back to Nairobi two days later, the baby elephant and his tin bath were inseparable and he was drinking milk by the gallon every day.

During these early days the nearest we ever got to building our house was when we would pitch our tent on the land we had bought at Langata and spend a few days there filming the game in what we told ourselves would one day be our garden. Then gradually we began to adjust to the pace of our new existence. Life was not quite such a rush. We found we could organise our filming a month and even two months in advance and inevitably we started thinking about our house in earnest.

As soon as Michaela and I discussed the form it should take it

was clear that we would both have to make some serious compromises if we were to avoid building two separate and totally
different houses. For Michaela loves space. She loves gilt and marble
and rich carpets and if she had had her way she would have built a
sort of oriental palace.

My ideas were the exact opposite. For me a house was a purely
functional thing like a boat or a taxi. I wanted something as simple
and as properly adapted to the African climate as I could find. So
my idea was to use the style of the South African circular *rondavel*
house, a traditional African building of mud and thatch that was
easy to build and miraculously cool in the hot season. I thought of
having several of these *rondavels* and joining them with passages to
give us the space we needed.

Michaela and I would discuss this problem endlessly, and it was
soon clear to me that unless one or the other of us did something
decisive we would go on living in tents and hotels to the end of our
days. So one evening, when we were staying in Nairobi during a
break between programmes, I announced to Michaela that I was
going to design the house.

"But you can't design a house," she said.

"Why not?" I asked.

"Because you're not an architect," she replied with profound
female logic.

I, who have spent my life accomplishing things for which I have
no professional qualifications, was not going to accept that. I had
never designed a house before, but then, until that year, I had never
made a film for television either. So that very evening I took some
squared paper, a pencil and a ruler, and proceeded to become an
architect.

The main problem, as far as I was concerned, was to work out
some compromise between Michaela's ideas and my own, so I
started with the idea of a living-room. Here I had to agree that
Michaela's plans had a lot to be said for them, so I decided that
thirty feet by twenty feet would be a reasonable measurement to
start with. On my paper I measured off twenty squares in one direction and thirty in the other. We were building for a country with
plenty of space and I thought that the house should reflect something

of the same spirit, so I drew in a good big staircase at one end of the living-room, placed a large dining-room beyond and ran a veranda along the side of the house that would face the hills, to make the most of the view.

Another compromise we had to make in the design was between planning it as a place to live in and a place to work in. Michaela was interested in having a house. I was more concerned with providing garage space for four or five cars and room for an office, for a film-cutting room, for a sound-recording studio, and for storage space for the mass of equipment we had already begun to accumulate.

The problem was to keep the two worlds of ours from interfering with each other and somehow to combine comfort and good living with an efficient headquarters for a complete television production unit.

As far as I could see, the only possible solution was to place the living-room and the dining-room on the first floor, whilst downstairs the entire ground floor would become a working area where we could edit and record in peace. By placing the living-rooms upstairs they would also enjoy the advantage of more light and air.

Once I had started on this plan of mine I became quite enthusiastic about it, and was soon deciding that instead of walls between the dining-room and living-room, I would have two large arches to make the whole first floor appear even more spacious and airy than ever.

It is one thing to amuse yourself for an evening designing your dream house: it is quite another to convince a down-to-earth builder that the design is a possibility. So to be on the safe side, I took the plan to a good architect I knew in Nairobi.

I was expecting him to say, "Ah, yes, Mr. Denis. Very interesting, but we must be practical, mustn't we?" And proceed to redesign the whole place. Instead, he took my slightly dog-eared sketch and looked at it without saying anything. Then he turned it upside down and still went on looking at it.

"Seems all right," he said at last. "Seems like a good house to me. Let's build it."

So build it we did, almost exactly as I planned it originally;

Who will move first?

*The only way to get the baby elephant to a sufficient supply
of cow's milk was in the back of our car*

Voodoo, the hooded vulture. "I have always been annoyed by people who speak of the 'ugliness' and the 'evil' faces of vultures"

Outside our house near Nairobi before setting off to make another
television film — and on safari

The author with Michaela on the upstairs veranda of the house which he designed for them

A Marabou Stork, one of the two menaces to newly hatched baby crocodiles

Crocodile. "One of the things we wanted to find out was the
role the mother played in hatching the eggs"

A Monitor Lizard, the other threat to young crocodiles, about to take an egg. Below, the camouflaged raft built for filming crocodiles

and the strange thing is that although the house grew out of a compromise, Michaela and I have enjoyed living in it so much that if ever we had to build another, I think we would have it almost exactly the same.

It was not until we started building that we really understood what a perfect site we had found. We chose the highest point on the ridge and sited the house so that it faced right across the valley. Building was easy here. The rocky outcrop we stood on came almost to the surface, so that there was no problem of drainage or foundations for the house. At the same time, although this area was so unspoiled, we were close enough to Nairobi to be able to draw on the city for our light and water.

With great excitement we watched our walls rise. They were built from stone cut from an old quarry we had found on our own land. For the floors, the African carpenters used the local mvule wood, a wood that polishes well and reveals a rich, beautifully clear grain. When the walls were finished, we found the texture of the rough stone so satisfying that we would not have it covered with plaster. Instead we had the walls painted white, inside the house and out.

For although I had given up my idea of a *rondavel* house, I did not want this building of ours to turn into a weak imitation of a traditional English house, any more than I wanted the garden to look like the majority of Kenya gardens—a neatly cultivated corner of old England.

So we had the house roofed with the rough local tiles that have mellowed now into a delicate shade of orange, and when we had had an area of twenty yards around the house cleared as a protection against snakes, we moved in.

We soon found that the best months to be in the house were in January and early February. By then the rains have finished. The stream is still full, the forest is green, and Michaela and I always try to arrange our safaris so that we are home at this time every year to enjoy the house and everything it has to offer. Although we are practically on the equator, the house is over 5,000 feet above sea level, and whilst it gets hot at this time, we never find it oppressive, as it would be nearer the coast.

When we are home during these months, we begin the day early. I like to rise at six and put in at least two hours work in the film-cutting room before breakfast. We breakfast at eight—usually on the veranda—and I always enjoy the superb fruit like paw-paw, mango and golden grenadillas that Michaela buys for breakfast from the local Kikuyu farmers.

After breakfast we work hard for the rest of the morning, but we have both got into the habit when we are at home of taking the dogs for a long walk after lunch, down through our forest to the river.

In July and August the weather changes. It is often cloudy then with the sort of temperatures you expect in a normal English summer. If we are at home then we sometimes find the evenings a little chilly, but although I actually had two open fireplaces built into the dining-room and the living-room, we have never used them yet and hardly suppose we ever will.

Of course, once the house was built, it soon became a matter for one of those unacknowledged husband and wife struggles that go on in even the best regulated households. Michaela, being a woman, naturally wanted the house as neat and as elegant as possible and was always buying expensive antique furniture and oriental rugs for it, from the auction rooms in Nairobi.

I, on the other hand, still try to maintain a certain amount of contempt for anything as self-indulgent as a house of my own. I miss the wonderfully unencumbered sense of the old days when there was never a house to claim our loyalties, and we were free at a moment's notice to pack our bags and be off to the other end of the earth.

I suppose that the truth is that we have both converted each other a little. I hate admitting it but there are times when I enjoy living at home enormously, whilst Michaela is usually as excited as I am at the challenge of a new safari. Meanwhile, the chief concession she gained from me has been over the garden. Both of us, of course, intend to keep the forest as it always has been, but recently Michaela has been paying more and more attention to the area immediately around the house. From being a stretch of grass cleared to keep the snakes away, it has been rapidly turning into the most elaborate of tropical gardens. To start with she was content with planting an occasional bush of hibiscus or oleander or frangipani, but these were soon doing so well that her ambitions as a gardener began to grow with them. Recently she has begun laying out ornamental ponds between the house and the road. They are very handsome ponds with water lilies and banana palms and banks of great papyrus reeds, so that if you come up the drive when the yellow thorn is in bloom and the bougainvillæa is ablaze against the wall, you will think you have come to something more exotic than the headquarters of a hard-working film and television unit.

But we built our house near Nairobi because we thought it would be a good centre for our work and it has been as a centre for work that it has really justified itself. Without it we could never have made the films. We have acquired so much equipment that it makes me shudder to think how we could ever get it transported if we lived in London and had to have it packed and put aboard a plane every time we decided to go off abroad. Even so we never seem to have anything like enough space for the camping equipment and the trucks, the cameras and the recording gear that at times look as if they are going to invade the entire house.

Also, if we did not have the house, I have no idea what we would do with our animals. For since we have lived there we have become a sort of orphanage for every imaginable animal in the district from stray cats to eagles, and from sick pet monkeys to a baby hyena. Some animals stay on with us. Others go back to the wild. But all the animals seem to enjoy living here and the house obviously gives them all a sense of security that they would miss if ever we had to leave. Michaela's mongoose, Minnie, owns the veranda. The giant South American ant-eater sleeps in the dining-room, and the dogs regard the living-room as their own domain.

Meanwhile, the longer we have lived here, the more Michaela and I have come to love this most beautiful of all the regions of Africa. We travel as much as ever, quite apart from our safaris, and usually have to get to London and Paris and New York at least once a year on some business or other. But we never feel we want to stay there.

We have built our life here in Africa. It is the cities that now seem unreal and whenever we have visited them the most exciting moment of the journey always comes when we catch sight of the white walls of our house standing out against the valley, and know that we are really back in Africa again.

24   *A Television Series is Made*

THERE is one question I am always being asked and never really know how to answer—how do we make our television programmes? Not that there is any particular mystery about the way we work. I do have a few tricks of the trade which I have picked up over the years and prefer to keep to myself, but these are not the reasons I find these questions so difficult.

There is no point in my answering with a lengthy description of the equipment we use, since I have almost made a fetish of keeping our equipment down to a minimum. Ever since I made my first film in Bali with an obsolete, wooden, hand-operated camera, I have always been reacting against the standard Hollywood idea that a good film depends on elaborate cameras and expensive apparatus. There is probably no one making regular films for television who uses less actual equipment than we do when we set off on safari.

Our much-used Bell and Howell cameras are still carried along but most of our work is done with Des Bartlett's Arriflex cameras. Des uses them of course to photograph any scenes in which we appear. He also owns an incredible variety of still cameras; he seems to collect them as other people collect stamps. Nowadays we pay a great deal of attention to still photography—a thing for which there was literally no time in our first years of television production —and Des revels in this: his eagerness to take pictures is only matched by his reluctance to appear in them himself. Apart from the cameras, there are the tripods, the lenses, the light meters and the cans of exposed and unexposed cine film that we always keep in waterproof aluminium boxes. We also carry a pair of reflectors with us—large plywood panels with aluminium paint on one side that can be stood in position around the more static subjects we film to reflect the sunlight on to them and lighten up the shadows.

Two of our four Land-Rovers are equipped with thousand watt and fifteen hundred watt generators and straightforward portable lighting equipment to enable us to light a simple scene. Apart from our two tape-recorders, this is virtually all the equipment we carry.

Another reason why I find questions about our technique of film-making so difficult to answer is that each film we make seems to call for a new set of rules and every animal for a different approach. There is never a great deal of sense in elaborate plans or preparations before we set off on a trip for the perfectly simple reason that we are never entirely sure what animals we are going to find when we get there. If there is a secret in the sort of films we have made, it really lies in the way we have exploited the chances that presented themselves quite unexpectedly as we went along.

One of the best examples of this cropped up in an early film we made for television on the life cycle of the crocodile.

I had known about the crocodiles of the Murchison Falls for years. They used to breed along the headwaters of the Nile between the foot of the falls and Lake Albert and to-day are probably the biggest single colony of crocodiles in Africa. Elsewhere crocodiles have been hunted so intensively for their skins that they have actually disappeared from many African rivers, but these crocodiles seem to have escaped the general massacre, and the foot of Murchison Falls remains a sort of crocodile paradise.

The Falls themselves are one of the sights of Africa. This is the place where the great volume of the waters of the Nile surges through a cleft of rock so narrow that an Olympic or hare-brained athlete could jump across. The surrounding landscape is impressive, and the impact of the water as it hits the foot of the falls is tremendous.

I had realised what a good subject these crocodiles would make for a film ever since 1952 when I first visited the Falls. On that occasion I had been almost to the foot of Murchison Falls in a small boat on the lower river. But although I had tried to film the crocodiles I found that the boat was not stable enough for my camera and the film had not been a great success. But I had kept the idea of filming the crocodiles at the back of my mind ever since, and at the beginning of 1958 began to think seriously of how we could do it.

For the shots I wanted we clearly had to have a boat, but I knew by now that this would have to be a particular kind of boat and that I would have to build it myself. I experimented with several models first. The boat we wanted had to be extremely stable and extremely light, for in those days the present road to the Falls had not been built and everything would have to be transported by truck across rough country.

Finally I designed a sort of light wooden raft that could be bolted across a couple of collapsible canvas dinghies, and that would take an outboard motor on the back. This took us only a few days to build and by the end of February we were on our way.

When we approached the foot of the Falls, we spent some time camouflaging our craft by tying large bunches of reeds all round it. Then we fixed our camera and tripod aboard, started the motor, and chugged our way slowly up river to the foot of the Falls.

It was a stately journey and surprisingly enjoyable despite the herds of hippos swimming all round us. They worried me more than I liked to admit for it needed only one of them to take exception to us or even to bump against us and our raft would have capsized. But apparently the hippos had other things to worry about and we were so well camouflaged that we were able to get to within five feet of some of the biggest fresh-water crocodiles I have seen in my life. They must have been between twelve and fourteen feet long, and were remarkably handsome. Their colours were superb and their size made them doubly impressive.

But while we were filming them it occurred to me that we were seeing only one part of the story. With so many crocodiles about, the actual place where they laid and hatched their eggs could not be far away and I worked out that this should be about the season when the baby crocodiles made their appearance.

So we beached our raft on a stretch of shore as far from any basking crocodiles as we could find, and went cautiously in search of their nests.

This sounds rather more dangerous than it actually was, for the African crocodile, despite the stories that are often told about him, is not at his most aggressive on land. As long as you stay away from the edge of the water and keep your eyes open you are reasonably safe. Also the mother crocodile, although she stays near her eggs when they are about to hatch, has no particularly strong maternal feelings to outrage and generally does not show much inclination to defend her eggs.

In fact, the role the mother crocodile played in hatching the eggs was one of the things we wanted to find out, and when a crocodile suddenly darted out in front of us from a bank of sand to plunge with a splash into the river, we walked over to investigate. It looked as if she had been digging; at any rate the sand had been disturbed to a depth of several inches and when I scooped a dozen handfuls of sand away I came upon the round hard surface of an egg. Michaela joined me and together, keeping a wary eye open just in case the mother crocodile decided to return after all, we dug up thirty-two crocodile eggs before we were finished.

I think that the role the mother crocodile normally performs is to start digging them up just about the time they are due to hatch. The female crocodile we had disturbed must have been engaged in this when we first saw her. This digging is of course purely instinctive; it seems that its purpose, or rather its effect, is to give the baby crocodiles inside the eggs a gentle reminder that life is about to begin in earnest and that it is time they started breaking their way out into the world. The baby crocodiles are provided with an "egg tooth" at the end of their snouts to enable them to break through the shell, and they have to get out of the egg by their own unaided effort. While Michaela was actually holding one of them, we both heard faint scratching sounds inside it. She held on to it gently, and then had the strange experience of having a young crocodile come to life in her hands. We had disturbed the eggs in much the same way as the mother would have done. This had given them the signal they had been waiting for and, quite rapidly, one after the other, the rest of the thirty-two eggs started to hatch.

This hatching of the crocodiles was an exciting sight. It was wonderful to see how completely nature provided for the babies from the very instant they appeared. They were most elegant creatures, these second-old crocodiles, with their golden eyes and their gleaming olive and black skin. They issued from their eggs like young dragons and all their aggressiveness was there from the very start. They were about eight inches long but their first action after clambering out of the shell was to try to nip our fingers, and they would jump at us, mouths wide open, showing all their sharp little teeth.

We had wondered how long it took them to adapt to life, but it was obvious that they were born with all the instinctive abilities they needed. From the moment they hatched they could cope quite adequately with all the problems confronting a crocodile for the remainder of his life. They could swim, they could fight, they could use their limbs perfectly and they could eat.

With so much apparently in their favour, it seemed strange that the river and Africa itself, for that matter, were not overrun with crocodiles. Each female laid thirty or forty eggs in a season, so that here on this river bank there must have been thousands of these powerful, well-equipped young crocodiles hatching out every year. Yet we worked out that unless the numbers of crocodiles were to increase astronomically, only about one in fifty of them could grow into an adult animal. The numbers were not increasing, so what fate overtook the other forty-nine?

We discussed this casually, but as we walked farther along the bank, and saw several nests recently opened and filled with broken shells, and yet could find no baby crocodiles alive, our curiosity became really aroused. We had splendid film material already on crocodiles and their young, but there was a mystery here which we wanted to solve, and which might add an entirely un-expected episode to our film.

The first thing to do was to wait. By walking along the bank, we had disturbed the crocodiles and made it difficult to observe anything. If we were to find out what was happening to the baby crocodiles, we were going to need considerable patience. So we went away and came back early next morning with a portable canvas hide so that we could watch a nest while the eggs were hatching without any animals being aware we were there.

Waiting in a hide like this with crocodiles wandering around within three or four feet of you can be uncomfortable. At close quarters crocodiles have a strange smell and this, coupled with the flimsiness of the hide, makes you wonder if this time you have not got just a little too close to your wild animals. But if you tried getting out you would be worse off still, and after a while, when the animals still take no notice of you, you stop worrying.

We stayed cooped up in this hide the whole of one day. We had suspected that the baby crocodiles had some deadly enemy making short work of them as they hatched, but we soon saw that there was not one enemy but at least two. Right from the start the odds against a young crocodile surviving more than a day were appallingly high.

It was Michaela who spotted the first of the animals preying on the young crocodiles.

"Look," she said. "Those storks over there by the bank. What are they up to?"

I looked where she was pointing and saw half a dozen marabou storks picking away busily with their beaks at something just beyond the reeds. These storks with their long beaks and the strange orange-coloured sack hanging from their throats perform much the same function for the wild life of Africa as the vultures. They are scavengers but they are not equipped to tear meat. So they clean up the refuse left behind when the other animals have made their kill. Now, through our binoculars, we could see that these six marabou storks were waiting like grim sentinels for the young crocodiles to hatch out. As soon as one did, there would be a swift peck and just for a moment we could see the crocodile squirming in the bird's beak. Then the stork would gulp and that would be one more young crocodile that would not live to grow fat on the fish carried down by the Murchison Falls.

During the next day we got some dramatic close-up shots of the storks in action; but while we were watching them we gradually realised that they could not be accounting for all the crocodiles on their own. Several times we found the remains of the actual crocodile eggs with traces of yolk still inside. There was some other animal that was attacking them before they hatched. We did not know what it could be and once more the only way to find out was to wait.

We realised what was happening when we saw a large green monitor lizard making his way along the sandy patches by the shore. At first he looked as if he was sniffing, much as a dog would. But this was not really the case. It was not his nose but his long snake-like tongue, incessantly flickering that was guiding him, and he was obviously using it to tell exactly where the eggs were buried. It was only then that we realised that these lizards were the killers we were looking for and that they were digging up the eggs before they were hatched. These lizards are up to five feet long and that day we filmed as many as four of them together raiding a nest. When they found an egg, they would all fight over it, and the lizard that won would hold the egg down with his claws and tear it open with his powerful jaws. They worked methodically, until the nest was empty, gorging themselves full on the squirming infants until they could hardly scuttle away.

Put down like this in black and white, this whole scene probably sounds more unpleasant than it really was. Of course it was cruel and brutal, but then, in many ways, nature is cruel and brutal. In this case if it had not been, the river would have been overflowing with crocodiles. One was tempted to marvel that the forces of destruction should have been weighted so exactly against the crocodiles' chances of survival, with the result that the number of crocodiles in the river continue much the same as ever.

Not long after we filmed our crocodiles, chance again presented us with another strange film sequence of animal life when we were least expecting it. We had been driving through the desolate wastelands of North Kenya on our way to Ethiopia. This sort of country has always appealed to me—hot, empty, with little vegetation and with blue ranges of mountains along the horizon. The sense of space and freedom here is uncanny. You can drive for days at a time and never meet a soul, and the idea of finding in these surroundings any animal scenes which would be good subject matter for our films seemed unlikely. Because of this I was puzzled when I noticed spurts of sand leaping a good foot into the air, from a small hole in the ground just ahead of the truck. I stopped the car and walked over. There were several holes, obviously entrances to burrows, but only one was spurting sand. Whatever the animal was that was inside must have been working away like mad, for the sand continued to spurt out like soil thrown up by a mechanical digger.

Our driver, at the time, was a Somali, familiar with this desert area. He knew all about the holes and the spurting sand. This, he said, was the burrow of a small animal who lived underground and was found only in places like this, miles from anywhere. The creature was blind; he had absolutely no hair at all, and he never stopped digging with his teeth. Needless to say, Michaela and I were excited by this. Neither of us could think what animal this could be, so we obviously had to catch him and find out.

This was rather easier than we had imagined. We used a pickaxe to cut off the animal's line of retreat in his burrow, and one of the oddest creatures I have ever seen poked his nose out of the hole.

Our driver's description of the strange creature had been surprisingly accurate. It had no hair. It had enormous teeth, and its minute eyes were screwed up tight against the light of day. It was a species of desert mole-rat and we spent hours with it, marvelling at its incredible energy. For these "naked mole-rats"—we found this to be their correct name—spend their time burrowing through the earth, and they really do use their teeth as our driver described. As soon as we put our captive on the ground he would immediately start digging with neurotic frenzy. He struck me as one of the saddest, loneliest animals I had ever seen, living this frightened life in the middle of nowhere where his only instinct seemed to be to disappear from view. We timed him, and from placing him down on the ground it took exactly forty seconds for him to dig himself out of sight.

He must have lived on roots and occasional insects and larvæ that would exist even in this most inhospitable of landscapes, but I still cannot understand how he ever found enough to eat to sustain his amazing output of energy. However he did it he took his secret with him, for we decided that this was one animal that even Michaela would not be able to make into a pet. So when we had finished filming him we put him back by his burrow and watched as his first bursts of sand told us he was back where he so obviously wanted to be beneath the desert.

Another subterranean animal we came upon by chance was an aardvark. This is a large species of ant-eater occurring in most of Central and South Africa. We were in the Transvaal filming weaver birds when we spotted this one. He was a strange, clumsy, slightly unprepossessing fellow, rather like a pig, but with large upright ears, a long nose and enormous claws on his feet. The name "aardvark," by the way, means "earthpig" in Dutch.

We were so busy watching the birds we were filming that we did not notice him until he was nearly on top of us. Luckily he had something on his mind as well—ants—and he started digging for them practically in front of our hide. He made a great business of digging, lying on his sides and practically on his back to widen the hole, and he went on quite oblivious of us until it was really dark and we went back to camp.

Next morning almost the first thing Michaela said when we woke up was, "Let's go and see what's happened to the aardvark." So we went back, and although we could find the hole he had made, there was no sign of him at all. But when I put my ear to the hole I could hear him scratching and digging away somewhere deep in the earth, so I said to Michaela, "We'll never get another chance like this to photograph an aardvark. Let's go back to camp for some shovels and dig him out."

When I said this I had no idea just how far and how fast an aardvark could dig, for although we came back with three men, all of us armed with shovels, we spent nearly the whole day digging after him. Backwards and forwards we went, making trench after trench in the hope of cutting into his burrow. We moved mountains of earth. Finally, late in the afternoon, when we were nearly worn out and the whole place was trenched like a battlefield, we caught our aardvark. He was still digging away, about eight feet underground, when we unearthed him, his feet working like power-shovels; we had to grab him by the hind legs and tail, and it took the full strength of three men to pull him out of the hole.

He fought like a demon, but we managed to get him wrapped in

301

a tarpaulin and carried him back to camp. I thought there was no point in keeping him long. He was clearly not over-sociable, so I simply intended taking a few shots of him and then turning him loose. But when we turned him out of the tarpaulin he behaved in the most civilised manner imaginable. He made no attempt to fight. He gave no sign of attacking anyone. Instead he simply wandered round, sniffing disapprovingly at each of us in turn.

I thought to myself, "This is very odd, but very interesting. I've never heard of a tame aardvark, but perhaps this one is the exception. Perhaps we can feed him and keep him and see what sort of pet he makes."

So I tried preparing him some food, but he showed not the slightest interest in it. One day passed, then another. The aardvark would not eat, but neither would he leave us; he hung around the camp, still sniffing suspiciously at anyone or anything he saw. Michaela by this time was hard at work collecting ants to try and tempt him to eat, but not even these would arouse his interest.

Finally I rummaged in my suitcase, and found a complicated recipe someone had given me in South America for the feeding of ant-eaters. It called for a lot of cream, raw meat, a dozen eggs, and several other less common ingredients, and I spent a long time preparing it. I placed it hopefully in front of the aardvark, but not even this interested him. He sniffed at it once or twice, turned his back to it, ostentatiously kicked some dust into it and walked away.

I was beginning to despair when suddenly he changed his mind, trotted back to the food and started to eat.

At once I called to Michaela. "Look," I shouted, "look! The aardvark is eating. He likes the stuff. It's wonderful, we've a tame aardvark at last."

"Yes," she shouted back, "we can take him home with us. We can take him to America. No one has ever seen a tame aardvark in America before. He'll be famous."

But while we were so busy congratulating ourselves, the aardvark stopped eating. It was almost as if he had understood exactly what we were saying. For he gave us one long disapproving look, turned around and again kicked dust into the mixture I had so painstakingly prepared, and then he trotted off, with never a backward glance, in a straight line for the forest. That was the last we ever saw of our tame aardvark.

Luck, of course, is important in filming animals in the wild, but there are also times when you need a great deal of patience as well.

This was particularly the case with our film of the leopard larder. For many years I had heard how the leopard, when he has made his kill, and has eaten all he can for the time being, drags the carcase of the animal up into a tree where it stays safe from the jackals and the vultures until he is hungry again. He is supposed to be able to drag up animals almost double his weight, and to make his "larder" thirty or forty feet above the ground.

Although we had occasionally seen the remains of carcases where leopards had left them it was not until one summer, when Michaela and I were in the Serengeti, that we had a chance of filming a leopard storing its larder. We were waiting near a small stream when Michaela spotted a large object hanging in one of the topmost forks of a tree on the opposite bank. I looked at it carefully through the binoculars. It was not a large ants' nest or wasps' nest as I expected. As far as I could see, it was the remains of a large antelope and I had never heard of antelope climbing trees. Then I remembered the stories so often heard and began to wonder excitedly whether this could be the almost legendary leopard's larder.

We spent the rest of that day watching the tree. Nothing happened. There was no sign of a leopard. It was the same the following day. But on the third day when we turned up, rather later than before, we spotted a leopard actually in the tree. He was on his way down and as soon as he saw us he leapt to the ground and sped away through the high grass. We waited most of the morning for him to reappear, but he did not. Instead a vulture swooped down and alighted about thirty yards from the tree on the body of a freshly killed antelope that we had not noticed in the high grass. Surely, I thought, this must bring the leopard back, if only to defend his kill. It did not, but the vulture did not have long to enjoy his meal. Another leopard, whose presence we had not suspected, appeared on a branch half-way up the tree and, keeping a cautious eye on us, came very slowly, hesitantly, down the trunk of the tree and chased the vulture away.

Then for several minutes it was as if he could not make up his mind what to do with this dead antelope, and we were waiting anxiously for the moment to start our camera. After this long hesitation, the leopard suddenly grabbed the dead antelope by the neck and, with surprising ease, began dragging it to the foot of the tree.

We had only some forty feet of unused film in the camera and so now had to decide whether to let it run or to keep it for later. We have so often made the wrong decision, and run out of film just at the crucial point of a sequence. . . . We let the camera run on. Luckily the leopard had made up his mind. He braced himself with the body of the dead antelope still in his jaws and then, with an amazing leap, he was up into the tree. Several times he stopped to gain his breath and take a fresh hold on the heavy carcase, but each time he would continue climbing, hanging on to the tree with his four feet, the antelope hanging down between him and the tree.

Once the leopard had finally got his animal safely wedged in a fork high up in the tree, our job became much easier. For it is a strange thing about the psychology of leopards that they behave very differently when they are in a tree from when they are on the ground. On the ground they are exceedingly nervous and difficult to photograph. They are also dangerous: their reaction is usually to run away—but not always. It may well be to attack.

Once he is up in a tree a leopard becomes almost a different animal. I am sure I know the reason for this. In a tree, the leopard believes himself to be invisible. He relaxes, feeling safe because of the difficulty anyone would have in spotting him, his coat so exactly matching the pattern of the sunlight on the leaves. Often a leopard will just lie all day stretched full length on a horizontal branch, his head peeping over and his paws hanging down on either side of the branch. I have been beneath a leopard like this, scarcely fifteen feet from him, and actually seen him looking down at me with the calmest face in the world: he was completely sure that I could not see him.

As a result of this sense of security, the leopard we were watching

One of the residents at our house in Kenya

*Recording an anteater and, below, the 'earth pig' or aardvark,
"a strange, clumsy, slightly unprepossessing fellow"*

Leopard. "*On the ground they are exceedingly nervous and difficult to photograph*"

"Once he is up a tree the leopard believes himself to be
invisible. He relaxes." Below, a graceful leap

*Poached ivory and, above, the elephant with a foot
almost severed by a poacher's snare*

A Njemp girl from the Lake Baringo country

"Riding an Indian elephant is one of the stateliest experiences I know. You are so high up that you feel you dominate the world"

"Our travels will go on. There is still so much of the world to see . . ."

now became much easier to film and we were able to approach closely and to photograph him as he ate. This was extremely interesting: leopards are fastidious eaters; they have a peculiar habit of licking, at prolonged length, an area of their victim's skin before they bite into the flesh. Their tongues are rough enough to take off all the hair on this patch of skin, and they do this carefully, spitting out the hair as they go; we watched this leopard doing this for several minutes before he actually tore at the skin, made a hole in the carcase and began to eat.

This carcase lasted him several days, and during this time, Michaela and I were the most devoted of audiences. We soon discovered that this leopard was a male and that he had a whole family hidden away in the tree. The leopard we had seen originally disappearing into the grass was his mate and they had three cubs.

On several occasions we were able to watch the whole family eating forty feet above the ground, and although the cubs could not have been much more than a month old, we were interested to see that they were quite able to feed themselves. One of the things that struck us most was the great difference in the table manners of this leopard family and those of most of the lions we had filmed in the past. In comparison with the dainty leopards, lions are greedy and bad-mannered eaters; when a lion family turns up at a kill it is really a free-for-all, with frequent outbursts of impatience and temper.

The leopard, on the other hand, seems to have a natural elegance in everything he does and a natural sense of poise and dignity. During the days we watched the leopard family eating from its larder, we never saw the slightest sign of unbecoming behaviour from the cubs, or of disharmony between their parents.

Outlook for the Animals

IT would be wrong if I gave the impression that we have liked everything we have seen while we have been in Africa. We love the country and we love to work in it. But the sights we have seen while we have been making our programmes have not all been peaceful. There have been times when we have been angry and times when we have felt helpless and times when we have been close to despair at the needless destruction of wild life that has been allowed to occur.

There was the morning in January, for instance, three years ago, when we had been on safari in Uganda close to the Congo border, filming the herds of elephant as they crossed this great area of savannah country. We had started early. To the west we had a rare and magnificent view of Ruwenzori, the Mountains of the Moon, and although we drove for more than two hours through high, rich grass, we saw nothing except baboons and a few hyena. Of all the elephants that we had been told were in the area there was not a sign.

This was mysterious. Game does not usually disappear like this without a cause, yet there was nothing we could see to account for it.

It was just before noon that we spotted our first elephant of the day. It was a nearly full-grown cow, and as soon as we saw her we could tell there was something wrong with the way she was walking. We stopped about half a mile away from her and looked at her through the binoculars to see what was the matter. It was not difficult to see the trouble. About eighteen inches above the foot ran a thin steel wire encircling her leg. On the end of it trailed an eight-foot long wooden stake that she had somehow managed to pull out of the ground. But the wire had been drawn so tight that it had bitten deeply into the flesh and the whole leg had festered and swollen up like a balloon.

It was intensely moving to see the way the elephant accepted this terrible injury and carried on, limping uncomplainingly after the herd that was probably miles ahead of her by now.

We had never seen anything like this before, but Michaela and I both knew all too well what had caused the injury. For several months past we had been hearing reports about the steady increase of elephant poaching, not only in this area but almost everywhere in Africa where elephants occur. Even in the Tsavo National Park in Kenya, the number of elephants being killed each year by the poachers was beginning to run well into hundreds. Poaching was becoming a business. The poachers were being organised into gangs, sometimes operating in Land-Rovers from semi-permanent camps. They would set these murderous snares of theirs indiscriminately for any animals they could catch.

We pulled close to within a hundred yards of the painfully limping elephant.

"She's been snared, but it looks as if she's broken away," I said to Michaela. "That wire would have bitten through to the bone by now."

"But what can we do to help her?" asked Michaela.

"Nothing now," I replied. "We're too late. She could never recover from an injury like that. The leg is rotted. She must have been like this for weeks."

As I spoke, it was almost as if the elephant heard what I said. She stopped, faced us and trumpeted forlornly. For once I wished that we carried a gun with us. At least we could have put her out of her agony. As it was the only thing we could do was to drive back as fast as we could to the game warden's headquarters and get him to do it.

This took us most of the afternoon and it was nearly dark before we had found him and caught up with the elephant again. By now she had dragged herself on for about half a mile from where we had left her and then stopped.

She did not bother to trumpet when she saw us this time, but stood facing us passively. The ranger took his time over the shot and made a clean kill of it. When he fired she sank to her knees and died without a murmur.

I hate the death of any animal. Normally, however, you reason with yourself and realise that you have to accept the facts of death. Death is one of the laws of the wild and not something to get sentimental about.

This was something different. The waste and the appalling suffering of the animal disgusted us. We drove back with the game ranger.

" Is that a job you often have to do ? " I asked him.

He nodded. " There's always elephant poaching going on round here."

" But don't you ever catch the men who do it ? " asked Michaela.

"Of course we do, although it's getting more difficult these days than it used to be. The poachers are arming themselves now and they're much better organised than they were. Only last week one of my own men was shot in the leg by a poacher. He was lucky to be shot in the leg. He will recover. Lucky that was all it was."

"But what do you do with the poachers when you do catch them ?" insisted Michaela.

The ranger looked as if this was a question he had heard many times before.

"Well," he said, "you can put them in gaol, of course, but that doesn't do anyone much good. The Africans don't particularly object to a few month's free board at the Government's expense. It doesn't bring the animals back and it certainly doesn't turn the poacher into an animal lover."

"To tell you the truth," he went on, "the men I'm bitter about are not really the poachers. After all, they're local men. They've always hunted the game and they take a lot of risks I wouldn't like to. The people someone really should clamp down on are the merchants and the middlemen on the coast who finance the poachers and buy the ivory from them. If there was a bit more drastic action against them from above, we might start getting somewhere."

This conversation with the game ranger made a great impression on us both. If the Government was slow to act about poaching, we at least had the chance of making the people who watched our programmes aware of what was happening. That very night we decided to shelve our plans to film the rest of the elephant herds. Instead we would make a full-scale documentary film on the poaching of Africa's wild life.

It was not a particularly pleasant film to make. During the weeks that followed we saw sights too gruesome ever to show to any television audience. There were rhinos within twenty miles of Nairobi that had been speared to death and left rotting for the vultures. All the poachers had wanted had been the horns that they hacked out and sold to one of the local merchants engaged in the perfectly legal trade of selling rhino horn as a theoretical aphrodisiac to the Far East.

We saw zebras and wildebeeste that had been snared with steel wire, hamstrung, and then left several days to die. All the poachers could be bothered to take would be the wildebeeste tails to make into flywhisks that sell, again perfectly legally, to the tourists in the gift shops of Nairobi for a few shillings.

Worst of all were the completely useless deaths we encountered. Snaring is easy, but it is also indiscriminate, and the snares were placed so widely that for every animal caught that was any use to the poachers, there must have been dozens that were not. These would just be left where they were—female gazelles caught and left to die of starvation, their young waiting patiently beside them; warthogs and buffalo that had suffered a similar fate; rotting carcases too far gone even to identify. Once we found a giraffe that was still alive but had had a front leg torn off by a snare.

The snares' worst victims of all were not the animals that they killed, but those that managed to escape and survive. Twice during these weeks Des Bartlett came upon elephants that had been caught in snares by their trunks. One had broken away and was somehow managing to exist with only half a trunk, by grazing the grass on his knees. The other was less fortunate. When Des first spotted him he was floundering in a river, and he watched him actually feeding on floating weeds. This was all he could manage to get, for an elephant relies almost completely on his trunk for feeding and Des saw that this elephant's trunk must have been caught in a snare fot although it looked intact, it was paralysed and just hung uselessly.

I estimate that to-day there remains at the most only a tenth of the game that was in Africa before the First World War, perhaps much less than a tenth. The numbers are still declining, and still we are doing nothing to teach the African why he should behave better than we have with organised hunting over the years.

I felt all this even more strongly a few months later over the last hippos of Lake Baringo. Baringo is a small lake by African standards. About twenty-five miles long, it lies to the north of Nakuru in particularly wild country. Unlike Nakuru, Elementeita, Hannington and Magadi, the big salt-lakes of the Great Rift Valley, Lake Baringo has fresh water. In this respect, it is like Lake Naivasha and, like Naivasha, it used to support a large and flourishing population of hippo. After the war these hippo and the rest of the game that used to surround the two lakes began to be seriously threatened by indiscriminate shooting and spearing. By the time the hippo were declared Royal Game five years ago, the hippo of both Baringo and Naivasha had been brought close to extinction.

In the whole of Lake Baringo, there could scarcely have been more than a hundred hippo left; and about this time another danger came to threaten this pitiful remnant. For several seasons drought or scanty rainfall brought disaster to the surrounding area which had already been ravaged by overgrazing and injudicious burning of the grass and bush. Two years ago the hippos had to live through a period of several months of virtual starvation, and last year conditions were even worse.

Soon the hippos were so weak that they could scarcely stagger a few hundred yards from their lake, and within that limited radius they would wander searching for the dry seed pods that fell from the thorn trees and that were all that was left to give them the illusion of food.

Michaela and I heard about the plight of the hippos when we were staying with our friend, David Roberts, who has the fishing concession of Lake Baringo, and lives there with his family on the western shore. He had been particularly affected by the plight of eight hippos that had lived for a long time on the edge of the lake within sight of his house.

As the weeks passed without sign of rain, these eight hippos had become weaker and weaker. At night they used to wander through the remains of his parched-up garden in search of food and soon they became so thin that their ribs showed and they staggered as they walked. Instead of disappearing out of sight in the lake during the day, as these animals usually do, they would simply lie exhausted on the bank, a sitting target for any African hunter who cared to take them.

Finally, when David found the bull of this small herd actually in the porch of his house, sniffing at the remains of the food he had left out for the dog, he decided that the time had come to make some attempt to save these eight hippos.

Hay was the only food that he could get for them in sufficient quantities and this he put out. To start with the hippos were clearly puzzled by the new food. The first night they nuzzled it and scattered most of it along the shore. But they ate a little and, within a few days, they were eating three to four full bales a night.

The hippos began to put on weight again, and although they still looked emaciated, they clearly had a chance of surviving until the rains came. Their favourite food of all was fine lucerne hay, with star grass hay and oat hay running it a close second. At first they would also accept Rhodes grass hay and ordinary wheat straw, but then they became fussier about the food they would take and tended to leave this uneaten. As a result, David was having to spend more than he could afford on good quality hay to keep the eight hippos alive, and Michaela and I offered to help by starting a small fund for the hippos of Lake Baringo. The Wild Life Society headed the subscription list with a gift of £50 and although we received contributions from as far afield as the United States, most of the money came from conservationists we knew in Kenya. Within a few weeks we had enough money to guarantee the hippos' food for as long as the drought lasted.

Soon we saw a remarkable difference in the habits of the hippos. They began to develop confidence in people. Normally, hippos spend most of the day well off shore and land only at night, but these soon started lying in the shallow water during the day, not more than twenty or thirty yards from the men loading the fish into David's freezing plant.

In the evening they would come out of the water, start eating long before dark, and stay out until day-break. One evening I actually saw David pat one of the hippos on the back as it waddled past on the way to the house for the day's ration. All this was very satisfactory except for one thing that began to worry David as the drought went on.

He knew the Africans well who lived around the lake and he understood how the drought was hitting them. They were beginning to go hungry too, and he knew that the longer the drought lasted the more of a temptation these nearly tamed hippos would become. He knew just how serious this danger was when he saw one of the hippos with a spear sticking out of its back. It was not a bad wound and David was able to get the spear out.

But the day came when David had to leave home for a week. When he returned he found that the big old bull had been speared to death in his absence. A few weeks later, another followed. Then a female was killed and her baby caught in the mud and choked to death. Within a matter of weeks, the last of the eight hippos we thought we had saved had been killed, and the animals exterminated from one more African lake.

Ultimately several of the Africans responsible for the killings were arrested and imprisoned for a while, but, in this case, the sentence struck me as being almost as pointless as it was unfair.

Despite all our opportunities we have failed to teach the African to value the wild life of his country.

Take first the continuance of licensed hunting in East Africa, which seems to me such arrant stupidity at the moment. Quite apart from any question of cruelty to the animals, it makes the sheerest nonsense of any attempt to teach the African to value the game of his own country. As long as the white man is allowed to hunt, any attempt to suppress the poacher will always appear mere hypocrisy in African eyes.

Consider next the fact that for the ordinary African villager the two things that matter more than anything else are land and cattle. Wild animals, not surprisingly, appear to him as a threat to both and he has always been encouraged in this attitude by the wholesale campaigns of game extermination which the Europeans in Africa have carried on under one pretext or another over great areas.

In Uganda, for instance, countless zebra and antelope have been methodically destroyed on the grounds that they are dangerous carriers of sleeping sickness. The whole theory behind this has been disproved by every reputable scientist who has studied the subject, but the slaughter still goes on. The wild animals killed in various areas in the last ten years for so-called "tsetse control" run into hundreds of thousands.

Because of such examples when European authorities do try to set aside an area for the protection of game it is not surprising if Africans regard it simply as a means of robbing them of land on which they should be allowed to settle themselves. Many times I have heard the National Parks referred to as land stolen from the African and the preservation of animals is usually regarded as a perverse white man's hobby.

As a result, the herdsmen and the African settlers have felt themselves within their rights in moving into many of the areas of the National Parks and hard pressed local administrators have all too often accepted this way out of the problem of providing more land for an ever-growing population. In this way, whole areas have been irretrievably lost. The Ngorongoro Crater where Al Klein and I watched some of the largest game herds in Africa less than twenty years ago is now being settled by a steady influx of Masai nomads and their cattle. The crater is still officially a "Conservation Area" but it is difficult to see what conservation is being practised there or what chance the animals really have of surviving for long.

Worst of all, the land itself is changing and turning against the wild life as it is in so many other parts of the world. The cattle and the goats increase each year. The sparse land becomes overgrazed. Grass dies. Trees are felled. The thin soil of the bush erodes even more quickly than the soil did in the American Middle West, and like the Middle West, much of Africa is already rapidly turning into a dust bowl.

The world is littered with deserts of man's own making and unless something drastic is done soon, most of the East African plain will soon join them. The great drought we recently experienced was a warning. More recently still we had flooding on a greater scale than ever before in Kenya's history; still worse is to be expected now that the balance between soil, climate and forests is being so remorselessly destroyed.

Clearly, in the end, it will be not just the wild life of Africa that will suffer; but it is the wild life that goes first. Almost mysteriously the animals disappear. In the area we see from our house for instance, there has been no serious poaching or hunting but the herds of game we used to watch crossing the plain towards the Ngong hills come no longer. The wild animals near our house are becoming rarer each year. One day they will simply cease to be.

What is happening in Africa is happening to wild life throughout the world. The threat is universal. After a lifetime in contact with the wild, I know it is no use underestimating the forces we are up against. If all protection were to cease I would give the giraffe a couple of years at the most. After that it would become extinct. The rhinoceros might last five years—the lion just a little longer. A remnant of the elephants would retreat to the forests and survive there for a period. The rest of them would perish, and with them would go the buffalo, the zebra, the wildebeeste and the antelope until the plains of Africa became empty of the life they had known.

If this is to be prevented, man must step in now and step in fast. A crash programme is needed. In the short run we must have a first-aid policy to save the animals that are most gravely threatened. The game laws must be enforced, hunting finally stopped and the men behind the poachers dealt with as rigorously as they obviously could be.

At the same time, this cannot be successful without an effective campaign to convince the Africans who are taking over their governments that here, in their animals and wild life, lie some of the most valuable natural resources their lands possess. Wild animals are the capital of Africa. What the mountains are for Switzerland, wild life could be for Africa, and if the tourist traffic were organised here with a fraction of the efficiency with which it has been organised in Switzerland, it could be the salvation of many an impoverished area of Africa.

The enthusiasm with which wild life programmes like ours on television have been received outside Africa shows that there is a potential market of immense proportions for tourism to Africa. With chartered flights and properly organised camps and hotels, Africa could come within the reach of ordinary people and the country is still large enough to absorb a heavy flow of tourists without being spoiled in the process.

At the same time, the game will need intelligent control as well as protection. Where certain animals are overgrazing and destroying the habitat, their numbers will have to be culled. Where others are failing to maintain their numbers it may be necessary to introduce new strains from elsewhere, as has already been done successfully in South Africa where several areas are being re-populated with white and black rhino many years after these animals had been exterminated there by the hunters.

Similarly in time of drought and famine the animals will have to rely on the help of man if they are to survive, while the continuation of particularly threatened species may be possible only by establishing breeding colonies of animals under carefully controlled conditions in countries where they have never been known before. In time we might see a colony of rhino living in Australia or of elephants in South America.

I speak about East Africa because it is here that I see the danger to wild life at first hand. But the same forces are threatening wild life throughout the world. Because of this I am convinced that the real hope for the animals lies, not in any single plan but in the revolution that has been taking place in the attitude of people throughout the world to wild life. Animal conservation is no longer just a cause for a few enthusiasts. World opinion has finally become concerned and I believe that the most important thing I have done in my life was to become the first to put the case for wild life on television.

Recently I was lecturing for the National Geographical Society in

Washington on the need for animal conservation, and the organisers seemed very pleased when seven thousand people turned up to the two performances I gave. But I worked it out afterwards that if I had wanted my message to reach the same number of people that see a single one of our television programmes in England, Germany, France, Canada and the rest of the twenty-six countries where we regularly appear, I should have had to lecture twice a day for the next twenty years.

There are grave drawbacks to television and I would be the last to underestimate them, but the mass wave of sympathy and understanding it has produced for wild life during the last ten years must certainly be counted among its positive benefits. Even the popular idea of a "wild animal" is changing. Instead of being regarded as things to be fought and destroyed, wild animals are beginning to be thought of as creatures to be observed and understood. When young people think of a lion to-day they associate it with a camera rather than with a gun.

For me there has been a particular excitement at being involved in this change. When I started my career such a swing of public opinion was inconceivable. The early films I made could only be a record of a world that I believed was doomed. Our television programmes are propaganda for a world I know now can still be saved.

Another reason why I am grateful for television is that after a lifetime enjoying animals, it has given me the chance of turning this strange, apparently haphazard life of mine to a definite purpose—the preservation of the world I believe in. For if there is one thing my life does prove it is the supreme satisfaction that the untamed parts of the world offer to those who would understand them. I have had more than my share of the pleasures our civilisation can offer, but the moment I always look forward to most is when the aircraft door slams behind us and we know that we are finally off on a new expedition.

The sense of peace and calm is complete. There are no more telephones to ring, no more schedules to arrange and however difficult or unpleasant an expedition may appear at times, it always seems to offer this strange peace of mind that I have never been able to find in the life of the city. You meet each problem as it arises. If your truck gets stuck in a hole you have nothing else to worry about until you have got it out again, and it is the same with every other difficulty you encounter.

The real worries of life only start when you are back in civilisation.

Of course, I cannot deny that I have been attracted by the excitement of wild animals quite as much as any hunter. But I would claim that it is far more thrilling to film animals than to shoot them. There are the hours of long stalking through the grass. There is the additional excitement of knowing that you are not armed and that your safety depends purely on yourself and your knowledge of the animal you are watching. There is the fact that to get the picture you really want you must approach far closer than any marksman who merely wants to kill.

But when you do succeed, the satisfaction of filming a wild animal well is unbeatable. If you had shot it, you would have its corpse to look at and the knowledge that the earth was that much poorer. Instead you have not destroyed—you have created. The film you have made is the best possible trophy you ever could bring back and—if you value such things—the best proof of your personal daring.

For me there have always been other satisfactions as well. From the start I have always enjoyed the technical problems of filming and sound recording which provide something of an outlet for what inventive skills I possess. I enjoy the detail of arranging an expedition and get back my old schoolboy enthusiasm for travel whenever we set out on safari. And I am still happiest when I am with animals, particularly if I can tame them or live close to them in the wild.

Against this, I consider that I have definite defects for the sort of life I have lived. I am incurably lazy and always have to drive myself to accomplish anything. I also think of myself as a slow sort of person. I am obstinate rather than quick-witted and feel that I have inherited more than my share of my Flemish ancestors' mental solidity. For a medium like television this is a great disadvantage, and unlike Michaela I have always disliked the idea of appearing live before the cameras, although when I have done so the result has not always been as disastrous as I expected.

Perhaps it is because of this mentality of mine that I have always admired the exact opposite in people and in animals. The one quality I never cease to envy is complete and effortless excellence. Acrobats, jugglers, professional billiard players or accomplished public speakers, for instance, fill me with almost childish jealousy and much of my feeling for animals comes from an instinctive admiration for their superb efficiency. I love the cheetah for his speed, the baboon for the casual grace with which he can climb, and whenever I see a human ballet I feel an irrepressible desire to laugh because I cannot help comparing its performance with that of the gibbons, that can leap forty feet without the slightest apparent effort.

When I think back over my life, I can never remember a time when I planned the shape it was to take. The only principle I have ever worked to has always been to do whatever interested me at the time. I have gambled quite consciously with myself and with my career, and I am lucky that the gamble has paid off. But in case any-one feels like following my example, it is only fair that I should give the same warning that I always give to any new cameramen who join me. I tell them that if they come with me they will enjoy them-selves. They will savour the satisfaction that wild life has to give, but they will also change. For once they have tasted a wild exist-ence, they will never be really satisfied to settle down to the life of the cities again. The canker of restlessness will be within them for the rest of their lives. Only in the wild will they ever be really at peace with themselves.

I realise now that this happened to me over thirty years ago when I first saw Bali. I have moments of wondering if I should regret the settled, comfortable life I might have led as a research scientist, but I console myself with the thought that if I had stayed on in my laboratory instead of taking the gamble that I have been living ever since, I would have led a life that hundreds of other people could have lived equally well.

Instead I have lived a life that, whatever its faults, has been unique. Even during the last few months, when I have been trying to cut down on commitments and shut myself away in the house to work on this book, the unexpected has kept cropping up to give me an excuse to get away from my desk. Last October, when the drought ended and we had finished most of the filming for our current television series, I thought I would have some time to myself. But no sooner had the rains come in earnest than I found the roof leaking extensively over the dining-room. Such things take on the proportions of major problems in Africa. It took us all several days to deal with it. Then when the rains continued more heavily than anyone could remember, bringing widespread floods to Kenya, Michaela and I were invited to film the R.A.F. relief operations bringing supplies to beleaguered African villagers.

I had planned to have this book finished by Christmas to give me time to think about an exciting new venture—"Animals," the colour magazine that I am editing. But I write slowly. There has been all our routine work of scripting and editing for our next television programme to do at the same time, and with so many delays I found that I had to finish the last few chapters after our journey to Barotseland at the end of February. Neither of us wanted to miss the unique chance of filming the spectacular Kuomboka ceremony when the chief of the Barotses is rowed down river by his warriors in his great canoe of state.

But now that this book is finished I have the feeling that it only skims the surface of my life. If we were not leaving for Suriname in a few days I would go on until I had written a book twice the size, covering our safaris and adventures of the last few years. There were our two safaris to South Africa. There was our trip to the Hadhramaut, that strange, parched land where Arabia meets the Gulf of Aden. And there was our highly eventful recent safari to the Far East. If I had time, I would describe the honey bear who became our constant companion on that trip, and the snake farm outside Bangkok where Michaela and I thought our last hour had come.

But a book must end somewhere. Suriname cannot be postponed. And when we are back from Suriname . . . our travels will still go on. There is still so much of the world to see and so many of its animals to record.

One of the first things I learned as a traveller was never to see all of a country on one visit, but to leave one part untried to provide an incentive to return. I have visited Italy many times, but I have never been to Venice. Purposely I have hoarded this as somewhere special for the future and have always looked forward to the day when I will actually go to Venice for the first time.

As with Italy, so with the rest of the world.